READING THE GLOBAL

READING THE GLOBAL

Troubling Perspectives
on Britain's Empire in Asia

SANJAY KRISHNAN

COLUMBIA UNIVERSITY PRESS   *new york*

COLUMBIA UNIVERSITY PRESS

Publishers Since 1893

New York   Chichester, West Sussex

An earlier version of chapter 2 was published in *Boundary 2* 33, no. 2 (2006). An earlier version of chapter 4 was published in *Novel: A Forum on Fiction* 37, no. 3 (2004), copyright © NOVEL Corp. 2004. Reprinted with permission.

Columbia University Press wishes to express its appreciation for assistance given by the University of Pennsylvania toward the cost of publishing this book.

Library of Congress Cataloging-in-Publication Data

Krishnan, Sanjay.
    Reading the global : troubling perspectives on Britain's empire in Asia / Sanjay Krishnan
        p. cm.
    Includes bibliographical references and index.
    ISBN 978-0-231-14070-6 (cloth : acid-free paper)—ISBN 978-0-231-51174-2 (e-book)
        1. English literature—History and criticism. 2. Globalization in literature. 3. Great
Britain—Colonies—Asia—History—19th century. 4. Asia—In literature. 5. Imperialism
in literature. 6. Capitalism in literature. 7. Smith, Adam, 1723–1790—Criticism and
interpretation. 8. De Quincey, Thomas, 1785–1859—Criticism and interpretation. 9. Conrad,
Joseph, 1857–1924—Criticism and interpretation. 10. Abdullah, Munshi, 1796–1854—
Criticism and interpretation.   I. Title.

PR149.G54K75 2007
820.9'3552—DC22

                                                                                2007000289

♾ Columbia University Press books are printed on permanent and durable acid-free paper.
This book is printed on paper with recycled content.

Printed in the United States of America

c 10 9 8 7 6 5 4 3 2 1

BOOK + JACKET DESIGN BY VIN DANG

CONTENTS

ACKNOWLEDGMENTS

This book could not have been written without the help of many friends and colleagues. I am grateful to John Archer, Rita Barnard, Stuart Curran, Janadas Devan, James English, Christopher GoGwilt, Geraldine Heng, Jean Howard, Andreas Huyssen, Sharaad Kuttan, Lee Weng Choy, Betty Joseph, Ania Loomba, Sumit Mandal, Karuna Mantena, John Mowitt, Pascale Montadert, Dorothea von Mücke, Aamir Mufti, Rob Nixon, John Richetti, Susan Stewart, Tim Watson, Chi-ming Yang, and Deborah White. I am indebted to Gayatri Chakravorty Spivak's teaching. Gauri Viswanathan provided intellectual guidance and support. Early on, Milind Wakankar, Sunil Agnani, Sanjay Reddy, and Chenxi Tang impressed me with how much I needed to learn. Conversations with Qadri Ismail kept me going as I wrote the book. Throughout the process, Colleen Lye was skeptical and supportive in the best way possible. Siraj Ahmed was the ideal reader. Suvir Kaul's extraordinary generosity and insight were of great help in the final stages of writing. Jennifer Crewe and Michael Haskell at Columbia University Press shepherded the manuscript with great professionalism. Finally, to my constant companion and interlocutor, Teena Purohit, I owe much more than I can tell.

READING THE GLOBAL

INTRODUCTION:

HOW TO READ THE GLOBAL

I. READING MATTER

In this book I study "the global" as an instituted perspective, not as an empirical process. The term "global" describes a way of bringing into view the world as a single, unified entity, articulated in space and developing over (common) time. I show how the global as a frame and an operation constitutes or produces the region it claims merely to describe, taking as my point of departure a group of prose narratives composed during the rise and consolidation of the British Empire in Asia. Through an elaboration of this peculiar and powerful style of thematization as it is variously manifested in the work of four authors who engage with the "East Indies" from the late eighteenth to the twentieth centuries—Adam Smith, Thomas De Quincey, Abdullah bin Abdul Kadir Munshi, and Joseph Conrad—I advance an approach to the comparative study of cultures that is attentive to the claims of contextual unevenness and heterogeneity. Such an approach, I contend, may serve as the point of departure for a more complex and nuanced style of literary and historical analysis.

My argument challenges the ways in which the "global" has been uncritically assimilated, in the humanities and social sciences, to a transparent comprehension of the world. Inasmuch as scholars have failed to engage the historicity of this term, they tacitly perpetuate the naturalization of a frame that was elaborated as an instrument of modern imperial expansion. The problem is epistemic. As parts of the global, things and peoples are subjected to a form of representation in which they are laid before the comprehensive gaze of the trained viewer, but the figures, concepts, and schemata in which such description takes place are not considered a part of, or implicated by, the historical web that they thematize. The conceit of objective description—in which language is deployed as if it were a transparent vehicle of communication—underpins all proper descriptions of the world today.[1]

A central task for a literary or cultural analysis that seeks to understand globalization as a historical process is exploration of the formal struggles and textual strategies through which the global is instituted as a perspective. The eighteenth- and nineteenth-century texts I study here were produced in the context of modern European aggrandizement in Asia. Because the discursive template of the global plays out in these texts as a recoding or transvaluation of older ways of making sense of the world that took place over a period leading to the consolidation of British power worldwide, a reading of texts as they institute this perspective can also reveal the formal patterns and idioms through which this "correct" way of seeing lends itself to being displaced or recoded. This would require inculcating a practice of reading that puts the global in its place, as a part of the historical weave it seeks to thematize from afar. The value of this approach becomes apparent in the texts I study, whose descriptions and analyses are set to work *through* a suppression of marginalized or subaltern perspectives. To read is to show how the truth effects enacted in these texts are constitutively dependent upon these suppressed subject positions. By activating these marginal perspectives and reading them against the grain of the global, I provide examples of how cultural study can interrupt or reconstellate the frames through which the world is made available for thought and action.

In recent discussions of globalization, the adjective "global" is tacitly assumed to refer to an empirical process that takes place "out there" in the world.[2] The "global" in global history, for instance, indexes the disparate and complex ways in which the events and institutional configurations of a "real" and self-evidently given world can be transparently displayed or narrated. Debates on "globalization" have accordingly centered on disagreements between historians and social scientists over whether global history began with Western capitalist expansion of the sixteenth or eighteenth century, or if it refers to the uniquely "deterritorializing" power of finance capital and satellite technology of the late twentieth century.[3] In line with this empirical conception of "global," the term is also often used in a manner suggestive of normative ideals, as with "global community," which refers to a loose collectivity whose values and ethical ideals are (or should be) binding everywhere. In the febrile atmosphere generated by such discussions, the "global" has come to be equated with comprehensiveness: thus, "global history" is distinguished from "world history" by virtue of the fact that under the former rubric the world is grasped as a single entity, all its coordinates mappable onto a single grid. Such comprehensiveness, it is implied, is also the condition of truth or historical adequacy. Consider the words of C. A. Bayly:

> The concept of globalization—a progressive increase in the scale of social processes from a local or regional to a world level—became fashionable because a variety of disciplines came to realize that the study of the village, province, nation state or regional bloc of human communities was inadequate to capture causation even within the 'fragment'. Economists concluded that international flows of capital were becoming so massive that no single government could control them. Anthropologists realized that even small and apparently isolated communities were now directly linked to each other and to the wider society through television, the mobile telephone, the internet and population movements.[4]

The "global" in this description refers at once to a physical process and an objectively transparent method of understanding that process. What this conflation of process and description elides is the perspective from which such a formulation is produced.

Bayly says that his is a non-Eurocentric account of globalization that avoids the "rigid teleology" of world-systems theorists like Immanuel Wallerstein, "show[ing] that the [non-European] agents of archaic [i.e. proto-capitalist] globalization could become active forces in the expansion of the Euro-American-dominated world economy and even survive and transcend it" (Bayly, "Archaic," 48). By incorporating a "wider range of agents" in Asia and Africa—nearly all of whom turn out to be elite mercantile or metropolitan communities that grafted themselves onto colonial capitalist institutions—Bayly asserts that globalization can be conceived of as a hybrid form "cannibalized" by non-European agents.[5] His approach is to be admired for many reasons. Drawing on an extraordinary knowledge of the economic histories of modern Europe, Asia, and Africa, Bayly shows that "globalization" is not merely a phenomenon rooted in the technological breakthroughs of the twentieth century but is inextricably linked to the transformative institutional force of European global imperial expansion that began in the sixteenth. By extension, he also shows how the different regions of the world are historically linked through complex forms of cultural and economic exchange involving diverse peoples who shaped and were shaped by the historical processes in which they were implicated.

However, despite his assertion that "'globalization' is a heuristic device, not a description of linear social change," Bayly's account tacitly assumes that collective processes all over the world tend toward the historical condition broadly described as capitalist modernity. For all his desire to give full play to the plural constitution of world history, a rhetoric of "transition" to capitalism underpins his discourse. Practically speaking, Bayly's approach presupposes the existence of or tendency toward "globalization" in the sense used today. Without judgment it should be said that what Bayly describes, in the first passage quoted above, as an adequate methodological frame is in truth informed by a perspective that discerns a single and homogeneous tendency underpinning all economic practices in the modern era. It is within the confines of this unspoken set or direction that the diverse economies of the world are described as "cannibalized" by non-European agents.[6] Historical narrative and "agency" are produced within these prejudged terms. Bayly's work, like that of other "global" historians, raises the question of the unacknowledged perspective that informs the production of a narrative in which global capitalism is assumed to be the necessary telos of diverse forms of cultural and economic activity across time and space.

In contrast, I argue that the global describes a mode of thematization or a way of bringing the world into view. It does not point to the world as such but at the conditions and effects attendant upon institutionally validated modes of making legible within a single frame the diverse terrains and peoples of the world. A "global perspective" ought not simply be taken to mean that the world is grasped in its entirety but should alert the reader to the way in which the world is constituted—rendered visible and legible—through a particular style of perspectivizing that is as useful as it is dangerous. In the modern era, which was for the majority of the world's population defined by European forms of territorial and commercial imperialism, the global stands as the dominant perspective from which the world was produced for representation and control. As importantly, this perspective set the terms within which subjectivity and history came to be imagined. The institutionalization in imperialism of this powerful mode of thematizing the world has resulted in the naturalization of this perspective as "correct" seeing: with its naturalization the global ceases to be a perspective and is thought to give access to things in themselves. It is perhaps no exaggeration to say that this unexamined use of "global" informs every empirical study of globalization.

If the global names a historically produced way of seeing that generates "reality effects" with profound material consequences for people, the literary critic engages the means by which such a perspective, and the way it frames truth, is set up. The ability to constitute a global perspective, as the mid-nineteenth-century Malay-language writer Abdullah bin Abdul Kadir implied, was the minimal precondition of historical and political agency. This ability to *produce* fact, rather than the facts themselves, is what interests me. It bears repeating that whereas historians and social scientists generally consider such thematization to be a matter of correct analytic "tools," reading attends to the matter of representation. In my study of the global, therefore, language does not function simply as a medium through which information or meaning is communicated.

Two points follow from this. First, the univocal and unilinear character of the global as perspective is *part* of the web it thematizes; that is, the representational structures through which the world is objectively given for sight and everyday actions are irreducibly a part of the weave they purport to set before and describe. For this reason, it is crucial that any critical discussion of globalization foreground the texture in which historical or social scientific truth claims are produced. Later in the chapter I will elaborate this insight by way of Heidegger's important discussion of the *form* of representational intelligibility, what he calls the "world as picture."

Second, in order to cultivate the attitude that more than one outcome for history is possible or desirable, the global must be conceived not as an empirical process but as an instituted perspective. Practically speaking, this does not involve rejecting the empirical claims of social scientists or positing alternative truth claims. What it involves is an attention to how truth is produced in the dominant style, learning how to displace or unsettle its lines and rules of perception in order to activate other, less conformist ways of thinking about the world.[7] My textual engagement with the writings of Adam Smith, Thomas De Quincey, Abdullah bin Abdul Kadir, and Joseph Conrad is made possible by reading those elements in each text—and the sites invoked—as singular and interruptive engagements with the general discourse of history.

This introduction focuses on the recent historiography of empire and economic histories of globalization because such works illustrate most clearly the tacit and dominant presuppositions that students of literary and cultural studies take for granted.[8] Historians and social scientists most frankly display the epistemic reflexes assumed by many metropolitan literary and cultural critics.[9] This is not an accusation; Eurocentrism is less an ideologically motivated misrepresentation than the condition of knowledge production. It cannot be jettisoned at will. Conversely, because the univocal character of the global as perspective is itself an embedded historical form (not the disinterested, disembodied eye that it poses as in the discourse of social science), it is necessarily woven into—encompassed by—the texture it thematizes. The trick is to explore this prior configuration and to show how to loosen it through a reading of its formal conduct.

II. THE GLOBAL AND ANTI-EUROCENTRISM

I first want to go back to the discussion with which I began this chapter, in order to delineate more precisely the issue of perspective that goes unthematized in Bayly's comprehensive grasp of the world. The question of perspective in Bayly is intimately linked to his inattention to the fact that all such grasping takes place in language, which is not merely a medium of communication or a repository of information. In a more explicit reflection on the matter, Bruce Mazlish draws attention to this problem in his discussion of the "global" in globalization. He correctly notes that "words are not just what individuals say they mean; they have a historical nature":[10]

> Our "imaginings" must leap from world history to global history. In making the jump, a look at the etymology of the words, *world* and *globe*, is helpful. Words are not just what individuals say they mean; they have a historical nature. *World* comes from the Middle English for "human existence;" its central reference is to the earth, including everyone and everything on it. Worlds can also be imaginary, such as the "next world," meaning life after death, or they can designate a class of persons—the academic world, for instance. For many, the discovery of the New World marked the advent of world history. More recently, a first, second, and a third world have been discerned, demarcating different levels of development.
>
> Such usage ill accords with the term *global* (one cannot substitute New Globe for New World in 1492, or third globe for third world today). It occupies a different valence, deriving from the Latin, *globus*, the first definition of which is something spherical or rounded," like a "heavenly body." Only secondarily

does the dictionary offer the synonym earth. *Global* thus points in the direction of space; its sense permits the notion of standing outside our planet and seeing "Spaceship Earth." (Incidentally, earth is a misnomer for our planet: as is evident from outside space, our abode is more water than earth. This new perspective is one of the keys to global history.)[11]

This appears at first sight to signal a different approach from that adopted by Bayly, whose tacit equation of the global with comprehensiveness arguably results in a lack of attention to the epistemic issues involved in such a mode of thematization. However, despite Mazlish's acknowledgment of the constitutive role of "perspective," he, too, naturalizes the metropolitan perspective. Perspectives alien to his account of the global are either ignored or assimilated through an invocation of the endlessly co-optative power of modern technology ("1 billion people watched the first step on the moon on their television sets—and they can go from one end of the globe to the other in less than a day").[12] Satellites, computer linkages, the globalization of culture, "especially music" (in which Mazlish finds a notable example of "local" difference at work) are similarly invoked. Thus Mazlish's argument serves as an instance of the global as an absolutist perspective that effectively occludes or effaces viewpoints that cannot be made to cohere with its computations.[13]

Similarly, it should be noted that Mazlish's conceit of "standing outside" is hardly a perspective unique to people born in the age of satellite dishes and space travel. Mazlish is himself aware that the possibility of imagining the world as a globe has been available at least since the era of early modern cartography. We can therefore use the term "global" to describe a train of thinking that has, *mutatis mutandis*, been in operation long before the word "global" came into popular use. There are obvious if unacknowledged affinities between Mazlish's convocation of a value-free global history and the stadial theory of the Scottish Enlightenment, which I will come to in a moment:

> Hence, global history examines the processes that transcend the nation state framework (in the process, abandoning the centuries-old division between civilized and uncivilized, and ourselves and the "other"; "barbarians" that is, inferior peoples, no longer figure in global history, only momentarily less developed peoples).[14]

It would be trivial to label such assertions "Eurocentric," for the mode of perspectivizing suggested in the Mazlish passages resonates formally with the approach and attitude of a number of influential revisionist or anti-Eurocentric global histories recently published. Thus, notwithstanding the valuable critique of histories that assume Western exceptionalism in Andre Gunder Frank's *ReOrient: Global Economy in the Asian Age*, this work is informed by a conventional understanding of historical process. Crudely put, he criticizes European-centered narratives of progress so as to install "Asia" as the new hero in place of the old one. In Frank's account of globalization, the global economy did not begin in Europe; rather, European merchants were latecomers who tapped into an already existing "world system" centered on China and India. More significantly, he assimilates this center to the institutions peculiar to market economies of the present day. He thus evinces a strategy adopted by critics of Eurocentrism in the age of globalization:

> The implications of this book are that the "Rise" of East Asia need come as no surprise just because it does not fit into the Western scheme of things. This book suggests a rather different scheme of things instead, into which the contemporary and possible future events in East Asia, and maybe also elsewhere in Asia, can and do fit. This is a global economic development scheme of things, in which Asia, and especially East Asia, was already dominant and remained so until—in historical terms—very recently, that is, less than two centuries ago. Only then, for reasons to be explored below, did Asian economies lose their positions of predominance in the world economy, while that position came to be occupied by the West—apparently only temporarily.[15]

The substitution of historical protagonists only confirms how firmly its mode of evaluation remains in place. Drawing on the work of scholars like Frank, Robert Markley criticizes postcolonial studies for its obsessive ideological critiques of colonial domination. Not only do such efforts "reinforce myths of European . . . superiority," they cannot account for the centrality of a "Sinocentric world," the study of whose wealth, power, and advancement is the best way to prove that Europe was never really the power it claimed to be.[16] Like Frank, Markley believes that his discovery of China as the true center of global economic culture in the early modern era will dispel the distracting fixation, on the right and the left, with the myth of European exceptionalism:

> In Japan and China during the early modern era, something close to the inverse of common sense propositions seem to have been the case. As Claudia Schnur-

mann puts it, "compared to the Far East's progressive medicine, industry and *savoir vivre*, even the Dutch, although highly sophisticated from a European perspective, at best measured up to what today would be considered 'third world' inhabitants in Asian eyes." Behind this statement lies a complex history of the early modern world.[17]

Behind this statement lies an entrenched system of evaluation. Unlike Frank and Markley, R. Bin Wong's more circumspect *China Transformed: Historical Change and the Limits of European Experience* does not seek to dethrone Europe and place Asia at the center. Wong reveals instead the enunciative rules that organize his factual claims.[18] He assumes that human beings everywhere desire the material and socioeconomic arrangements found in the metropolitan centers of the North and South:

> While the world remains unevenly developed economically, it is generally agreed that the expansion of material wealth has been largely a positive development. Most criticisms of materialist excess and anxieties over ecological balances take for granted certain advantages of an industrialized economic system even as they lament and rail against features they find problematic or dangerous. General agreement about the direction of economic change and its basic advantages confirms that at least in this realm people across cultures associate quality of life with material security and abundance. The multiple dynamics of economic change since industrialization all point in a single direction of increased productivity and greater material wealth. This is a shared condition of modernity. The situation in politics is different.[19]

All history may not culminate in liberal democracy, but the pragmatist definition of economic "growth" holds sway as the end-all of human possibility. In the current world order, this definition of progress is tacitly endorsed as much by the elites of the "developing" South as the "developed" North.[20] It implicitly defines what qualifies as "global." In Bayly's as much as Wong's necessitarian view of historical development, there is an instance of "myth" in the sense described by Roland Barthes, precisely not in the received sense that it is false, but as the unthematized point of departure for the production of truth effects. Obscured are the perspectives of the majority of the world's population, who are excluded from the upward mobility that supposedly follows from "growth," but whose labor is required to sustain the truth effects produced by this framework of evaluation.

Within and without the university, it is now politic to dress the legiti-
mation of capitalist teleology in the rhetoric of anti-Eurocentrism. This is
an indication of the degree to which critiques of European exceptionalism
have been embraced by policymakers as well as the metropolitan intellectual
mainstream. In a famous World Bank Report entitled *The East Asian Miracle*, what used to be described in the colonial nineteenth century by the name
"East Indies" is given the empowering title of "East Asia," whose essentially
capitalist traits, it is suggested, precede the arrival of the Europeans:

> How much of East Asia's success is due to geography, common cultural charac-
> teristics, and historical accident? Certainly some—but definitely not all. Ready
> access to common sea lanes and relative geographical proximity are the most
> obvious shared characteristics of the successful Asian economies. East Asian
> economies have clearly benefited from the kind of informal economic linkages
> geographic proximity encourages, including trade and investment flows. For ex-
> ample, throughout Southeast Asia, ethnic Chinese drawing on a common cul-
> tural heritage have been active in trade and investments. Intraregional economic
> relationships date back many centuries to China's relation with the kingdoms
> that became Cambodia, Japan, Korea, Laos, Myanmar and Viet Nam.
>
> In South and Southeast Asia, Muslim traders sailed from India to Java,
> landing to trade at points in between, for several hundred years before the arrival
> of European ships. Thus tribute missions and traditional trade networks, rein-
> forced in the nineteenth and twentieth centuries by surges of emigration, have
> fostered elements of a common trading culture, including two lingua francas,
> Malay and Hokein [*sic*] Chinese, that remain important in the region today.
>
> In our own century, key Asian ports were integrated into the emerging world
> economic system as the result of European military and trade expansion.[21]

What is striking about this description is the fact that the description of
the Asian context involves something like an "Asia-centric" perspective that
tacitly supposes a transhistorical "East Asian" identity seamlessly secured by
geography and kinship networks even as it elides the role played by European imperialism and Cold War geopolitics—relegated to a single mention
of "European ships"—in the emergence of market societies in the region.[22]
The World Bank turns to its own uses the revisionist scholarship of anti-
Eurocentric world historians in order to make identitarian or culturalist
claims underpin an alternative narrative of the emergence of indigenous
capitalism. It suggests that indigenous trading networks and political institutions yielded a natural and unforced transition in the twentieth century,

when Asian ports were gradually "integrated" into the capitalist world economy. Whereas in an earlier era dominated by modernization theory, neoclassical economists might have used the language of "transition" or "takeoff" to describe Asian economic success, metaphors of a more empowering multiculturalism shine through in the World Bank's emphasis on autonomously derived progress.

Hence, unlike the bad past of modernization theory, where Asians had to be inducted into capitalist values and habits for their own good, in the happier era of neoliberal globalization, Asians are discovered to have always had a propensity for capitalism. In the new dispensation, the trope of transition relied on by social scientists is replaced by a concept-metaphor closer to metamorphosis: Asian cultural forms and indigenous structures are now taken as evidence that precapitalist networks could be easily integrated with the "world economic systems" of the twentieth century. The report's authors suggest that the integration of these economies has less to do with European colonial capitalism than with kinship, geography, and informal trading practices.

One can almost anticipate the templates in which histories will be written in view of the much anticipated "Asian Age" to come. Imperialism was not a prerequisite for modernization in *this* Asia because it was always already becoming capitalist of its own accord.[23] Hence a global vision is deployed to account for a euphoric vision of history in which formerly colonized subjects may feel empowered to narrate their "rise" in such revalued terms. Ironically but aptly enough, many accounts that presume Britain's imperial grandeur make a point of noting its lowly beginnings as a Roman colony. Gibbon's *Decline and Fall of the Roman Empire* and Conrad's *Heart of Darkness* are two works that come to mind. Future novelists and world historians based in Shanghai or Bangalore may well learn to lace their account of Asia's unique greatness with correspondingly edifying allusions to their own humble past.

III. TROUBLING PERSPECTIVE

Given that the "Asian Century" is apparently set to rival, if not unseat, Western world-historical dominance, and in particular the "American Century," it would help to focus on the global (as) perspective not simply as a tool of European imperialism but as it enacts a powerful style of representation that can be reproduced in ever-changing ways in diverse places. The usurpation of Euro-American dominance by "Asia" may not be cause for celebration if, with the appearance of new historical protagonists, given modes of thematizing and representing the world remain in place. This should be kept in view even as one learns from counter-hegemonic efforts to uncover "agency" or "resistance" to political and economic domination, on the one hand, or to celebrate alternative centers or "modernities," on the other. Similarly, the critical proliferation of "hybrid" agents and "local" sites of contestation, with their "intersecting histories" and "discrepant detours and returns," must engage the perspectivization within whose frame historical meaning and political agency are conditioned.[24] For the formerly colonized subject as much as the colonizer, the proper or adequate analysis of the world is without ideological content: it is an indispensable way of seeing that has to be learned and practiced as a matter of course. And in the case of more recent historical scholarship, perspectival stability appears to hold in place what would otherwise seem an ideologically disparate group of thinkers. It is worth reflecting on how this mode of thematization "holds" across such differences of historical and ideological assignment.

In an essay entitled "The Age of the World Picture," Martin Heidegger examines the unthematized but operative presuppositions in all acts of modern knowledge production.[25] What interests Heidegger is the prior move or operation through which individuals come to naturalize their representations of the world and are trained to conflate how they see with what is "out there." No age in history, least of all that epoch beginning in the sixteenth century, is exempt from this rule. Heidegger argues that "procedure" in scientific research

> does not just mean methodology, how things are done. For every procedure requires, in advance, an open region within which it operates. But precisely the opening up of such a region constitutes the fundamental occurrence in research. This is accomplished through the projection, in which some region of (for example) natural beings, of a ground plan (*Grundriss*) of natural processes. Such a projection maps out in advance the way in which the procedure of knowing is to bind itself to the region that is opened up. This commitment [*Bindung*] is the rigor of research.
>
> ("Age," 59; "Die Zeit," 71)

In the representational form underpinned by such calculation, the world is defined in advance as the "always-already-known." Truth appears as an effect of this framing. Heidegger argues that the region to be known is, as it were, rendered visible in the terms made available or "given" by this prior comprehension, which is a kind of template or ground plan (*Grun-driss*): "Every natural event must be viewed in such a way that it fits into this ground-plan of nature. Only within the perspective [*Gesichtskreis*] of this ground-plan does a natural event become visible [*sichtbar*] as such. The ground-plan of nature is secured in place in that physical research, in each step of investigation, is obligated [*bindet*] to it in advance" (60).

Although these involved or embedded conditions presuppose and make possible all description, objective description requires that such conditions be dissimulated. This dissimulation is then taken for the condition of correct or adequate representation, that is, an objective representation that transcends the contingencies attendant upon any embodied perspective. Thus the power of the global derives from the fundamental conceit that it transcends perspective. Heidegger notes that modern representation is informed by a peculiar version of this metaphysics, in which the world is grasped as a picture, that is, as something set before or against the observer. The capacity to represent (in this manner) is what defines the subject of history:

> In distinction from the Greek apprehension, modern representing, whose sig-nification is first expressed by the word *repraesentatio*, means something quite different. Representation [*Vor-stellen*] here means: to bring the present-at-hand before one as something standing over-and-against, to relate it to oneself, the representer, and in this relation to force it back on oneself as the norm-giving domain [*das Vorhandene als ein Entgegenstehendes vor sich bringen, auf sich, den Vorstellenden zu, beziehen und in diesen Bezug zu sich als den maßgebenden Bereich zurückzwingen*]. Where this happens man "puts himself in the picture" concern-ing beings. When, however, in this way, he does this, he places himself in the scene; in, that is, the sphere of what is generally and publicly represented. And what goes along with this is that man sets himself forth as the scene in which, henceforth, beings must set-themselves-before, present themselves—be, that is to say, in the picture. Man becomes the representative [*Repräsentant*] of beings in the sense of the objective.
>
> ("Age," 69; "Die Zeit," 84).

Heidegger shows how objects have to appear in order to qualify for his-torical and scientific truth (and falsehood). In thus becoming the subject of history, man also becomes subject to a particular mode of making the world available. The discourse on globalization remains operated by this modal-ity of representation as truth, which is a general condition of knowledge production.

Rather than pretend that it is possible or desirable to reject this mode of seeing and saying, I argue that it can be turned around and put to different imaginative use by means of an encounter with literary reading. It is possible in this way to make the global respond to perspectives that are suppressed or invalidated by its overt claims but activated through its matter of representation. Reading helps cultivate reflexes or habits of thought and action that resist the conformism reinforced through the representational strategies employed in institutions of knowledge production and the popular media today. A textured reading shows how global analyses and narratives are situated by a broader weave of difference that is caught or implicated by that other in ways not comprehended by the mastery affected by the global perspective.

A modest task that literary or cultural study in the era of globalization can set itself is to cultivate critical reflexes that actively interrupt the global perspective. Such "resistance" aims to enrich the global through the repeated interruption of its frame. Given that as modern subjects we are "hardwired" to equate comprehension with success and interruption with failure, the beginnings of change to our critical reflexes may come by learning how *not* to see in the preceding sentence a contradiction or a paradox. Far from being a rejection of the global, this approach must be thought of as its interruptive embrace.

From writers of the eighteenth century come some of the most explicit and sophisticated discussions of the world comprehended as a single, interconnected entity developing over time, that is to say, as an effect of the global as perspective. In part the consequence of the sudden acquisition by Britain of a polyglot territorial empire in Asia, Africa, and the Americas, the global served writers such as Adam Smith as a way of making heterogeneous spaces and nonwhite subjects "legible." I quote a famous description of the world as an effect of this instituted perspective, capable of simultaneously surveying the past and the future: "The discovery of America, and that of the passage to the East Indies by the Cape of Good Hope, are the two greatest and most important events recorded in the history of mankind."[26] Drawn from Smith's *Wealth of Nations*, these words are produced in the political context of imperial rivalry between the British and the French in Asia. In this light,

Smith recalls an earlier phase of imperialism through the two discoveries, belonging to the Spanish and the Portuguese, respectively. For all the writers that follow in Smith's wake in this book—De Quincey, Abdullah Munshi, and Conrad—it is tacitly supposed that the narrative of Western capitalist expansion is coterminous with history *as such*. The word "discovery" in the Smith quotation is used in a manner that presupposes that frame and operation. Given this discursive restriction, neither the Amerindians nor the Arabs can be regarded as agents of "discovery." Discovery is implicitly cast in Smith's text as an exclusive feature of early modern European journeys of trade and exploration, not least because they are part of a narrative that links them to the mercantilist system, which characterizes the British colonial system whose reform is key to Smith's vision. Made to appear as an effect of this frame, it is difficult to see how the Arabs, Indians, or native peoples of the archipelago—despite their ubiquitous presence in the trading world of an "Asia before Europe"—can be read as historical agents. It is noteworthy that in Smith's narrative, only the Portuguese and Spanish are cast as precursors of the British empire, never the Chinese or the Mughals, despite their power and opulence.[27] Smith informs us of the material preconditions of the global imagination when he implies that it is genealogically derived from the legacy of Portuguese and Spanish imperialism in the early modern era.

Whether or not British imperialism is like that of the Spanish in its ideological makeup and policies, the perspective organizing Smith's conception of the global, the frame or code through which the world comes into view, is indebted to the material and discursive possibilities set in motion by these European conquests. The global is an effect of empire of a particular kind (the Mughals and the Chinese had empires, but they are not global in that their conquests or expeditions cannot be assimilated to capitalist development). The claim to speak for the global or to see the global implications of any thing is intimately linked to the perspective, its code and rules, of the imperial metropolitan West. It is in this sense that the global as manifested in Smith's text is the mobilization of a perspective and an operation produced within a particular history of economic and military expansion. Conversely, the knowledge that America was populated before the arrival of the Spanish or that the Portuguese were latecomers to the complex trading networks in Asia is of little consequence to a competent reading of the *Wealth of Nations*. These other perspectives cannot be discursively validated as "discoveries."[28] The global therefore is not just a peculiar mode of thematization: it is aligned to a conception of historical development unique to European colonial capitalism.

In the chapters that follow I draw upon Smith's *Wealth of Nations* as an inaugural text, a framework that at once exemplifies and highlights the mode of thematization common not only to the colonial and the postcolonial periods but also the age of "globalization" as it has latterly been constituted. Smith's masterwork executes an imaginative and perspectival shift through which the different parts of the world could be effectively articulated as a "system" that progresses through time as a single entity. Partly as a consequence of Smith's influential enframing, nineteenth-century discussions of free trade were typically cast as a moral obligation of empire or, in Thomas De Quincey's phrase, as Britain's "gift" to the world. In short, Smith does not merely offer a new interpretation of history: he inducts the reader into a comprehensive epistemological and ethical framework. For the English and Malay writers I study, he is the precursor who laid down the attitudes, styles of argumentation, and imaginative lines that shaped their seeing and thinking as an effect of which the global was produced and productively (mis)taken as naming a self-evident object.

Who were the agents of the global as a mode of thematization and from where did the literary and historical narratives derive their conceptual and imaginative frame? A conventional narrative would point to the rise of a comparative method of social-scientific evaluation. This "train of thinking" developed after the mid-eighteenth century alongside the acquisition of a heterogeneous—nonwhite, non-Protestant, non-English-speaking—territorial empire in Asia, Africa, and the Americas, and it was only intensified with the loss of the white Protestant North American colonies at century's end.[29] This is an example from a modern historian's description of two influential figures from the eighteenth century:

> English readers at the end of the eighteenth century were being fed with new assessments of Asia in which the mysterious and the exotic were being pushed further back into poetry and pantomime sets. Elsewhere what contemporaries often called the Natural History of Man was triumphing. Marsden [author of the *History of Sumatra* (1783)], who hoped to make the study of man a 'science, like all the others' resting on 'a regular series of authenticated facts' was a representative Natural Historian of Man. John Millar of Glasgow was another. His obituary recorded that: 'He wondered at nothing.... Instead of gazing, therefore, with stupid amazement, on the singular and diversified appearance

of human manners and institutions, Mr. Millar taught his pupils to refer them all to one simple principle, and to consider them as necessary links in the great chain which connects civilized with barbarous society.' For Marsden, Millar and others like them, the Natural History of Man was essentially comparative. The peoples of the world were given places on a universal scale of human progress ranging from the savage to the polished. Scottish 'conjectural history', with its pattern of historical development through economically determined stages of society, was the most intellectually coherent of such scales.[30]

The juxtaposition of William Marsden, a brilliant scholar-official of the British East India Company stationed in Bencoolen (in southwestern Sumatra), with John Millar, a central figure of the Scottish Enlightenment, offers us a glimpse of the entanglements between knowledge production and imperialist agendas. The imperial conditions in which modern knowledge production often took shape are only part of the interest of this passage. What is of equal significance is the way it illustrates a comprehensive grasp of reality that shapes the very means by which the world is endowed, as it were, with substance and life and vitality. This way of grasping reality exceeds the historical moment of European imperialism; the global style of thematization is by no means a monopoly of the colonial scholars and officials who served as its conduit. A kind of "traveling theory," it becomes part of the equipage of elite nationalist and anticolonial discourses of different stripes in Asia.

It is instructive to note here that in Marshall's view the approach outlined in the passage quoted above is best likened to a creative or imaginative way of *producing* the world through a set of framing devices within which objective description, analysis, comparison, and evaluation might over time be refined into diverse social-scientific methods for the presencing of the object. In the course of the nineteenth and twentieth centuries, such descriptions would become less schematic and rigid, subtly incorporating self-critical modes by which descriptions could be refined: new "knowledge effects" would be created for more discriminating ages, not least because native elites who had once been objects of taxonomic science were now being incorporated as *subjects* of a new and powerful knowledge production.[31]

Within this new and fluid dispensation, I explore how this perspective informs and is played out in a group of diverse texts on the British "East Indies" (a geopolitical category referring to territories and commercial routes stretching from India, through the Malay Archipelago, to the ports of southern China). The authors I study write in the context of the world-wide European expansion of territory and trade. In this dispensation an older kind of racially and culturally homogenous empire in British North America collapses and a newer one is gradually rebuilt elsewhere around ideas of racial difference and universal "improvement." The literary texts I read assume the perspective of a global that is already attuned to this novel ideal of imperialism in Asia and Africa. In different ways, their writings reflect the new mechanisms, institutions, and practices by which the colonial territories were shaped as part of an ethical project of empire, most notably through the rhetoric of "free trade." In line with a broader agenda of enlightenment progress, their representations assume universal commensurability as a consequence of commodity production and exchange in different parts of the East Indies.[32]

The emergence of a global perspective coincides with a new kind of territorial and commercial empire in Asia and a new ideology of imperial governance based at once on greater formal state control and free trade. In this context, the Malay Archipelago was brought into discursive view by Adam Smith and others as a geopolitical and commercial zone defined by the sea route between the two great imperial prizes of Asia: India and China. Located midway between Calcutta and Canton, key ports of the Malay world were given this tacit valence by writers of this period. The Malay Archipelago has long been home to a diversity of social groups, among them indigenous peoples, Malays, Javanese, Bugis, Chinese, Indians, and Arabs, most, if not all, of which would be better described as "creolized" communities. But national entities such as Malaysia, Indonesia, Singapore, and Brunei, like the "Southeast Asia" of which these countries are currently deemed part, do not refer to natural or hygienically bounded objects but to the partitions produced in large part by the utilitarian demands of colonial geopolitics and knowledge production.[33] The truth effects produced through colonial pedagogy continue to play a fundamental role in shaping the material and institutional vocabularies within which the people have been and will be trained, in shifting and contingent ways, to imagine the nation and region.

At one level, then, the peripheral status of the Malay Archipelago in current discussions of globalization helps me to take my distance from the discussions in which "India" and "China" are taken to refer to self-evident and monolithic entities (I have already noted my unease with this tendency in revisionist global histories, but the same problem is pervasive among so-called Indian or Chinese scholars, revisionist or otherwise). At another level, the constructed character of the nations carved out of the Malay Archipelago by colonial powers in the aftermath of the Second World War, as well as persisting debates about the "identity" of the region as a whole, offers a way of problematizing the global. I begin with the assumption that knowledge production by officials in the archipelago served the needs of refining and expanding the conditions for colonial surplus extraction. From Smith and De Quincey to Abdullah and Conrad, this is the unacknowledged frame within which the Malay Archipelago in particular and Asia in general were rendered legible. In a variety of ways, each writer obliquely invokes the region as an object for the global imagination: free trade (in *The Wealth of Nations*); global civil society (in *The Confessions of an English Opium-Eater*); the perspectivizing "I" (in *Hikayat Abdullah*); and the autonomous ethical subject (in *Lord Jim*).

In chapter 1, I consider how Adam Smith's account of world history in the *Wealth of Nations* (1776) is crucially dependent upon a conceit: a model of material progress guided by nature. He claims, without empirical corroboration, that the natural human "propensity to truck, barter and exchange" the world over was cruelly undermined by the first age of European imperial plunder. Smith argues that it is the ethical obligation (and in the interest) of the British state to *restore* the world to this original path of improvement, which will culminate in a mutually profitable universalization of production and exchange for the market. Hence, he at once imagines and prescribes a future empire of free trade that will graft itself without violence or coercion onto the subsistence or nonmarket economies of the world, thereby serving as a mere catalyst in a natural process of "improvement." In Smith's ethically informed vision, empire is at once a servant of and supplement to nature. However, I argue that a discourse of "subsistence" arises in the *Wealth of Nations* to subvert the necessitarian and homogenizing arguments made by Smith on behalf of free trade.

Whereas Smith writes at a time of imperial crisis marked by the prospective loss of the American colonies, Thomas De Quincey's imagination is fired by the vision of a globe being transformed in the triumphal wake of the Napoleonic Wars. Britain's victory over France in 1815 guaranteed the security of its Asian empire in India, and the policy aimed at securing the trade route to China also led to intensified British involvement in the Malay Archipelago, culminating in the founding of Singapore (1819) and the partition of the region into imperial spheres of influence as a consequence of the Anglo-Dutch Treaty of 1824. It is against this volatile context of imperial finance and geopolitics that I explore the significance of opium in De Quincey's *Confessions of an English Opium-Eater* (1821), a commodity grown by the British in Bengal and transshipped to the Malay ports for sale in other parts of the archipelago as well as in China. I show how the dual function of opium as commodity and opium as drug in the *Confessions* has a powerfully disorienting effect on the nature of imperial relations. De Quincey offers a strange parallel between the regenerative powers of opium (as narcotic) for the artist and the analogous role played by opium (as commodity) in revitalizing a British economy undermined by an alarming loss of silver bullion to pay for Chinese tea imports. However, the distortions induced by opium as narcotic in De Quincey's narration result in a nightmarish vision of the East Indies through the figure of the Malay who visits De Quincey in 1816. Through a dramatization of how global commodity production and exchange are given different forms of value, the Malay is imagined as a subject whose presence enables a revaluation of the standpoint De Quincey advocates.

From Smith and De Quincey's metropolitan perspectives I turn in the third chapter to an account written in mid-nineteenth century Singapore of the arrival and expansion of the British presence in Southeast Asia. Abdullah bin Abdul Kadir's *Hikayat Abdullah* (1849) and *Kesah Pelayaran Abdullah* (1838) are widely regarded as pioneering works of modern Malay literature. A child of the Tamil-Arab trading community of Malacca, Abdullah tells us that he sees the spread of commodity production and exchange as the key to bringing the virtues of civilization and progress to the colonies. In contradistinction to conventional readings, which invariably find in Abdullah's realistic style a "modern" figure,[34] I read Abdullah's works as attempts to engage with the frame by which they are produced in the colonial archive. Abdullah's autobiographical writings are attempts to induct his readers into representing the world correctly, that is, from a global perspective. It is in this process that Abdullah tries to project a writerly subjectivity based upon a novel conception of an autobiographical "I" (*saya*) commensurate with the subject of European civil society. But his account repeatedly finds itself displaced by the claims of the polyglot, culturally and historically diverse context from which some of his own idioms and perceptions derive. It is in this sympathetic description of an encounter with imperial culture that Abdullah discovers in the global a distinct vector by which the native community can be imagined differently. In its rich evocation of a precolonial trading network of Arabs,

Tamils, Chinese, Jews, Malays, and indigenous peoples, *Hikayat Abdullah*'s sympathetic vision of a "modernizing" and global imperial market system is acted upon by that which it thematizes and intends to improve.

In chapter 4 I elaborate a different way of reading individual subjectivity and historical change in the colonial capitalist context of Joseph Conrad's *Lord Jim* (1900). This continues a theme elaborated by Abdullah in his autobiographical narrative: the individualized subject is made the locus of ethical responsibility and historical possibility, as he or she is distinguished from a community overcome first by a representational structure that is rarely thematized. Whereas chapters 1 and 2 focus on the role of market production and exchange as the condition of subjective and perspectival transformation, in chapters 3 and 4 I explore this broader representational form as it takes place through the figure of the individual moral and historical subject shaped by this great transformation. Starting with an elaboration of the relationship that the narrator, Marlow, draws between subjective interiority and historical progress, I demonstrate that Marlow's conception of ethical responsibility is ironically premised on a failure to view the Malays as moral agents. Reading against the grain, I juxtapose Jim with native figures (Malay steersmen on the *Patna* and the polyglot immigrant communities of Patusan) that are likened to animals in their incapacity for autonomous reflection and for progressive temporal development. I link this problem of subjectivity to the question of world-historical progress as it articulates Marlow's attempt to contrast the world of Malay-Muslim pilgrims and immigrants to the European world. Turning around the unsympathetic metropolitan perspective Marlow brings to bear upon the native world, I show how Jim's metropolis-trained mindset undergoes a powerful transformation through his encounter with these diverse groups.

In the argument that runs through the whole book, the representational shifts charted from Smith to Conrad can be summed up as the consolidation of what Heidegger calls the "world-as-picture." The representational structure or template for historical narrativization that Smith uses to revalue empire becomes, by Conrad's day, the naturalized frame for the manifestation of reality. I would go as far as to say that this mode of thematization remains securely in place today. But even as the authors of these texts ostensibly aim to shore up the global perspective, I am interested in the way these texts teach us to activate radically heterogeneous movements that enable other ways of imagining this history.

My style of reading in each chapter may be described by way of the concept of "defamiliarization," a translation of the Russian *ostranenie*, that Viktor Shklovsky used to demonstrate that a key trait of literary language is its ability to make strange: the literary use or activation of language breaks with or interrupts the naturalization of everyday actions and perspectives into which we are otherwise conditioned.[35] The term can also be used to demonstrate that attention to the texture of linguistic and other cultural media is not an impediment to but the condition of contextual interpretation. When Shklovsky's insights are applied to the way in which the naturalization of the global perspective effaces the texture of the reality it purports to describe, it is possible to see how it is through a defamiliarization or interruption of this perspective that the global comes to find a richer and more complex character.[36] In the context of colonial capitalism, as much as that of neocolonial globalization, to engage the uneven uses of a word or turn of phrase *in all its aspects* is an invitation to imagine how the effaced subaltern perspectives of the non-European world stand in for subjects who are capable of deploying these terms in distinct ways.[37] This happens where a term or a phrase describing the non-European object is activated in ways that are not immediately translatable into the value-added vocabulary of historical truth as defined by the global as perspective.

By way of a defamiliarizing engagement that elaborates and unsettles this perspective, other textual effects and historical possibilities allow themselves to be brought into view and seen with different eyes. Here I am drawing on Gayatri Spivak's interruption of this normalized or naturalized perspective by deploying what she deliberately calls a "mistaken" reading. She posits as reader a subject position that is not available for archival recuperation:

> Such a reading is of course also "mistaken" because it attempts to engage the (im)possible perspective of the native informant, a figure who, in ethnography, can only provide data, to be interpreted by the knowing subject for reading. Indeed, there *can* be no correct scholarly attempts to transform into a reading-position the site of the "native informant" in anthropology, a site that can only *be* read, by definition, for the production of definitive descriptions. It is an (im)possible perspective.[38]

Spivak calls her reading "mistaken" because it seeks to figure forth—without claiming to retrieve as facts—perspectives "foreclosed" by the rules of seeing and saying instituted in dominant texts. Such perspectives cannot be resolved into the language of historical representation because her reading of the figure tries to activate them as readers or agents, rather than merely providers of "data" for the social scientist or literary critic. Arguably for Spivak, such figures are the ultimate judges of the style of representation in which they have been systemically effaced.[39] Her attempt to imagine the "native informant"—a position necessarily foreclosed by the seeing which she too must assume as the condition of knowledge—as reader puts into practice an "(im)possible perspective," in which the effaced perspective is re-imagined as possessed by an interruptive agency. Yet it is the maneuver through which Spivak can supplement, or interrupt, the "world-as-picture" that, Heidegger notes, frames the way in which the world is made visible and legible for knowledge production.

Spivak's enactment of the impossible "perspective" of the native informant inflects my reading of Heidegger's elaboration of "perspective" in "Age of the World Picture." If Heidegger is concerned to draw out how the world is brought into view, Spivak's strategy of reading aims at opening up such instituted modes of truth production to the claims of difference by way of interruption. My use of "perspective" obviously draws on the different uses to which these two thinkers put this word. The point is to look at the artwork as not simply representing the real but as producing the given frame in or through which the real is "given." If Heidegger provides a way to understand the lineaments of that (by now) naturalized sight, Spivak suggests strategies for its displacement or revaluation by way of an engagement with the terms of its setting up, its "texture," to use a phrase introduced, after all, by the formalists. Read with and against each other, they suggest a task for literary or cultural criticism in a globalizing age: to learn how to loosen and reconstellate the rules by which the world is correctly brought into view.

1

ADAM SMITH AND THE

CLAIMS OF SUBSISTENCE

I. INTRODUCTION

The serenely ironic tone of Adam Smith's *Wealth of Nations* (1776) is belied
by the climate of anxiety over the future of the British empire in which the
work was composed. Smith's ambivalent analysis of the imminent revolt in
the North American colonies (whose eleventh hour incorporation delayed
the work's publication) and his scathing references to the failures of the
British East India Company in the newly conquered Indian territories indicate that he wanted to show how Britain's fledgling territorial empire might
be reformed with distinctly more hopeful ends in view. Unlike twenty-first-
century readers, Smith's contemporaries did not have to be informed that
his account of the causes of the wealth of some nations and the poverty of
others unfolds in the context of financial instability at home, territorial expansion in Asia, military rivalry in Europe, and political unrest in America.[1]
After all, the *Wealth of Nations* was composed in the aftermath of the Seven
Years War, in the context of a suddenly rapid acquisition of heterogeneous
colonies around the world.[2] As a corollary to this sense of uneasy victory,
recent military triumphs in Asia and America seemed to set in motion an
imperial logic that took on an alarming (if bizarrely comic) life of its own
as Britain responded fitfully to the geopolitical imperatives of a territorial
empire on the rise. In the words of one historian:

The very nature of strategic planning created a snowballing process of expansion: to be safe in the valley the overlooking hill must be controlled, to be secure on the hill the next valley must be taken, and so on. As prime minister Lord Salisbury observed, 'the constant study of maps is apt to disturb men's reasoning powers', and he more than once complained that his naval and military advisers would have liked to 'annex the moon in order to prevent its being appropriated by the planet Mars'.[3]

Imperial historians have noted that the British East India Company's conquest of Bengal and Bihar in the 1760s led to a period of prolonged territorial expansion within the subcontinent. Beyond the subcontinent, a much wider set of geopolitical concerns emerged. In order to preempt the resurgence of French ambitions (which was considered a threat until 1815), the British urgently sought a naval base to protect the southern coasts of India. As a result of spiraling administrative and military costs, this project in turn expanded into a regional quest for a transshipment port to secure the vital trade route between India and China. And because the shortest way between these two great prizes of the imperial imaginary was via the Straits of Melaka, it became clear by the 1780s that such a port would have to be located in the Malay Archipelago. This strategic thinking is implicit in Smith's description of how the demand for Chinese tea had to be paid for with revenue from the Indian colonies. In any event, the safe passage from Calcutta to Canton could only be made secure by means of Britain's imperial presence in the Malay-speaking world:

> The East India trade of all these [European] nations . . . has been almost continually augmenting. The increasing consumption of East India goods in Europe is, it seems, so great, as to afford a gradual increase of employment to them all. Tea, for example, was a drug very little used in Europe before the middle of the last century. At present the value of the tea annually imported by the English East India Company, for the use of their own countrymen, amount to more than a million and a half a year; and even this is not enough . . . the consumption of the porcelain of China, of the spiceries of the Moluccas, of the piece goods of Bengal, and of innumerable other articles, has increased very nearly in a like proportion.
>
> (*Wealth of Nations*, 1.11.g.27)

In the context of a political crisis, *The Wealth of Nations* powerfully reimagines British imperialism as an ethical institution whose purpose is to enable its colonized subjects to freely partake in their material improvement through free production and exchange worldwide. It is in response to a failure of imperial institutions—most spectacularly described by the threatened loss of the American colonies—that Smith draws upon the rhetoric of "free trade" to configure the world as a single, interconnected, and unified entity, developing in common space and time, that is, as *global*.[4] A style of activating and constituting relations between different parts of the world, the global emerges as a self-conscious response to two distinct but related historical events, the loss of Britain's colonies of settlement in America and the acquisition of colonies of trade in Asia.

The global perspective turns on Asia and it is articulated at the temporal cusp of what imperial historians refer to as the First and Second British Empires.[5] The global is at once a reaction to a crisis in America and a call for a new and more hopeful imperial beginning in Asia. Smith's narrative of global free trade takes place against the backdrop of the emergence of Britain's territorial empire in India. Smith's global perspective therefore takes as its empirical condition of possibility the fact that this region is brought under British control. The Malay Archipelago is not the object of his analysis but is instead the condition for narrative objectification. As his arguments in *The Wealth of Nations* reveal, Smith's formal vision of the global presupposes the necessity of making the secure Malay Archipelago the linchpin around which Asia can then be imagined or produced as part of a novel vision of empire founded upon free trade. For although the Malay Archipelago does not qualify for extended analysis in Smith's discussion of the global, it makes possible the elaboration of a global perspective coincident with the gains in India, on the one hand, and the threatened loss of America, on the other. Smith's narrative presupposes the historical conditions whose institution it urges.

The Wealth of Nations is a text of imperial reform. Smith produces the global as the perspective that realizes the project of a good and just imperialism. He implies that this perspective cannot be put into effect or serve as the frame through which the world is comprehended as long as exclusive trading companies like the British East India Company exacerbate the crisis of imperial governance around the world through their selfish and cruel policies. These exclusive companies were in the process of destroying the British Empire they claimed to serve, not least because under the merchants the

British Empire had come to be synonymous with thoughtlessly cruel and rapacious imperial rule. The natural basis of free and consensual exchange between diverse peoples of the world could not take place in this historical context. In Smith's view, these exclusive companies had to be dismantled.

In keeping with his aim to make empire an instrument of justice and improvement, Smith's fundamental response is to delineate the global as a way of perspectivizing, as a representational style and form in which the disparate parts of the world and its diverse and heterogeneous peoples and actions are comprehended as a single, bounded, unified, and interconnected entity developing in common time. The global does not refer to an empirical thing or process; it is the frame in which empirical facts are made to appear and are given their particular and contextual assignments. Smith deploys anecdotes, perspectival shifts, historical comparisons, and commensurating mechanisms in order to create this effect of reality. He shifts the terms of historical narrative and evaluation by rejecting out of hand the view that the world is made up of competing individual nations or self-contained entities that can grow rich only at the expense of others. He argues that if the world is viewed globally, that is, as a single interconnected entity, history becomes synonymous with universal progress. Smith thereby turns his critique of the cruelty and greed of monopolistic trading companies into a novel vision of progress. His aim is less to write history than to frame the interpretive and analytic protocols in which all future histories will be written. The *Wealth of Nations* is a revolutionary text in that it does not merely provide another interpretation of the situation it describes: it seeks to change the very terrain on which description and evaluation take place.

II. THE GLOBAL AS PERSPECTIVE

Smith's articulation of a global perspective produces as its object an Asia defined by a free commercial exchange that is built on the overthrow of mercantile imperialism. Although much commentary has traditionally assumed that the American "troubles" constitute the entirety of the colonial question in the *Wealth of Nations*,[6] I argue that Smith elaborates a vision of a different and novel kind of empire by configuring Asia as its expressive locus. A conjunction is suggested in Smith's narrative between the mode of seeing—what I am calling the global as perspective—and the actual objects thematized for the purposes of a reformed imperial project. It is within this configuration or "picture" (see the introduction) that the Malay Archipelago is made available as an object for representation.

Smith's position aggressively distinguishes itself from the putatively hegemonic claims of the mercantilists. But even as he excoriates the exclusive trading companies like the East India Company for their excesses in Bengal and the Malay Archipelago, he ruefully surveys that region with an eye to the profits that a proper system of imperial rule might have secured. He remarks that although British dominion in the "East Indies"—the name for a geopolitical imaginary stretching from India, through the Malay Archipelago, to China—ought to have led to a trade more profitable than that from America, that did not happen because of the corruption that results from monopoly. Smith is equally attuned to the economic potential of diverse non-European sites: he creates a hierarchy by placing China and India on a different scale of civilization than Mexico and Peru. This mode of thematization is prelude to his claim that the imperial project be at once reformed and intensified. What comes through is a surveying eye that speaks in the language of an imperial order it nonetheless criticizes:

> The discovery of a passage to the East Indies by the Cape of Good Hope, which happened much about the same time, opened perhaps a still more extensive range to foreign commerce than even that of America, notwithstanding the greater distance. There were but two nations in America in any respect superior to savages, and these were destroyed almost as soon as discovered. The rest were mere savages. But the empires of China, Indostan, Japan, as well as several others in the East Indies, without having richer mines of gold or silver, were in every other respect much richer, better cultivated, and more advanced in all arts and manufactures than either Mexico or Peru. . . . But rich and civilized nations can always exchange to a much greater value with one another than with savages and barbarians. Europe, however, has hitherto derived much less advantage from its commerce with the East Indies than from that with America. The Portuguese monopolized the East India trade to themselves for about a century, and it was only indirectly and through them that the other nations of Europe could either send out or receive any goods from that country. When the Dutch, in the beginning of the last century, began to encroach upon them, they vested their whole East India commerce in an exclusive company.
>
> (4.1.33)

Smith's tone is harsher elsewhere: "Of all the expedients that can well be contrived to stunt the natural growth of a new colony, that of an exclusive company is undoubtedly the most effectual" (4.7.b.22). He polemicizes against and produces a caricature of the so-called mercantilists, whose destructive policies are informed by the naïve belief that wealth is found, not created.[7]

Smith at once argues against the current political establishment and sees in it the opportunity for a revitalized and just empire. His perspective is filled out with an account that justifies replacing the bad imperialism of the commercial system with the good imperialism of a British government that will enforce contracts and guarantee individual security so that free production and trade can thrive between Britain and her colonies. He argues that not only is reform in India morally imperative, it is also conducive to increased revenue for Britain (5.3.91). In this connection, he draws attention to some fundamental differences between America and India:

> Though the Europeans possess many considerable settlements both upon the coast of Africa and in the East Indies, they have not yet established in either of those countries such numerous and thriving colonies as those in the islands and continent of America.... In Africa and the East Indies, therefore, it was more difficult [than in America] to displace the natives, and to extend the European plantations over the greater part of the lands of the original inhabitants.
>
> (4.7.c.100)

Notwithstanding the enormous utility of the Indian territories, no colony of settlement is possible there because of its large indigenous population. In view of the possibilities opening up in the Indian territories and related opportunities held out by the China trade, Smith balances his evaluation of new settlements in Asia with an exploration of well-positioned ports from which the British government might oversee the induction of natives into production and exchange for the market.

Smith's gaze comes to rest on the two Dutch fortified settlements of the Cape of Good Hope and Batavia (Jakarta). And in view of Britain's troubled circumstances in India, as well as the obvious importance of the China trade, he is in all likelihood alerting his readers, state officials as much as private citizens, to the necessity of dislodging the Dutch from Batavia and the Cape of Good Hope if the British are to consolidate their precarious gains on the Indian subcontinent. Let us recall that the elaboration of Smith's vision of the global, and the vision of a reformed empire committed to promoting free trade, is dependent upon the securing of the Malay Archipelago inasmuch as it defines the India-China sea route:

The Dutch settlements at the Cape of Good Hope and at Batavia are at present the most considerable colonies which the Europeans have established either in Africa or in the East Indies, and both these settlements are peculiarly fortunate in their situation. The Cape of Good Hope was inhabited by a race of people almost as barbarous and quite as incapable of defending themselves as the natives of America. It is besides the half-way house, if one may say so, between Europe and the East Indies, at which almost every European ship makes some stay, both in going and returning. The supplying of those ships with every sort of fresh provisions, with fruit and sometimes with wine, affords alone a very extensive market for the surplus produce of the colonists.

(4.7.c.100)

The reader is here introduced to the formal operation of the global perspective as it is irreducibly linked to the agendas of an imperialist power on the rise. Smith's description of the strategic and commercial value non-European ports is assimilated to this tacit dimension presupposed by knowledge production.

Smith writes with an obvious awareness of Britain's increased involvement in the East Indies and Britain's intensifying search throughout the 1770s and 1780s for a port in the Malay Archipelago.[8] By focusing on the importance of the ports of the Malay Archipelago to the India-China trade, he not only reveals the emerging centers of imperial interest but also provides a way to cognitively map and compare the geopolitical and commercial significance of far-flung spaces to one another by a measure not available in a prior imperial imaginary. If the merchants are to be replaced by the British state as overlords in India and elsewhere, the following perspective must be adopted before success can be contemplated:

What the Cape of Good Hope is between Europe and every part of the East Indies, Batavia is between the principal countries of the East Indies. It lies upon the most frequented road from Indostan to China and Japan, and is nearly about midway upon that road. Almost all the ships, too, that sail between Europe and China touch at Batavia; and it is, over and above all this, the centre and principal mart of what is called the country trade of the East Indies, not only of that part of it which is carried on by Europeans, but of that which is carried on by the native Indians; and vessels navigated by the inhabitants of China and Japan, of Tonquin, Malacca, Cochin-China, and the island of Celebes, are frequently to be seen in its port.

(4.7.c.100)

Nothing short of an epochal shift is signaled by these remarks. To anyone familiar with the momentous importance accorded the Cape of Good
Hope in *The Wealth of Nations* (4.1.33, 4.7.a.6, etc.),[9] the comparison with
Batavia indicates the linchpin role of the all but invisible Malay Archipelago to Smith's discussion of how Britain's gains in India and projected profits
through the China trade will be the means by which the British Empire will
make up for the likely loss of its American colonies.[10]

The historical site, "the East Indies," whose representations I study in this
book therefore appears in Smith's argument as part of a vision of imperial
reform that discursively prepares the way for an idea of trade that is global
and free. It inaugurates the vision of a second, and more hopeful, phase of
British ascendancy. The imperialism of the novel, cosmopolitan variety that
Smith subtly elaborates will, far from being coercive or rapacious, lay the
historical and institutional conditions for liberty and prosperity the world
over. And whereas the First British Empire was made possible by the round-
ing of the Cape of Good Hope and the discovery of America, the second
imperial epoch will, in Smith's view, be founded on territorial possessions
subordinated to the interests of a free trade centered on Britain's colonies
in Asia.[11] Smith argues that colonies should no longer be held for the sake
of maintaining monopolies (4.7.c.64). Rather, they should be taken out of
the control of the exclusive merchant companies and placed in the hands
of the British state, which will ensure their "proportionate" growth. Because
the revenues of the sovereign are drawn from that of the people, Smith argues,
it is vital that "an extensive market be opened for the produce of the [colony]"
and that there be "perfect freedom of commerce in order to increase as much
as possible the number and the competition of the buyers" (4.7.c.102). Modeling himself in part on the example of ancient Greek colonialism, Smith
believes that the newly gained Asian territories can be turned into trading
partners with imperial tutelage. After monopolies are abolished by the state,
a secondary role will devolve to the merchants as helpers in enhancing the
foreign commerce and natural development of the British colony:

> The settlements which different European nations have obtained in the East
> Indies, if they were taken from the exclusive companies from which they at
> present belong and placed under the immediate protection of the sovereign,
> would render this residence both safe and easy, at least to the merchants of the
> particular nations to whom those settlements belong.

> (4.7.c.99)

If empire has thus far been responsible for destroying free trade, the reform of empire will be responsible for its restoration. In Smith's text, the global is the setup within which the crisis of empire is posited and resolved through the institution of free trade, with Asia as its geopolitical referent.

The global is a mode of perspectivization, and free-trade imperialism is its institutional correlate. If, however, it is evident that Smith's style of seeing and saying has had a profound influence on metropolitan models of global progress, it is also worth noting that such univocal arguments have emerged as a result of a narrow focus on Smith's "message," at the expense of the rhetorical dimensions of his great work. This is the reason Smith has been cast as a market fundamentalist by neoclassical economists, whereas in the accounts of historians he appears as a disinterested thinker opposed on rational or ethical grounds to British imperialism.[12] I argue instead that even as Smith advocates the global as a universal template of representation, the formal conduct of his text creates divergent effects. It is in the rhetorical dimension that *The Wealth of Nations* indicates ways of imagining the global that are not determined solely by the very metropolitan agenda that exercised him so greatly. The reading I offer is unorthodox, but it is my belief that the sinuous and mixed historical forms through which Smith conceptualizes historical progress invites such a revaluation. In this way Smith's great text can also serve as a thoughtful challenge to the socially and ecologically destructive fundamentalisms that shape mainstream political and economic discourse in the metropolises of the North and South. To this end, my discussion does not seek to evaluate the argument of *The Wealth of Nations* in order to praise Smith as bearing no responsibility for the ideological excesses of global capitalism, or to accuse him of being its pioneering apologist. Rather, I attend to its texture to ask how it can teach us to redo the very mode of perspectivizing—as useful as it is dangerous—it has instituted. (This distinction is important; it also has "practical" uses.) This shift can only be demonstrated by working slowly through Smith's way of seeing and saying, at once respecting its movement and displacing or turning it in other directions.

Take Smith's need to establish an absolute moral distinction between his system of natural liberty and the old colonial system. To separate his vision of a just global order from the old colonial system, Smith searches for an alternative origin for his system of natural liberty, that is, an origin altogether uncontaminated by the legacy of the old colonial system. He makes this separation by claiming an extrahistorical origin for it. He appeals to the purity and goodness of "nature" to distinguish his system from the corruption of the old colonial system. Simply put, whereas mercantile imperialism is "historical," his system of natural liberty is "natural." Smith argues that, unlike the currently powerful forms of imperial rule, which have their origins in "human institutions," free trade has its origins in "natural inclinations" (3.3.1). The historically instituted merchant companies distorted the natural development of the savage societies they encountered around the world.

Smith makes this extrahistorical origin, and the narrative of a natural and good historical development it authorizes, the transcendent basis of the global perspective. By such means Smith excludes the worldwide ascendancy of the British East India Company from any claim to the global. The global is instead produced in the exclusive affinity between the system of natural liberty—on which free trade is based—and the nonmarket economies that are in Smith's day being pulled into the circuit of colonial capitalism. In a different context, Joseph Schumpeter archly notes a "judiciously diluted Rousseauism" in Smith.[13] Unlike Rousseau, Smith is not allergic to civil society or the concept of historical development. However, because he believes that nonmarket societies originally gave priority to subsistence, Smith declares them more natural *and therefore* governed by a spirit that is closer to the ideals of global "free trade" than any of the opulent civilizations of Europe. For this reason, in the movement of Smith's axiomatic conjoining of free trade with nature there is a conception of the global derived from values that are quite distinct from the pragmatic, policy-oriented argument by which Smith is generally engaged. These values are used to provide an absolute moral justification for a British Empire of free trade. This is seen in Smith's reliance on "subsistence" as an absolute good: "As subsistence is, in the nature of things, prior to conveniency and luxury, so the industry which procures the former, must necessarily be prior to that which ministers to the latter (3.1.2). The priority of nature over history is reflected by the priority, "in the nature of things," of subsistence over luxury. Whereas mercantile capitalism is unnatural because it promotes trade in long-distance, luxury goods that benefits the few at the expense of the many, Smith argues, the system of natural liberty is guided by the propriety and goodness of subsistence.[14] Subsistence is the transcendent standard by which Europe's historical development will be judged; it is the trace of nature in history. Hence the global is tacitly elaborated in Smith's account as a normative perspective that is justified by virtue of its adherence to nature.

His stated intention notwithstanding, my aim is to track Smith's analytic and rhetorical moves because I wish to show how his reliance on subsistence enables a divergent and reconstellative interpretation of the global. It allows us to turn the global from a synonym for comprehensive overview into a lens that focalizes different, if less familiar, ways of imagining the world. I do so by dislodging the vision of subsistence from the narrative of linear and univocal progress for which Smith tries to marshal it. Let us first consider how Smith turns the global perspective into a way of thematizing world history from its natural, idyllic origins to its present disastrous conditions under the baleful sway of the exclusive trading companies. Smith's attack shades into a sweeping historical account in which the merchants of his day are depicted as the inheritors of the commercial interest responsible for the distorted economic development of medieval Europe (book 3). On an equally grand scale, Smith posits an identity of interests between fifteenth-century figures like Columbus and the rapacious officials of the exclusive trading companies in control of eighteenth-century Bengal and Java (book 4).[15] It is not so much that Smith brooks no dissent as that he *sets up*, with the license of a masterful artist, the frame wherein dissent and assent are newly made available: a novel matrix of meanings and significations, new grounds of evaluation and justification are produced by this means. In this sense the mercantilist position is not rejected as much as given a formulaic charge within Smith's economy of meaning: its degeneracy is opposed with neat symmetry to his tale of wholesome human improvement.

This revaluation is most powerfully seen in the way the commercial interests are caricatured as forces that distort or thwart the natural course of history and human progress.[16] Whereas in their natural form markets are a benign manifestation of the inherent human "propensity to truck, barter, and exchange," historically they stand as a melancholy reminder of the genocide of the Amerindians, the enslavement of Africans and Asians, as well as the worldwide violent transformation of natural habitats and social practices to serve the greed of the commercial civilizations of modern Europe. Smith's global perspective ostentatiously dissociates itself from the forces associated with such institutionalized injustice.[17] These forces cannot by definition grasp the world as a unified and harmoniously interconnected entity. Speaking of the imperial record of his own nation, Smith claims that the British East India Company is responsible for the "want, famine and mortality" that beset the territories over which it rules:

> This perhaps is nearly the present state of Bengal, and of some other of the English settlements in the East Indies. In a fertile country which had before been much depopulated, where subsistence, consequently, should not be very difficult, and where, notwithstanding, three or four hundred thousand people die of hunger in one year, we may be assured that the funds destined for the maintenance of the labouring poor are fast decaying. The difference between the genius of the British constitution which protects and governs North America, and that of the mercantile company which oppresses and domineers in the East Indies, cannot perhaps be better illustrated than by the different state of those countries.
>
> (1.7.26)

Smith locates the origins of the contemporary crisis in a structural feature of the merchant companies. He brilliantly shuttles between a demystification of the mercantilists' version of past events and a narrative of how history ought to have developed. In doing so, Smith achieves an effect that is missed by those who concentrate exclusively on the content of his argument: whereas he claims to be merely explaining the past in light of the facts, he installs or sets up a new way of perspectivizing. He trains the reader into a new way of producing truth.

This strategy is elaborated further in a passage where the tension between the beneficence and horrors of global markets is mediated by an account of the first European encounter with the inhabitants of South America. Smith's prose trains the reader to reimagine the history of European imperialism through the evaluative lens of the system of natural liberty. He notes first that what the British are doing in Bengal is merely a repetition of the atrocities committed by Columbus in South America several centuries earlier:

> The discovery of America, however, certainly made a most essential [change]. By opening a new and inexhaustible market to all the commodities of Europe, it gave occasion to new divisions of labour and improvements of art, which, in the narrow circle of the ancient commerce, could never have taken place for want of a market to take off the greater part of their produce. . . . The commodities of Europe were almost all new to America, and many of those of America were new to Europe. A new set of exchanges, therefore, began to take place which had never been thought of before, and which should naturally have proved as advantageous to the new, as it certainly did to the old continent. The savage

injustice of the Europeans rendered an event, which ought to have been benefi-
cial to all, ruinous and destructive to several of those unfortunate countries.

(IV. i; 25)

It is apparent, however, that this violent denunciation of mercantile imperialism is a stalking horse for a more fundamental agenda, which is an
alternative and counterfactual narrative of history spun out of a belief in a
continuity between the historical institution of free trade and exchange as it
takes place in earlier or less developed stages of human society. Inasmuch as
this connection legitimizes his vision of historical development, this transcendent element underpins Smith's global-imperial perspective. It allows
him to lay claim to the historical fantasy that the bad imperialism of the
Spanish in the West Indies may be rectified by the good imperialism of the
British in the East Indies. In condemning the forms of exchange imposed
by the merchant-adventurers, Smith aims to rescue the normative ideal of
free market exchange by associating it with something close to "natural,"
premarket exchange. In this way, the mercantilists are given a new charge
in Smith's discourse: they are the scapegoats whose sacrifice facilitates the
fantasy of a historical continuum connecting the primitive or "natural" exchange of the Amerindians with the terms of the free-exchange economy
that Smith is so anxious to justify. In this oblique way, the imperialism of
free trade is given a natural pedigree.

The rhetorical conduct of Smith's prose makes clear how the conditions
for historical interpretation are newly configured. In the passage from *The
Wealth of Nations* just quoted, it is notable that violence was never written
into the original encounter between European and Amerindian: it is "the
discovery," not "the discoverers," that is responsible for the "opening" of native markets that appeared and would have continued to flourish had they
been allowed to.[18] The discovery is an event that actuates without coercion
a transformation in the native economy; that is to say, the discovery takes
place on the discursive terrain of "nature," not "history." This is perhaps because the goodness of the colonial market in its initial state has, in Smith's
view, nothing to do with imperial violence. Rather, the original development of the market—its natural "opening"—was only subsequently turned
to distorted ends by "the savage injustice of the Europeans." Embodied in
the merchants' actions, history is as brutal as it is unnatural. Hence the
opening of the native market takes place independently of human agency, a bringing to fruition of an inherent potential or tendency: the radical

reorganization of the native economy to serve the exigencies of production for the market can, in this way, be represented in the language of (kind) nature rather than (cruel) history.

"The discovery"—the subject of the sentence is an abstract noun—"gave occasion to new divisions of labour and improvements of art" and to "a new set of exchanges." In Smith's words the European discovery of the Americas did not cause but passively enabled the natural metamorphosis of nonmarket into exchange economies, as an endogenous process, although one that may have been hastened by external elements. However, instead of coaxing or developing this already existing tendency to its full potential by means of mutually profitable exchanges—actions that would not have required coercion or force—the Spanish subjected the natives to the horrors of slavery and plunder. History thereby intervened in nature, distorting the natural progress of opulence. By suggesting that the Amerindians were already naturally participating in a version of the system of natural liberty, Smith establishes an absolute separation between his system and that of the mercantilists he caricatures. Consequently, he posits a continuity between the nonmarket and free market economies in their common antipathy to the merchants, who represent the aberration from the norm.[19] In this vision, Smith's longing for a natural order founded on agriculture is clear, as is his endorsement of an imperial project that seeks to restore the world to its path of natural progress, in which the market is viewed as an extension of the nonmarket. On the one hand, the non-European world is now brought into view by means of a natural free-trade system, and, on the other, the terms of the exchange economy are grafted onto the nonmarket economies of the Amerindians. Smith claims an affiliation between his system and that one existing in the Americas prior to the catastrophic appearance of Columbus. The mutually profitable trade that "began" to take place was destroyed as a result of Spanish aggression. By separating the bad market of the mercantilists from the good market of free trade, he sets up the representational framework within which the system of natural liberty (4.7.c.44) is deemed commensurate with already existing tendencies in the native society.

Subsistence is the natural origin of free trade. It carries a moral charge because it serves the material needs of the people, not the greed of a well-placed few. It is through the figure of subsistence that Smith's conception of free trade separates itself absolutely from mercantilist values. Given the priority of "subsistence," the word represents for Smith something more than the bare state of survival it has come to connote today. It does not simply name backward or impoverished economies that are in need of modernization. Subsistence connotes the natural realm of obligations and responsibilities from which the system of natural liberty derives its moral legitimacy.[20] I will show, however, that it is Smith's attempt to link free trade with the originality of nonmarket systems that opens *The Wealth of Nations* to historical possibilities other than those delineated by a metropolitan perspective. Whereas for Smith this relationship is empirically defined by the stewardship of agriculture, a different conception of the global—one that is not tacitly centered on Europe's or Britain's imperial progress—emerges around the figure of heterogeneous forms of production and exchange elsewhere in the world.

With the figure of subsistence in the foreground, *The Wealth of Nations* marginalizes the merchants by arguing for a condition that satisfies both the claim that free trade is a priori natural—even to Amerindians and Bengali peasants—and that a just form of imperial rule will facilitate the natural and proportioned development that is simply waiting to unfold in the Asian colonies.[21] Already in the case of Europe, Smith suggests that whereas the mercantilist system arose from the distortions of human institutions, the free market system grew naturally out of subsistence economies.[22] It is in this light that Smith's repeated tendency to posit a relation between the free market and the subsistence economy gains its full significance. In *The Wealth of Nations* the market is not instituted by means of a violent rupture with the "rude" or "savage" past—that is what the evil merchants do—but is deemed to arise out of a differential relationship produced *within* the subsistence economy, that is, where subsistence is the ground of economy.[23] Against the forced imposition of production for the market by colonial merchants, it is the native economies that are deemed to be the source and origin of a future global economy based upon harmony and mutual benefit. Smith's repeated emphasis on "proportioned" development and his fear that monopolies disrupt the productive flows that characterize subsistence speak to this point (4.7.c.43). This is perhaps why Smith does not put the conquest down to a regrettable (but happily receding) past that the conditions of market society have decisively overcome. Instead, he harps on this brutal European legacy to underscore the continuing dominance of the mercantilist system that is "altogether unfit to govern its territorial possessions" in the East Indies (5.1.e.26). The following passage illustrates how this colonial system has distorted the livelihood of the natives of Bengal. What ought to have been a market system emerging naturally from an encouragement of native agriculture has been turned into its opposite:

> The English company have not yet had time to establish in Bengal so perfectly destructive a system [as the Dutch in Java]. The plan of their government, however, has had exactly the same tendency. It has not been uncommon, I am well assured, for the chief, that is, the first clerk of a factory, to order a peasant to plough up a rich field of poppies and sow it with rice or some other grain. The pretence was, to prevent a scarcity of provisions; but the real reason, to give the chief an opportunity of selling at a better price a large quantity of opium, which he happened then to have upon hand. Upon other occasions the order has been reversed; and a rich field of rice or other grain has been ploughed up, in order to make room for a plantation of poppies; when the chief foresaw that extraordinary profit was likely to be made by opium. The servants of the company have upon several occasions attempted to establish in their own favour the monopoly of some of the most important branches, not only of the foreign, but of the inland trade of the country.
>
> (4.7.c.101)

To the extent that Smith is motivated by a desire to justify the free market through the primordial figure of subsistence, his text also articulates a normative view that does not take economic "growth" to be an end in itself. In line with a vision of economic well-being grounded in the rich connotations of subsistence, Smith situates Europe in relation to diverse political and economic institutions at work in various parts of both the European and non-European worlds, where capital accumulation and the satisfaction of immediate social needs are not necessarily disconnected from each other. It is, however, the case that this strain in Smith's argument is subordinated to the more practical concern of imagining a more hopeful future for the British empire.[24] But by reading Smith's dominant agenda against the grain, a different vision of the global begins to take shape.

III. SUBSISTENCE AND THE DISPLACEMENT OF THE GLOBAL

In telling the story of the unnatural and unwelcome rise of mercantile capitalism that I refer to above, Smith notes that the capitalists have no regard for subsistence and care only for their own enrichment. This narrative is offered through an account of the rise of merchant power in Europe from the

end of the Roman empire. Historically, the inordinate power of merchants
is the result of the disproportioned development of European towns, which
grew powerful through manufacture and commerce in long-distance luxury
goods. These cities prospered at the expense of the "poverty and wretch-
edness" of the countryside around them, the consequence of which was
the current domination of the merchant monopolies, at home and abroad.
Smith provides counterexamples to European development, in which the
development of the city was proportioned to the subsistence of the country. Certain non-European societies are cited as exemplifying this preferred
form of development:

> There were, however, within the narrow circle of the commerce of those times,
> some countries that were opulent and industrious. Such was the Greek empire
> as long as it subsisted, and that of the Saracens during the reign of the Abba-
> sides. Such too was Egypt till it was conquered by the Turks, some part of the
> coast of Barbary, and all those provinces of Spain which were under the govern-
> ment of the Moors.
>
> (3.3.13)

Given that the forms of subsistence-linked progress are contextually determined, in much the same way that Europe's "inverted" development was a
feature of its own historical peculiarities, it is the univocally defined global
perspective that is necessarily displaced by Smith's ideal of normative development. In short, Smith's dependence on the figure of subsistence troubles
the global perspective that he deploys to justify a reformed British Empire
as the instrument of historical progress. It opens up the global to the engagement of the heterogeneous places it thematizes. In this light, the latter
can no longer simply be incorporated or subsumed into a single or universal
metric of "improvement." To the contrary, their institutions and values infect the self-sufficient terms in which the global is articulated. The appeal to
(and reconfiguration of) the global through the figure of subsistence in *The
Wealth of Nations* has the unexpected or wayward effect of highlighting the
uneven and heterogeneous character of the different societies that appear in
his account, which ranges from ancient Egypt and medieval Europe to contemporary North America and China. Although he obviously views the institutions and manners of European commercial society—which are absent
and unrealizable in these societies—to be the apotheosis of human possibility, Smith's invocation of these diverse histories in order to undermine the
role of the merchants, however, engages vistas that cannot be squared with

Smith's endorsement of the system of natural liberty, especially as it serves the instrumentalities of British imperial aggrandizement.

His narrative of progress invites interruption by calling for a reading of other sites, not merely as objects for a global mode of thematization but because the (con)textuality of such sites complicates and interrupts such sight. Although for the most part the thematic aim of Smith's narrative is to shore up a narrowly cosmopolitan view of the "progress of refinement" as it improves manners at home (civil society) and creates subjects abroad (empire), what is enabled by such a density of historical and geographical allusions is a sense of other institutions or vectors worldwide that cannot be accounted for within a ready-made discourse of the global. Smith describes "good" and "bad" spaces elsewhere in comparison to European commercial society chiefly because they clarify what course of action best serves Britain's aggrandizement. But what this simultaneously suggests is the way these spaces can be imagined, against the grain of Smith's vision, as populated by historical agents whose cultural media are complex in their own right:

> It is otherwise in the barbarous societies, as they are commonly called, of hunt-ers, of shepherds, and even of husbandmen in that rude state of husbandry which precedes the improvement of manufactures and the extension of foreign com-merce. In such societies the varied occupations of every man oblige every man to exert his capacity and to invent expedients for removing difficulties which are continually recurring. Invention is kept alive and the mind is not suffered to fall into that which, in a civilized society, seems to benumb the understanding of almost all the inferior ranks of people. In those barbarous societies, as they are called, every man, it has already been observed, is a warrior. Every man, too, is in some measure a statesman, and can form a tolerable judgment concerning the interests of the society and the conduct of those who govern it.
>
> (5.1.f.51)

If we can step away from a perspective that maintains "civilized society" as the center or point of reference, even when ostensibly absent from view, a textual abyss reveals itself in this passage.[25] Instead of remaining caught in the cosmopolitan fixation with fabricating historical topoi that indirectly confirm its self-importance—which is why we should not be distracted by Smith's criticism of civilized society in this passage—a task for the cultural study of globalization today might well involve a literalizing of this refer-ence by following through on the objectification of such groups in order to reimagine them as historical subjects.

I have argued that Smith legitimizes the vision of free trade by describing it as an extension of subsistence. Although Smith deploys this term to denote the sheer heterogeneity of the social and economic systems around the world, he repeatedly reins in this vision to serve the narrative of univocal, Europe-centered progress. In this sense, Smith ultimately closes off what I think of as the richest and most suggestive implications of his writing. Drawing on the uneven complexity that Smith's narrative so powerfully evokes, I seek in this section to turn his narrative tendencies to other, divergent conceptions of progress. My reading is parasitic on Smith's argument in that it follows the lines of perception he enables in order to turn them and explore other ways of imagining historical possibility.

"Subsistence," as I have read it, stands as a general term for the formidably diverse economies in which the disembedded or self-regulating market is not in place.[26] I have already shown how Smith asserts that the free market is an outgrowth of subsistence. Smith's system of natural liberty is offered as an elaboration of, rather than a break from, the belief that the economy serves the needs of human subsistence. This is the narrative presupposition that makes Smith's account of European history resonate unexpectedly with the non-European economies he describes, where the agents of value production are not fully or evenly inscribed within the mode of "general equivalence" expressed by the monetary form but rather belong to what Karl Marx would call the mixed or "defective" expressions associated with the "total or expanded form of value."[27]

Smith obviously sees the organization of material production and distribution in a market system to be quite distinct, but he insistently represents it in a differential and entangled relation with an order that is not reducible to the universal metric of market exchange. Whereas Smith relied on subsistence to anchor the global perspective in an unassailable moral discourse, subsistence can now be reinterpreted to stand not for nature but the diverse terrains where mixed forms of production and exchange take place. Subsistence names the numberless narratives of the world rather than the pure and unchanging space of "nature" by which Eurocentric norms may be asserted. The global is put into play by the very subsistence marshaled to confirm its perspective as normative. The global is made the effect of mutually interruptive and articulated perspectives, as these perspectives are given the general name "subsistence." By Smith's own logic, in this light, the "system of natural liberty" is itself one of many such heterogeneous instances of subsistence. The global perspective can now be viewed as a part, or a subset, of this heterogeneity rather than its external or objective measure.

The global perspective becomes inflected or colored by the numerous non-European, nonmarket societies that emphasize the development of the land and the sustenance of its inhabitants over the focus on positive balances of trade.[28] The vision of historical development outlined by Smith may therefore admit of local variation here, where market society is viewed as an effect of its contextual make-up. Put crudely, if "society" is put before or as the condition for "economy," or, what amounts to the same thing, if economic activity cannot be uncoupled from the needs of the collective order, the link Smith establishes between subsistence and the market here might equally suggest a link with the "economic" practices in the non-European world not yet fully articulated with the global exchange economy. Speaking to the question of productive labor, Thorstein Veblen addresses the "nutritive" agenda that drives Smith's vision of a market system that marshals its arguments by way of an undeclared affinity with the call of subsistence:

> So far as Adam Smith's economic theories are a tracing out of a causal sequence in economic phenomena, they are worked out in terms given by these two main directions of activity,—human effort and discretion directed to a pecuniary gain. The former is the great, substantial productive force; the latter is not immediately, or proximately, productive. Adam Smith still has too lively a sense of the nutritive purpose of the order of nature freely to extend the concept of productiveness to any activity that does not yield a material increase of creature comforts.[29]

Hence the commercial or mercantilist system may be read as a violent break not only with its own European past but also with a normative global order conceived through the figure of subsistence. It is with this in mind that Smith derisively labels mercantilism a "modern system" (4.1.5). Smith eschews the disjunction between commercial and noncommercial societies. Scholars have noted that even where he argues that the self-regulating market should not be interfered with—witness his opposition to the regulation of the internal corn trade—he does so with the needs of the collective in mind.[30]

From a worldwide perspective it follows that Europe is seen to cohere within a differential relationship with its counterpart societies in the rest of the world.[31] By this eccentric view the name "Europe" is not merely juxtaposed with the name "China," for Europe is itself internally differentiated

by the existence of unevenly articulated economies that brings such sites
into a relation with non-European spaces. At times it is even possible to see
Smith's critique of the misguided emphasis on foreign trade, particularly
its tendency to adversely influence productive labor in the hinterland, as
an expression of partiality to countries where long-distance trade does not
overwhelm agriculture:

> The wealth of ancient Egypt, that of China and Indostan, sufficiently dem-
> onstrate that a nation may attain a very high degree of opulence, though the
> greater part of its exportation trade be carried on by foreigners.... According
> to the natural course of things therefore, the greater part of the capital of every
> growing society is, first directed to agriculture, afterwards to manufactures, and
> last of all to foreign commerce.
>
> (3.1.7–8)

The attention to agriculture suggests that non-European spaces like China
or Egypt are well placed to improve of their own accord with the benefit of
reforms akin to those so urgently needed in modern Europe. Once again,
because agriculture pervaded social practices all over the world before the
emergence of mercantile capitalism, the figure of subsistence suggests a distinct vision of the global, at once heterogeneous to and supplementary of
the hegemonic forms of commercial capitalism of the day. In a powerfully
defamiliarizing description of existing market systems, Smith views European economies as historical grotesques, ahead only as examples of how *not*
to develop. Book 3 argues that Europe's material progress has been "entirely
inverted" (3.3.9).

Smith refers to agriculture as the "original destination of man"; he lauds
the worthiness of this "primitive employment" (3.1.3) over manufacture and
commerce, much as he praises manufacture only when it is "the offspring
of agriculture" (3.3.20). He never articulates the values associated with the
cultivation of the land, but there is no question that they provide the moral
basis of improvement. In this way, the market society Smith celebrates can
itself be imagined otherwise, that is, in differential relation with the societies that have existed elsewhere, in both time and space. Not only does this
trouble the naturalized form of the global perspective, it raises the uncanny
prospect whether the global may be conceived by way of its reconstellation
across different terrains.

How much more complex an account of the global is required when
Smith turns from the European theater to that of Asia or Africa? And

what of the mixed forms produced by capitalist colonialism and slavery, where the texture of the native economy undergoes violent disruption in a manner that is not assimilable to the language of "transition"? The task here is not to think up even more comprehensive solutions, on the model of an "expanded" global perspective. My aim is not to challenge the global perspective's failure to be adequate or comprehensive; it is to change the rules by which such standards of evaluation are naturalized. So instead, I ask how reading can serve as an invitation to take up perspectives that are disruptive of the very global template by which they are brought into view in Smith's text.

Indeed, I have shown that Smith's own historical arguments presuppose a particular imaginative act: the belief that free trade is natural and, by extension, that the market must be configured as an extension of subsistence. It follows, in my reading, that the history of the market is repeatedly waylaid and displaced in *The Wealth of Nations*, given the various historical instances of subsistence that Smith invokes. Smith interrupts the historical account with a series of counterfactuals—the realm of what "should have happened" or what would have been the natural outcome—so that the normative character of the global perspective itself becomes an effect of such virtualized differences: not only is the norm situated outside modern European development, inasmuch as the language of nature is deployed, it appears as a fantasy generated by the differential histories of development across space and time. The *global*—as opposed to the actual territories and markets around the world controlled by mercantile imperialism—now comes into view in its heterotopic rather than homogeneous form. The lines of internal division within each proper name—"Indostan," "China," "Peru,"—shift from delineating a thematized site—much like the imperial placeholder "East Indies" I noted at the outset—to index vectors of heterogeneity that are brought into view by a global that is itself being reconstellated.

It would appear that elements in *Wealth of Nations* do suggest possibilities that are not comprehended by the natural progress of opulence. If Smith's version of the market system distinguishes itself from the heedless plundering of mercantile imperialism that warns of the dangers of capital and is put to use in a manner disconnected from the needs of common people, Smith suggests once more that the precocious rise of market systems in Europe is actually a distortion of natural development. Here is an instance of the rise of the town as a center of commerce, connected to faraway places by long-distance trade but alienated from the natural subsistence of the country:

Sometimes [manufactures that are fit for distant sale] have been introduced, in the manner above mentioned, by the violent operation, if one may say so, of the stocks of particular merchants and undertakers, who established them in imitation of some foreign manufactures of the same kind. Such manufactures, therefore, are the offspring of foreign commerce, and such seem to have been the ancient manufactures of silks, velvets, and brocades, which flourished in Lucca in the thirteenth century.[32]

(3.3.19)

Smith then corrects this historical progress with a more "natural" development, where the market system appears as an outgrowth of the surplus that gradually accrues within the subsistence economy:

At other times, manufactures for distant sale grow up naturally, and as it were of their own accord, by the gradual refinement of those household and coarser manufactures which must at all times be carried on *even in the poorest and rudest countries.*

(3.3.20; emphasis added)

For anyone concerned with the matter of reading, it is necessary to resist the interpretive reflex—the result of a historical conditioning—to insert such poor and rude spaces within a univocal narrative of transition. Once again, my point is not to reject the truth claims implied by such narratives but to question the perspective in which such truths are framed. Smith's critique of the mercantilists can be used to imagine something distinct from what he or the mercantilists posit, whether framed in the language of good nature or bad history. What appears alongside the Europe-centered debate about good versus bad progress is a scenario of heterogeneous and unevenly articulated terrains within and between Europe, Asia, Africa, and America, given visibility and comparability by Smith's framework of "natural" development. Read differently, this frame can be used to displace rather than consolidate the metropolitan perspective by which the global is organized and projected in Smith's text.

The closer Smith's account gets to the contemporary period, the less conjectural history serves as a template for material progress. Instead, natural development seems hardly ever to have come to pass in Europe, as this *idealized* vision (which Smith invokes only to disavow) will attest:

[The cultivators] are thus both encouraged and enabled to increase this surplus produce by a further improvement and better cultivation of the land; and as the fertility of the land had given birth to the manufacture, so the progress of the manufacture reacts upon the land and increases still further its fertility. The manufacturers first supply the neighbourhood, and afterwards, as their work improves and refines, more distant markets. . . . In this manner have grown up naturally, and as it were of their own accord, the manufactures of Leeds, Halifax, Sheffield, Birmingham and Wolverhampton. Such manufactures are the off-spring of agriculture.[33]

(3.3.20)

As we have seen, this normative development was not realized in Europe. Indeed, given the influence of merchants, such development appears to have been conceivable only in places like China, whose government gave encouragement to agriculture, as well as Bengal and ancient Egypt (4.9.42–44).[34] The invocation of the Chinese, Indians, and Egyptians is partly aligned with the physiocrats' exclusive emphasis on agriculture as the source of wealth. The market system appears to be interrupted or supplemented to mixed, if not anarchic, ends. A series of variations, from England to China and Bengal and Egypt, inflects the "natural" form of development described in the passage above.

More to the point, the normative vision of progress presented above is a counterfactual account—generally what did not and could not have happened given the political conditions of medieval and early-modern Europe. The progress of commercial society serves less as evidence of Europe's actual superiority—in any case, the history of countries like ancient Egypt and China, notwithstanding their current "stationary" state (1.8.24), seems to fit this schema more closely—than as a story repeatedly undermined by actual events. Indeed, the stationary state of these societies cannot be taken to be a permanent condition. As Smith warns elsewhere, Britain itself risks becoming stationary, if not worse, as a consequence of having grown so dependent on the American market.[35] Smith notes that although China's peculiar advancement has been hindered by the lack of foreign commerce, its "home market . . . is, perhaps in extent, not much inferior to the market of all the different countries of Europe put together" (4.9.41). A related point is made of Egypt and Indostan:

The government of both countries was particularly attentive to the interest of agriculture. The works constructed by the ancient sovereigns of Egypt for the proper distribution of the waters of the Nile were famous in antiquity; and the ruined remains of some of them are still the admiration of travelers. Those of the same kind which were constructed by the ancient sovereigns of Indostan, for the proper distribution of the waters of the Ganges as well as of many other rivers, though they have been less celebrated, seem to have been equally great. Both countries, accordingly, though subject occasionally to dearths, have been famous for their great fertility. Though both were extremely populous, yet, in years of moderate plenty, they were both able to export great quantities of grain to their neighbours.

(4.9.45)

Such configurations suggest that the natural progress of opulence lacks a simple or straightforward historical referent because nowhere in the world does development happen as it should. "Natural-progress" narratives are the result of incorrectly, albeit productively, deployed metaphors. That is, they demand to be read rather than taken for historical fact. Empirically, such a narrative confirms only that the current form of development in Europe is "inverted" and that many institutional aspects of social progress in Asia and Africa and America are in need of situationally determined, or textured, responses. Inasmuch as most countries cannot presume becoming an imperial power of the kind that Smith's wishes Britain to be, it is more sensible to think of the global as encompassed and supplemented by the terms of subsistence in the sense described above. Were scholars in the humanities and the social sciences to train themselves to respond to the questions and possibilities raised by such a vision of the world, they might broach styles of thinking that could more accurately be called "global."

IV. UNEVENNESS AND HETEROGENEITY

Smith relies on this vision of heterogeneity in order to shore up the global perspective, which presents a reformed empire that fuses with the premodern societies it encounters so as to better prosecute the tasks of commercial and territorial expansion. As I have shown, however, the attempt to articulate this vision is undone as the diverse and hybrid histories he evokes indicate that the global denotes both the frame that makes such heterogeneity visible and the heterogeneity by which that frame is exceeded or displaced. Read in this fashion, Smith's account can be shown to unfold in wayward directions, that is, as it encourages "the global" to be rethought through the diverse contexts by which it is contaminated. For example, Smith's vision of colonial settlement in America draws upon an idea of experimentation and mixture more daring than that found in popular works such as Daniel Defoe's *Robinson Crusoe* (1719). Whereas Crusoe's identity as an Englishman and a Protestant is repeatedly emphasized in Defoe's novel, Smith's vision of American settlement describes a deliberate fusing of European know-how with the values of Native American subsistence economies. In his discussion of settler colonialism in America, Smith takes pains to suggest a continuity between the skills of the settlers and those of the native inhabitants. The skills of the Europeans are superior only in degree, not kind, to those of the natives. Rather than aliens intent upon a radical transformation of their new environment in ways altogether unfamiliar to the natives, Smith tacitly compares the settler colonists in North America to historical catalysts who expedite indigenous development. A fictive continuity is established between settler and native in the instituting of market society. The settler appears as a grafted indigene, bringing skills and customs shorn of the decadent trappings that have subverted the proper transition to commercial society in Europe:

> The colonists carry out with them a knowledge of agriculture and of other useful arts superior to what can grow up of its own accord in the course of many centuries among savage and barbarous nations. They carry out with them too the habit of subordination, some notion of the regular government which takes place in their own country, of the system of laws which support it, and of a regular administration of justice; and they naturally establish something of the same kind in the new settlement.
>
> (4.7.b.2)

This claim of continuity is reminiscent of Smith's description of ancient Greek settlements in southern Italy and Asia Minor, which he deems a desirable model of colonization. In the case of British settlers in America, the possibility of conflict is suppressed as the settlers harmoniously graft themselves onto the landscape and restore the land to its natural course of development. This is the "education" of the colonies for which the settlers, and not states or their merchant proxies, take full credit:

> In what way, therefore, has the policy of Europe contributed either to the first establishment, or to the present grandeur of the colonies of America? In one way, and in one way only, it has contributed a great deal. *Magna virum Mater!* It bred and formed the men who were capable of achieving such great actions, and

of laying the foundation of so great an empire; and there is no other quarter of the world of which the policy is capable of forming, or has ever actually and in fact formed such men. The colonies owe to the policy of Europe the education and great views of their active and enterprising founders; and some of the greatest and most important of them, so far as concerns their internal government, owe it to scarce anything else.

(4.7.b.64)

Thus the British market system arrives in America without violence: of a piece, as it were, with the natural development of the land. In contrast to the merchants, who cannot be accounted for except as an aberration from nature, or history as it should have unfolded, it is the settlers who develop the land in consonance with the normative idea of historical progress (3.4.18–19). This is as true of America as it was of the ancient Greek colonies in the Mediterranean. Smith's appeal to the ancients to bolster modern imperial policy, however, joins up with a broader and uneven movement which reconstellates the global:

> All those [ancient Greek] colonies had established themselves in countries inhabited by savage and barbarous nations, who easily gave place to the new settlers. They had plenty of good land, and as they were altogether independent of the mother city, they were at liberty to manage their own affairs in the way that they judged was most suitable to their own interest.
>
> (4.7.b.4)

Smith distinguishes between colonization in the ancient Mediterranean world, which was driven by the "irresistible necessity" of population pressures (4.7.a.3), from modern colonialism, which is motivated by "profits" and "avidity" (4.7.a.6). Ancient colonization was "natural" because, unlike modern merchant-led colonization, its institutions and practices were all in the service of subsistence. The historical template that Smith is drawing on here shows through in his attempt to find a way to bring British imperialism in line with this model of colonization. Once again he reveals the centrality of the trope of subsistence, although here it does not take shape around the figure of Native Americans in sixteenth-century America, but the ancient Greek colonists. In a brief but revealing digression, Smith notes that the ancient Greek word for "colony" is etymologically derived from the word for "home" (οικοσ). Greek colonization was embedded in institutions that were not driven by "avidity"; rather, they developed out of concerns that related to the well-being of the polity as household: "The Latin word (*Colonia*) signifies simply a plantation. The Greek word (αποικια), on the contrary, signifies a separation of dwelling, a departure from home, a going out of the house" (4.138). The ancient Greek colony was regarded "as a child" (4.136). The word for the household or home provides an obvious etymological link between "colony" (αποικια) and "economy" (οικονομεια), as it retains its original connotations of the management of the well-being of the household, not profit. Inasmuch, therefore, as the colony is seen as an outgrowth of the mother country, it deserves the proportioned development that underpins the sustenance or οικονομεια of the mother country, not a rapacious exploitation that leaves the colonial subjects in distress.[36]

Far from being precursors of market societies of the kind facilitated by modern British institutions, the English settlers in America are described as historical agents in that they resemble the ancient Greeks, who lived and worked within the rules of οικονομεια, that is, economic activity embedded within immediate needs. A different model of settlement and exchange suggests itself here, not least because the ancient Greeks in turn point to (other) non-European societies whose practices resembled theirs, insofar as these practices were diametrically opposed to the kind conjured with by the East India Company or the British state. It is by means of this reconstellation that *The Wealth of Nations* may be made to engage non-Europeans as historical agents, precisely as they do *not* partake of the global perspective in the narrow sense celebrated by Smith.

This distinct figure presents itself when, for instance, Smith refers to trade "carried on by the native Indians" in the Malay Archipelago and "the inhabitants of China and Japan, of Tonquin, Malacca, Cochin-China, and the island of Celebes" that are frequently seen in the Dutch port of Batavia (4.7.c.100) and other parts of the archipelago. Here we find a model of settlement and exchange that predates the arrival of the European and is not marked by the vertical integration of markets under imperial rule. According to a historical narrative made available by recent scholarship, these non-European historical agents had created networks and communities of settlement and exchange that were destroyed by European armed traders' attempt to capture the spice trade.

A strategic reliance on this other narrative enables a conception of the world in the heterogeneous senses noted above. It also allows us to figure, not retrieve, a "reading-position" for denizens of this world as they are unevenly brought into view by the global frame in the sense first described by Smith.[37] At the start of this chapter, I spoke of how Smith signaled the central importance of Batavia to his novel perspective. Batavia was central to the global perspective newly elaborated by Smith even as it was emptied of any contextual significance (much like "Cape of Good Hope" served for a previous generation of imperial theorists). Read as a historical place and not just a linchpin term, however, this trading world of an "Asia before Europe" would go some way toward explaining the otherwise mysterious appearance of the Malay in Thomas De Quincey's *Confessions of an English Opium-Eater*, which I discuss in the next chapter. This "native Indian" world also constitutes the background to the Malay-language writer Abdullah bin Abdul Kadir, whom I study in chapter 3. The struggles attendant upon growing European domination is the setting for Joseph Conrad's *Lord Jim*, populated by Chinese, Arabs, Indians, Malays, Bugis, and Eurasians, which I explore in chapter 4. Smith's perspective makes these sites legible and visible and the nineteenth-century narratives that I read in the chapters that follow tacitly draw upon it as the condition of "correct" representation. But inasmuch as his narrative subsumes without registering the texture and unevenness of these sites, this way of seeing and saying remains in need of supplementation.

Unlike the example of America, the indigenes are not effaced in this image, for the term "native Indian" as Smith uses it is an uncertain category, to an extent blurring the divisions between indigene and settlers who arrive from other parts of Asia, Africa, and elsewhere. What I seek to suggest by this image is that within the non-European world, such exchanges or historical interactions were already underway long before the arrival of the European. Unless we are committed to the belief that only capitalist or European settlement counts as historical, Smith's own argument would suggest that the native world must be taken as populated by value-producing agents. Long before the arrival of Europeans, the "indigene" of the Malay Archipelago (and the Americas) already incorporated the "settler." Smith's account of early European settlement in America can be read in a similar light: the settlers are historical agents insofar as they resemble the ancient Greek settlers, and, one might add, those hybrid races found in the Malay Archipelago. Seen in this light, the linchpin role of the Malay Archipelago in Smith's system can be imagined as a dynamic site of historical agency. It therefore helps to read these place names on the periphery not as serving to confirm the comprehensive power of a metropolitan system but rather as sites of active cultural media whose presence calls for a revaluation of the metropolitan mode of perspectivizing.

The distinction between "Europe" and "non-Europe" begins to blur, as European settlement in North America and elsewhere is seen as derived from a longer process of migrations and sojourning the world over.[38] The force of capitalist settlement is, in this case, no longer marked with exclusive world-historical significance but seen as parasitic upon and destructive of earlier historical relations. To read in this sense is to train oneself to see the "native Indian" as an agent, where the historical archive or the account perspectivize him or her as object for a progress whose spirit is located elsewhere. That the "native Indians" do exist and create is precisely what is attested to by this passage. Even though Smith can only see the depredations of the Dutch, this other movement is discernible, if only at the margins of the critique of a colonial capitalist system that is both rapacious and destructive:

> In the spice islands the Dutch are said to burn all the spiceries which a fertile season produces beyond what they expect to dispose of in Europe with such a profit as they think sufficient. In the islands where they have no settlements, they give a premium to those who collect the young blossoms and green leaves of the clove and nutmeg trees which naturally grow there, but which the savage policy has now, it is said, almost completely extirpated. Even in the islands where they have no settlements they have very much reduced, it is said, the number of those trees. If the produce even of their own islands was much greater than what suited their market, the natives, they suspect, might find means to convey some part of it to other nations; and the best way, they imagine, to secure their own monopoly, is to take care that no more shall grow than what they themselves carry to market. By different arts of oppression they have reduced the population of several of the Moluccas nearly to the number which is sufficient to supply with fresh provisions and other necessaries of life their own insignificant garrisons, and such of their ships as occasionally come there for a cargo of spices.

> (4.7.c.101)

A whole society stirs at the edges of this account, which cannot simply be occluded by the well-meaning denunciation of Dutch injustice. I do not, however, propose to portray the native as an agent of proto-capitalism or an "alternative" modernity. Instead, I ask how a different critical practice can teach us to read otherwise, to redo the seeing that normalizes or naturalizes the effacement of the other who cannot accede to the position of reader. This is to an extent commensurate with the task Smith set himself, in that *The Wealth of Nations* is an exercise in changing the terms in which the world is seen, that is, made visible and legible as such, as in this extraordinary passage:

> Many tribes of animals acknowledged to be all of the same species, derive from nature a much more remarkable distinction of genius, than what, antecedent to custom and education, appears to take place among men. By nature a philosopher is not in genius and disposition half so different from a street porter, as a mastiff is from a greyhound, or a greyhound from a spaniel, or this last from a shepherd's dog. Those different tribes of animals, however, though all of the same species, are of scarce any use to one another. The strength of the mastiff is not in the least supported either by the swiftness of the greyhound, or by the sagacity of the spaniel, or by the docility of the shepherd's dog. The effects of those different geniuses and talents, for want of the power or disposition to barter and exchange, cannot be brought into a common stock, and do not in the least contribute to the better accommodation and conveniency of the species.
>
> (1.2.5)

A defamiliarizing form of evaluation offers itself here; it makes the norm open to being displaced or supplemented by other readers who are "defective" or who fail to compute with the terms of the global conceived in its narrowly metropolitan and progressive form. The sheer heterogeneity of the animal world points to a conception of wealth to which Smith pays glancing homage. Smith's assertion that dogs possess a greater diversity of natural talent than men does not simply force a revaluation of social value; it can be made to resonate with a style of reading that solicits the conventions of modern historical narrative, which takes place exclusively within the narrowly utilitarian culture of capitalism. In Smith's view, the "genius and disposition" that distinguishes any two men is necessarily insignificant in comparison to that which distinguishes a shepherd's dog from a greyhound. The fact that humans make up for this natural poverty in a civil state only reveals that value is diversely constituted. In this light, market society represents one set of institutional arrangements evolved by that very species as a consequence of its natural poverty. But if, as Smith observes, an original deficiency can be turned into a great strength (most notably in the making of market society), the lesson surely is that no single perspective or mode of evaluation can possibly claim absolute superiority.

The comparison with the diverse genius of dogs points up the different forms of historical and cultural life that shape and inflect the putative lack of natural genius that is allegedly common to all human beings. Smith's assertion that animals are absolutely incapable of exchange in turn draws attention to the fact that exchange does not mean the same thing everywhere in the human world. The diverse forms taken by exchange make it hard, in turn, to agree to the utilitarian connotations of "common stock." The perspective of exchange and of common stock raises questions about history and culture that do not allow for the univocal narrative Smith proposes. Once again, an anecdote or comparison leads into divergent paths. Returning to the question of subsistence as it is mediated by the heterogeneous social systems being forcibly brought into one kind of "common stock" by the colonial capitalism of Smith's day, it is clear how the discourse of a normative modernity is grafted and metaleptically reproduced as the tale of the European settlers in North America or that of ancient Greeks in Sicily. As I have tried to show, Smith himself attempts to prove that the exchanges take different and mixed forms in these historical encounters. And although Smith finally absorbs these two sites into a homogenous narrative of global progress, it is clear that this ostensibly straightforward narrative is crucially dependent upon the diverse practices of exchange—where the quantitative calculus was informed by social and contextual form—in the Asian and African worlds that the British and the Dutch, like the Portuguese and Spanish before them, discovered as latecomers in Asia.

I have shown the important ways in which the figure of subsistence is deployed in Smith's narrative. But this figure also produces a different and unsettling effect on the univocal story of progress it is meant to secure. At once a central concept and uncanny residue, subsistence remains in place in both these senses through the most detailed empirical and pragmatic considerations in *The Wealth of Nations*. In the process, it creates effects that are not assimilable to the terms of a hygienic or self-identical exchange economy. In *The Wealth of Nations*, subsistence cannot be excised from a global perspective that it does not stop troubling.

What I have called, echoing Smith, the priority of subsistence occupies a place that is neither univocal nor undifferentiated; rather, it troubles the terms of a naively linear historical narrative of progress. Exchange is not necessarily a function of market exchange in the same way that the countless forms of nonmarket systems that Smith invokes reveal a global heterogeneity. This heterogeneity is in differential relation with rather than merely a derivative version of the market system. Subsistence comes to stand in for the diverse forms of exchange that are neither opposed to the terms of colonial capitalist exchange nor merely instances of "pre-" or "proto-" capitalism. As the imagination expands the epistemic assumptions of history, subsistence can serve as the general name for the diverse forms of exchange toward which any kind of economic development must be accountable. Subsistence puts Europe in its place within this broader set of heterogeneous yet related contexts; the global here simultaneously signifies a fundamental interruption and an affirmation of "the wealth of nations" in the robust sense of the phrase.

2

OPIUM CONFESSIONS

Narcotic, Commodity, and the Malay Amuk

I. OPIUM: NARCOTIC AND COMMODITY

Two years before the publication of De Quincey's *Confessions of an English Opium-Eater* in 1821, an ambitious young East India Company official named Stamford Raffles established a trading station on a tiny island at the tip of the Malay Peninsula. Soon to be known to the British as Singapore, it proved invaluable to Britain's maintenance of commercial and military hegemony in Asia, which lasted until the Japanese invasion of Malaya in 1942. In referring to the fall of colonial Singapore as the "worst disaster" and "greatest capitulation" in British history, Winston Churchill obliquely underscored the importance of the Malay Archipelago for any power aspiring to become the imperial overlord in Asia. If the fall of Singapore during the Second World War opened the precious natural resources of the archipelago to a Japanese war machine already in control of much of the Chinese mainland, it also yielded the launching point for the projected overland invasion of India.

The Malay Archipelago's centrality to any imperial project in Asia had been emphatically noted two centuries earlier by Adam Smith, most strikingly in his parallel between Batavia and the Cape of Good Hope. In the decades after the publication of *The Wealth of Nations*, the British East India Company established the first of several rival ports to Dutch Batavia in the archipelago. The first was Penang in 1786. In 1795, the company seized control of Melaka. In 1819, Singapore was founded. Finally, as if in confirmation of Smith's prescience, Batavia was overrun by the British in 1811 and then governed for six years by Stamford Raffles, who was devoted in principle to the ideology of free trade and to dismantling the hateful monopolistic policies of the Dutch East India Company so as to restore the natives of the Malay Archipelago to their "ancient" practice of free trade. It is not difficult to see that the key source for Raffles's rhetoric was *The Wealth of Nations.*

A contemporary of Raffles, Thomas De Quincey came of age during the Napoleonic wars and began writing in the aftermath of Britain's decisive victory in 1815. De Quincey wrote in the wake of the reforms that Smith so fervently urged in the name of good imperialism, reforms that resulted first in the elevation of figures like Raffles, who embodied, in principle if not in practice, the values of an enlightened state rather than those of a rapacious corporation.[1] In this light, De Quincey's fantasy of "Asia"—realized as the regularized extraction and circulation of commodities—assumes a moral valence. The planting of crops in India, their transportation to Singapore and Melaka, and their reshipment to other parts of Southeast Asia and beyond, to China, contribute to a vision of European colonialism as an instrument of human progress.

While Smith's argument centers upon the metropolitan diffusion of a strategy of good governance and exchange in the colonies, De Quincey's vision some fifty years later draws on the promise embodied by opium, a commodity produced in India by the British East India Company and sold in the Malay Archipelago. When we consider that De Quincey was himself addicted to opium, the relationship between the commodity through which the region is imagined and the narcotic that provides the conditions for such hallucinations become of more than passing interest. In this chapter, I consider the interplay of opium as commodity and opium as narcotic in De Quincey's global imagination of Asia. I spend the first two sections of the chapter charting out the peculiar character of De Quincey's artistic voice as it is shaped by his opium addiction. I argue that this imagination, which is marked by an attraction to alien or unfamiliar forces, is intimately bound up with the way he represents Asia. I show that he draws upon the strange power conferred by the heteronomous force of opium as narcotic to evoke the regularity of the movement of opium (as commodity) by means of which Asia is pictured and described as an object. Hence the literary imagination is dependent upon opium's two forms of appearance in the attempt to bring Asia into view. If Adam Smith had offered the template (free trade) through which Asia might be made visible, in De Quincey this visibility or legibility is read through the virulent force of a single commodity whose growth and distribution financed the consolidation of British colonial power in Asia.

In an echo of the East India Company's dependence for its survival on the export of opium as a commodity in the late eighteenth and early nineteenth centuries, De Quincey acknowledges how much his artistic achievements depended upon the effects of opium as a drug. Although the narcotic effects of opium consumption often led to the general incapacitation that was his publisher's despair, it seems also to have been the chief reason for the lucrative career De Quincey had as a magazine writer, beginning with his hugely successful *Confessions of an English Opium-Eater* (1821).[2] De Quincey's artistic identity was that of "Opium-Eater," a man whose fame and "gift" were conferred by his consumption of a mass-produced commodity sold on imperial markets. But in emphasizing the heteronomous power of opium (rather than the autonomy of the imagination) in the *Confessions*, De Quincey does not only distance himself from the rhetoric of objective description and sober judgment that Smith sought to link to a regime of commodity production and exchange secured by a just imperial order; he also notes the creative possibilities unleashed by the undermining of his subjective will.

De Quincey's description of opium resonates unexpectedly with the writings of some historians of colonialism, who have noted that the colonial capitalist order descended as an alien and externally imposed institution in non-European societies. Samir Amin, for instance, has argued that the institutional conditions of colonial capitalism systemically stripped the native workers of their "subjective will" by replacing the ideology of an existing "state religion" (tied to a redistributive or tributary system in which the political and the economic orders were not easily distinguished) with the ideology of impersonal, independent economic laws ("competition").[3] Whether or not the absoluteness of this distinction between market and nonmarket economies is accepted, as a form of narrativization it can be juxtaposed with Smith's belief that a system of free trade would restore native society to a state of clarity as regards the material relations that govern society. For Amin, the native was instead inducted into a new mode of production and subjected to new forms of mystification. The mystification caused by production for the market, he argues, is qualitatively distinct from that exercised by "native" forms because of its essentially abstract, nonsubjective character.

An analogous stripping of identity or will is suggested in De Quincey's *Confessions*: in this work he pays obsessive attention to the ways he is moved, often against his will, across different and unfamiliar terrains. Even spaces that once seemed familiar like contemporary London disorient and terrify him. De Quincey tells the reader that he has these experiences as a consequence of consuming opium, and opium is cultivated by Indian peasants drawn into the orbit of commodity production in Asia by the British East India Company. I propose to read this parallel between De Quincey's experience of opium as narcotic and a laboring native world tasked with the production of opium as commodity as they find expression in his encounter with the "Malay" who visits him in Dove Cottage. The discontinuously shared experience of a loss of individual agency and its consequent sense of disorientation enable connections to be made between the consumption of opium by De Quincey and its production by the unnamed Indian or Malay peasant.[4]

The opium vision is repeatedly described by De Quincey as a loss of subjective will, a passivity that produces errant insights into the larger world. In *Suspiria de Profundis*, De Quincey describes the capacity to dream as "a machinery . . . planted in the human brain," and elsewhere in the same work, he provides this peculiar description of the creative act:

> Any compliment I merited was due to the higher faculty of an electric aptitude for seizing analogies, and by means of these aerial pontoons passing over like lightning from one topic to another. Still it is a fact, that this pertinacious life of memory for things that simply touch the ear without touching the consciousness, does in fact beset me. Said but once, said but softly, not marked at all, words revive before me in darkness and solitude; and they arrange themselves gradually into sentences, but through an effort sometimes of a distressing kind, to which I am in a manner forced to become a party.
>
> (*Confessions*, 117)

The exteriorization of inspiration, "things that simply touch the ear without touching the consciousness," seems informed by an experience of or a "distressing" encounter with the shaping force of something unfamiliar. Opium forces a resonance between things alien or repugnant to one another in the opium eater's text, bringing with it also the possibility of a contamination or "infection."[5] Unable or perhaps unwilling to disavow the "detestable commerce" with the "horrid alien nature" opened up by the drug, De Quincey

describes his experiences as the peculiar material, "the writings in sympathetic ink" (68), through which the force of opium may be communicated.

Thus, opium's "character" can be negatively discerned in the traces it
leaves behind on the opium eater's thoughts and actions. Like the transformation in a chemical reaction that alerts us to the presence of an invisible
agent, opium's story may be deciphered through the wayward dreams that
take place through without belonging to the dreamer. It is in the attention
to the workings of these actions, loosened from a directing consciousness
to tell of distinct events and processes, that we see the true "hero" of De
Quincey's tale. If De Quincey writes of the effects of opium as drug, the
link to nonsubjective transformation implies that the worker newly trained
to produce opium as commodity is discontinuous but not altogether incommensurate with the terms of this imagination.

The drug experience informs his reasoning even when he is most lucid.
This self-subverting logic is evident the 1849 essay entitled "Hints Towards
an Appreciation of the Coming of the War in China" (18:155–56).[6] In this
fact-based, political essay that combines national economic concerns with
geopolitical considerations, De Quincey asserts that China is not free to
withdraw from trade with Britain and that the Chinese government may
not enforce the ban on the importation of Indian opium because it violates
a fundamental principle of free trade. After this, in an echo of a claim he
made several decades earlier in the *Confessions*, De Quincey describes tea
as a stimulant that has civilized the diet of the British as much as it has
enhanced the creation of polite society and a public sphere.[7] Just as British
identity has come to be profoundly dependent on such foreign commodities, foreign trade is now absolutely essential to the nation's constitution.
Britain's addiction to cheap goods from the outside must be fed by forcing
foreigners to take her exports. All this is said, as the title of the essay suggests, to urge the British public to recognize and embrace the inevitability
of war with China:

> Upon this world's tariff of international connections, what is China in relation
> to Great Britain? Free is she, or not—free to dissolve her connections with us?
> Secondly, first, then, China, viewed in its connection with ourselves, this vast
> (but perhaps not proportionably populous) country offers by accident the same
> unique advantage for meeting a social hiatus in our British system that is of-
> fered by certain southern regions in the American United States for meeting
> another hiatus within the same British system. Without tea, without cotton,

Great Britain, no longer great, would collapse into a very anomalous sort of second-rate power.

De Quincey's bluster ironically underscores Britain's dependency upon her colonial possessions; free trade takes the form of a new "tribute" in which impoverished or enslaved laborers and captive markets around the world supply the needs of Britain and support her luxurious and exploitative culture:

> In both of these cases [tea and cotton], it happens that the benefit we receive is unique; that is, not merely ranking foremost upon a scale of similar benefits reaped from other lands—a largest contribution where others might still be large—but standing alone, and in a solitude that we have always reason to regard as alarming. So that if Georgia, &c., withdrew from Liverpool and Manchester her myriads of cotton bales, palsied would be our commercial supremacy; and, if childish China should refuse her tea (for as to her silk, that is of secondary importance), we must all go supperless to bed; seriously speaking, the social life of England would receive a deadly wound. It is certainly a phenomenon without a parallel in the history of social man—that a great nation, numbering twenty-five millions, after making an allowance on account of those amongst the very poorest of the Irish who do not use tea, should within one hundred years have found themselves able so absolutely to revolutionise their diet as to substitute for the gross stimulation of ale and wine the most refined, elegant and intellectual mode of stimulation that human research has succeeded in discovering.
>
> ("Hints," 18:155)

Inadvertently reversing a conventional narrative, De Quincey announces that it is the imperial core that benefits from and is dependent upon the colonial periphery. By his reckoning, the national decision to "revolutionise" the British diet has resulted in a wholesome addiction that must be secured at any cost: if cheaply produced Indian opium will no longer be accepted in exchange for Chinese tea, there must be war. De Quincey's bellicose rhetoric is undercut by the anxious, if unintentionally derisory, description of Britain as "a very anomalous sort of second-rate power" were she deprived of the labor of slaves in Georgia and peasants in India or China; or that, unless she learns to act like a proper imperialist and declare war on China, she will be punished, forced "to go supperless to bed." This description of British power as an expression of vulnerability or dependency parallels the opium eater's belief that his addiction fuels his creativity. It proceeds from the opium eater's insight that the writing self is held in place, claims its integrity, as a result of discontinuous effects from the "outside." Read with the *Confessions* in mind, a shuttling effect is created: opium as drug, the heteronomous source of creative inspiration, is paralleled with opium as commodity, which pays for Britain's addiction to Chinese tea.[8]

II. ART AND TRANSPLANTATION:
A LITERARY INTUITION OF THE GLOBAL?

It is in his reflections on literary or creative writing that De Quincey makes explicit the peculiar force of this exteriority and the effect it has on his vision of the global. The opium eater, he first claims, consumes opium "in th[e] character" of a philosopher, to whom nothing is alien—"*Humani nihil a se alienum putat*":

> For amongst the conditions which he deems indispensable to the sustaining
> of any claim to the title of philosopher, is not merely the possession of a su-
> perb intellect in its *analytic* functions (in which part of the pretension, however,
> England can for some generations show but few claimants; at least, he is not
> aware of any known candidate for this honour who can be styled emphatically
> *a subtle thinker*, with the exception of Samuel Taylor *Coleridge*, and in a nar-
> rower department of thought, with the recent illustrious exception of *David
> Ricardo*)—but also on such a constitution of *moral* faculties, as shall give him an
> inner eye and power of intuition for the vision and the mysteries of our human
> nature: *that* constitution of faculties, in short, which (amongst all the genera-
> tions of men that from the beginning of time have deployed into life, as it were,
> upon this planet) our English poets have possessed in the highest degree—and
> Scottish Professors in the lowest.
>
> > (*Confessions*, 5)

The philosopher, in the sense of the poet, is exceptional in discerning the concealed and disparate significance of the evanescent words, actions, and gestures that animate the gross matter of everyday human activity. The "constitution of faculties" of such a figure is distinct in that it is, to follow a line of thinking opened up above, dependent upon outside forces for its power. If Britain's unique constitution is described by her addiction to tea, the philosopher's "subtlety" rests on his dependency on another alien commodity, opium.

In an essay composed soon after the *Confessions*, De Quincey briefly attends to the idea that art can facilitate an identification with the aggressor as opposed to the victim, in which scenario sympathy is defined by De Quincey as "the act of reproducing in our minds the feelings of another, whether for hatred, indignation, love, pity or approbation."[9] Art requires a prolonged state of acquiescence in which the audience "reproduces" within itself even feelings that are by convention or consensus thought repugnant or alien. De Quincey therefore declares it unfortunate that sympathy is taken for a synonym of pity: "hence, instead of saying 'sympathy *with* another,' many writers adopt the monstrous barbarism of 'sympathy *for* another.'" Such reproduction implies a passivity on the part of the reader: for its successful enactment one suspends judgment, thereby making oneself over as an element, or object, within the terms of this world. Needless to say, to give oneself over to the experience of the artwork is quite different from choosing to confer or withhold one's sympathy. There is instead an involuntary surrender, in which one finds oneself absorbed by another, just as an adequate response to Shakespeare's *Macbeth* must begin with the audience's having already entered unconditionally into the complex motivations of the two murderers. By acquiescing passively or being absorbed by the "retiring of the human heart and the entrance of the fiendish heart" (*Confessions*, 84), the spectator becomes complicit, as it were, with the murderer in that he comes to see this as the new world to which he must learn to respond, on its terms; the audience becomes a part of this other world:

> Another world has stepped in; and the murderers are taken out of the region of human things, human purposes, human desires. They are transfigured: Lady Macbeth is 'unsexed;' Macbeth has forgot that he was born of woman; both are conformed to the image of devils; and the world of devils is suddenly revealed. But how shall this be conveyed and made palpable? In order that a new world may step in, this world must for a time disappear. The murderers, and the murder, must be insulated from the ordinary tide and succession of human affairs— locked up and sequestered in some deep recess; we must be made sensible that the world of ordinary life is suddenly arrested—laid asleep—tranced—racked into a dread armistice; time must be annihilated; relation to things without abolished; and all must pass self-withdrawn into a deep syncope and suspension of earthly passion.
>
> (*Confessions*, 84)

In a strange twist on Lady Macbeth's "unsex[ing]," the reader is unselved, made to see the limits of his own vision. The extraordinary power of De Quincey's evocation here draws out the nature of sympathy as an undoing or making other of the self. As "the human" makes its "reflux upon the fiendish" with the knocking that returns the audience to the familiar world, the power of art lies revealed in having so overwhelmingly made the audience imaginatively partake of the atrocities committed by Macbeth. Although the knocking shocks them out of this complete surrender to and identification with the violence perpetrated by the regicide, it leaves a trace of the complicity between the audience and the "awful parenthesis" it now repudiates, from the ostensible shelter of the "everyday." This is the unresolved relationship between "this world" and "a new world" made visible by the artwork. The "new world" connotes both the realm of evil or aggrandizement that the audience, replicating the emotions of the regicide, covets, as well as the unfamiliar traits or emotions which contaminate them from, and, as it were, attract them to, another terrain.

Like the armed aggressor abroad, *Macbeth* stages the spectacularly violent way in which alien regimes are instituted and the ambivalent feelings of loathing and fascination elicited amongst audiences or spectators. In the everyday, this "awful parenthesis" may be rationalized as the condition for progress and improvement, much in the way De Quincey's essays revalue imperialism as the facilitator of global production and exchange. However, De Quincey's complex meditation on the aesthetic offers distinct insights into his own exploration of the relationship between the moral subjects of the core who indirectly benefit from even as they repudiate the imperial excesses committed in their name. In the sections that follow, I explore the manner in which *The Confessions of an English Opium-Eater*, read as an artwork in the sense suggested by De Quincey's reading of *Macbeth*, stages the "new world" of imperial Asia as it is brought into global view through the ambivalent figure of opium.

The force of this reading derives from the fact that the opium eater is alerted from the outside to the textuality of the self, that is to say, to the uneven and heterogeneous effects by which such an entity (or identity) is constituted. It could even suggest that the self is constituted as an effect of unbidden forms receptivity or absorption. In De Quincey's text, the ensuing contamination of the self generates a vision that is not premised on the putative homogeneity and stability of metropolitan norms. If imperial management and control seem indispensable in such a world of threatening differences, the possibilities of being moved, or transported, is as terrifyingly compelling to the dreamer. The literature of power yields a new and unfamiliar dream of the global:

The dreamer finds housed within himself—occupying, as it were, some separate
chamber in the brain—holding, perhaps, from that station a secret and detestable commerce with his own heart—some horrid alien creature. What if it were
his own nature repeated—still, if the duality were distinctly perceptible, even
that—even this mere numerical double of his own consciousness—might be
a curse too mighty to be sustained. But how, if the alien nature contradicts his
own, fights with it, perplexes and confounds it? How, again, if not one alien
nature, but two, but three, but four, but five, are introduced within what once he
thought the inviolable sanctuary of himself?

(*Confessions*, 201)

III. NIGHTMARE OF CONQUEST

"Not the opium-eater, but the opium, is the true hero of the tale; and the
legitimate center on which the interest revolves" (78). De Quincey's decla-
ration in the *Confessions* makes clear his belief that the opium eater's life
ought to be viewed as the lens or medium that brings into peculiar focus
the narcotic's effects. We might add that the singularity of De Quincey's
experience and personality are in no way vitiated by this approach. There is
no question that *this* opium eater is a necessary condition of the tale as it
unfolds; he is simply not its subject.

The "palimpsest" (68) of the dreamer's mind bears the imprint of material
events that are apparently unconnected to the intimate terrors of subjective
dispossession. In its other aspect, opium appears in De Quincey's dreams
as a commodity produced and distributed by the English East India Company. Grown in the newly conquered Indian territories of Bengal and Bihar
under the auspices of the company, the enormously profitable drug was sold
in Southeast and East Asia by private traders. Profits from opium helped secure the precarious gains of British administration and expansion in India in
the late eighteenth century. They also created the conditions for a more thor-
oughgoing commercial penetration of Southeast Asia in nineteenth century.

The "hero" of the *Confessions* alternately appears in the guise of opium as
narcotic and opium as commodity. These two aspects of opium play off each
other: whereas the vector of the narcotic pushes the self toward the terrors
and possibilities opened up by difference, the commodity functions as part
of a material process to make the diverse histories of the non-European
world homogeneous through mechanisms of discipline and "exchange."[10]

The full story of the *Confessions*'s "hero" cannot be told without a clear understanding of how the relation between narcotic and commodity is, in its divided unity, organized by the text. This double existence of opium is most economically brought into view by the events connected to the appearance of the Malay. The circumstances surrounding De Quincey's gift of opium to the Malay afford, in turn, a broader if oblique consideration of the effects of European imperialism in nineteenth-century Asia.

In the *Confessions*, a set of disturbing dream sequences culminate in an image that confronts the dreaming subject with a life of its own. De Quincey describes the dream first as if he were a spectator, then as if he would by empathy or remorse turn into one of the nameless many that "surge" with the ocean: "Upon the rocking waves of the ocean the human faces began to appear: the sea appeared paved with innumerable faces, upturned to the heavens: faces, imploring wrathful, despairing, surged upwards by the thousands, by myriads of generations, by centuries:—my agitation was infinite,—my mind tossed—and surged with the ocean" (*Confessions*, 72). To whom do these "human faces" belong and why does De Quincey admit to something like guilt here? The very same phrase is to be found in an earlier passage where the maritime image is obliquely anticipated:

> Some of these rambles led me to great distances: for an opium-eater is only too happy to observe the motion of time. And sometimes in my attempts to steer homewards, upon nautical principles, by fixing my eye on the pole-star, and seeking ambitiously for a north-west passage, instead of circumnavigating all the capes and head-lands I had doubled in my outward voyage, I came suddenly upon such knotty problems of alleys, such enigmatical entries, and such sphynx's riddles of streets without thoroughfares, as must, I conceive baffle the audacity of porters, and confound the intellects of hackney-coachmen. I could almost have believed, at times, that I must be the first discoverer of some of these *terrae incognitae*, and doubted whether they had yet been laid down in the modern charts of London. For all this, however, I paid a heavy price in distant years, when the human face tyrannized over my dreams, and the perplexities of my steps in London came back and haunted my sleep, with the feeling of perplexities moral or intellectual, that brought confusion to the reason, or anguish and remorse to the conscience.
>
> (*Confessions*, 47–48)

This hallucinated vision of a London in which an innocuous rambler turns ambitious explorer offers rich possibilities for interpretation. In keeping with the spirit of literal-minded inquiry, however, I confine myself to an elaboration of its obvious references. To begin with, the city is likened to an arctic region through which "ambitious" explorers navigate with hopes of discovering a quicker route from Europe to Asia. That is to say, the relocation of London to the frozen waters to the north of Canada and Alaska is authorized by the reference to the elusive "Northwest Passage," which stood in the collective imagination of English traders of the time as a metonym for the vast markets for opium in Asia.[11] The narcotic figure enforces an alternation between the subjective and the structural. London and the untapped Asian markets may here be likened to opposite ends of a Chinese fan, binding into a peculiar unity two spaces that seem absolutely separate and without relation.

The narcotic dream is presented through metaphors of surplus extraction. The city has become structurally (rather than empirically) unrecognizable as a result of the enormous profits repatriated from distant lands in Asia. Images of overabundance give London the simultaneous appearance of a rich wilderness awaiting exploitation *and* a city displaying the tangible rewards of a conquest realized.[12] The economic historians P. J. Cain and A. G. Hopkins have explored the relation between military adventurism and high finance that began in the late seventeenth century. They link the rise of complex financial services and state institutions in England to the political compromises of the Glorious Revolution of 1688, arguing that expansion abroad generated the surpluses deemed necessary by state elites to suppress likely uprisings at home.[13] Alongside the founding of the Bank of England and the creation of a state bureaucracy and civil service whose ranks were filled with sons of the landed gentry, the mercantile and financial interests of the city evolved crucial services related to banking, shipping, insurance, the professions, communications, and distribution. In the course of the eighteenth century, with the receding threat of Jacobitism and the growing opportunities of territorial expansion abroad, financial interests and the modern British state remade London into a qualitatively new space, secured politically and economically by invisible flows whose workings and benefits were opaque to ordinary men and women—hence perhaps the opium eater's humorously condescending reference in the passage quoted above to bemused coachmen and porters.[14] London seems to have become unrecognizable to the opium eater: as "*terra incognita*" its new institutions emblematize new territories that need to be husbanded for profit. But the same sentence at once carries a distinct if not opposed charge: the "knotty problems of alleys" and "sphynx's riddles of streets without thoroughfares" suggest the labyrinthine proliferation of complex new institutions and legislation to serve the needs of financial and territorial administration. Here the metaphor of "enigmatical entries" suggestively pulls together several distinct but mutually supporting activities of imperial Britain: the balance sheets of accountants and the census reports of colonial officials, as well as the jottings of naval explorers and cartographers.[15] In this double and contradictory image London is visualized as transit and terminus, at once wild and domesticated: it is both the heterogeneous, undeveloped empty spaces from which raw materials are extracted *and* the unseen boardrooms for a homogenous reckoning of profit and power.

The links made in the *Confessions* between opium's narcotic and commodity forms are oddly paralleled in received historical accounts of the relation between London and Asia. Contemporary Britain's craze for Chinese tea and silks in the latter half of the eighteenth century was the cause of a growing balance-of-payments deficit with China. Because of scant Chinese interest in British commodities, the latter were forced to pay for Chinese luxury goods in silver bullion. A solution to this alarming hemorrhage of funds was found in opium. The situation was corrected as a result of the English East India Company's export of opium grown in the newly conquered Indian territories of Bengal and Bihar to the southern ports of China.[16] Indeed, by the late eighteenth century, opium as commodity seemed to perform for the British economy what opium as narcotic did by De Quincey's reckoning for the human body, restoring equilibrium and generating a surplus of dynamic power: "But I took it:—and in an hour, oh! Heavens! what a revulsion! what an upheaving from its lowest depths, of the inner spirit! what an apocalypse of the world within me!" (*Confessions*, 38).

In less fulsome language, an economic historian makes a strikingly resonant claim for opium's effect on the British nation: it not only turned around and "composed" (Chung, "The Britain-China-India Trade Triangle," 40) the ailing fortunes of the East India Company (then struggling to finance and administer its territorial gains in India) but also miraculously served as a stimulant to manufacturing interests in the mother country. Adam Smith's global perspective is realized in microcosm by means the production and exchange of a commodity, which enables the viewer to comprehend the world as a single entity, secured by a system of imperial production and exchange. This is the mode of perspectivizing presupposed by the *Confessions*:

Opium accrued revenue for the British Raj, and simultaneously remitted back to England a part of this revenue which had become private fortunes. There was no better vehicle like opium which could transmit British fortunes homeward from India and simultaneously replenish the source of these fortunes. In this regard, Indian opium had a greater strategic importance in the trade triangle than Chinese tea and British textiles. The British manufacturing interests should have strongly resented the westward commodity movement of the triangular trade. But the double utility of opium as both the generator and transmitter of the Indian revenue harmonized the internal contradiction of Britain's China trade between its import-orientation and its urge of expanding British exports.[17]

(Chung, "The Britain-China-India Trade Triangle," 424)

There is a curious parallel between the disorientation felt by ordinary Londoners in a city transformed by imperial trade and the feelings of the explorer who seeks a way home from Asia, presumably laden with Chinese tea and silk gained in exchange for opium produced in British India. This parallel is intriguing in itself, but because the reference to the Northwest Passage quite pointedly dramatizes the structural transformation of the city as a consequence of the drug trade in Asia, one is led to inquire into exactly which route the trader-explorer takes on his return leg to Britain.[18] Such a move helps create a sense of "Asia" as a term that does not exist solely as an effect of European geopolitics and international trade.

Since the Northwest Passage was not discovered until the era of steam navigation, it is evident that the opium eater turned opium trader is forced to return to England through the longer but more familiar route of the "capes and head-lands" noted on his journey out. And since the only other route to China from Europe was via Southeast Asia—the vaunted India-China trade route—the implication appears to be that the opium eater sails home through the Malay Archipelago and that it is in this region that he encounters the troubling "human face." This literal "fix" makes it likely that the human face is encountered in the context of an imagined opium-trading mission specifically linking the financial structures of London to the untapped resources of island Southeast Asia. In this regard the voyage also points to the gift of opium to the Malay elsewhere in the text. The allusion to the human face connects two obscure points of the *Confessions*: the opium trade binding London to Asia and the historical context of De Quincey's encounter with the Malay.

IV. COMMON ACCOUNTS

De Quincey's youth was profoundly shaped by Britain's being plunged in a series of fateful imperial wars, from the Seven Years War (1757–1763) and the revolt of the American colonies (1774–1783) through the Napoleonic Wars (1795–1815).[19] Victory over France brought to a close more than fifty years of intermittent war in Europe and Asia, and it made Britain the pre-eminent military and economic power of the age. *Confessions of an English Opium-Eater*—the reference to the author's nationality is significant—was published at the end of the decades marked by these wars and by the English East India Company's search for a naval base in the Malay Archipelago. Passage through the Straits of Melaka in the archipelago made for the shortest distance between the ports of Calcutta and Canton, and it did not take much to realize that whoever controlled the Melaka Straits had an effective stranglehold on the immensely profitable China trade. The French and the Dutch also had designs on this trade route; in these circumstances the Malay Archipelago came under intense European scrutiny and pressure. Beginning in 1763, explorations for a suitable British base were conducted in the Melaka and Sunda Straits. Candidates included Aceh, Junk Ceylon, Balambangan, and the Nicobar and Andaman and Riau islands. It culminated in the founding of two ports in the Melaka Straits: Penang in 1786 and Singapore in 1819.[20] Both ports played key roles in the transshipment of opium grown in India for sale in the Malay Archipelago and China.

The opium trade caused profound dislocations throughout Asia.[21] The profits made in Singapore were the cause of the disparities of wealth in the region that led to the undermining of native authority in the peninsula. For the British, however, opium sales disbursed the cost of conquest and administration in the newly conquered territories of India and Java, and the profit paid for commercial expansion in island Southeast Asia.[22] By the end of the eighteenth century, the British governor of Melaka was writing his superiors in Bengal to say that "the people of Rembau, Selangor and Perak, like other natives, cannot live without opium."[23] This is not simply to offer a context for the stray encounter between De Quincey and the Malay; it is an indication of opium's programmatic significance to the transformation of the heterogeneous structures of the native world. For the key innovation of modern European imperialism may be described as bringing about a change in the "motive of action" in the members of native society through the institutionalization of profit as the rationale of social existence.[24] I have already noted that the encounter between De Quincey and the Malay is most productively read in the context of the subordination of society to the imperatives of a modern idea of economy. While the Malay Archipelago had long been part of an Asian "trading world" that was undermined with the onset of European armed trade in the sixteenth century, the systematic induction of the peasantry by the British into the mechanisms of global capital accumulation represented a departure from existing economic practices.[25] It also laid the foundation for a new commercial and political order, consolidating the British and the Dutch in their respective spheres of influence and the arbitrary partitioning of the archipelago (as described by the distinct political entities known today as Singapore, Malaysia, and Indonesia). De Quincey's appreciation of the significance of the Malay Archipelago to British geopolitical and commercial interests is indicated in an essay he published in *Blackwood's Magazine* some twenty years after the first appearance of the *Confessions*, in which he recalls with anger Britain's decision to hand back the colony of Java to the Netherlands V.O.C. in 1816: "We gave up to Holland, through unwise generosity, already one splendid island, viz. Java. Let one such folly suffice for one century."[26]

In this regard it is striking that De Quincey marks 1816 as the very year in which the Malay appears at Dove Cottage (*Confessions*, 61). Following the defeat of Napoleon, the date also coincides with the East India Company's resumed efforts to found a trading port in the Malay world to secure the opium trade between India and China: "One day a Malay knocked at my door. What business a Malay could have to transact amongst English mountains, I cannot conjecture: but possibly he was on his road to a seaport about forty miles distant" (*Confessions*, 55). In the familiarity with which the term "a Malay" is used here—and the breezy speculation over sea ports and business transactions—lies the East India Company's long presence in the Malay world and the enumerative and classificatory labor of its colonial scholar-officials.[27]

But who or what is a Malay? Even though influential colonial scholars like John Crawfurd, following William Marsden and Stamford Raffles, define a Malay as the inhabitants of the Malay Peninsula and parts of Sumatra and the coastal regions of Borneo, the imperial perspective was as liable in practice to equate the figure of the Malay with the material success of its trading ports in the Malay Archipelago. In a work published in 1855, Crawfurd refers to the astonishing success of Britain's port, Singapore, in these terms: "such prosperity of which there is no other example in the east, and which far more resembles that of an American than an Asiatic settlement" (*Descriptive Dictionary*, 401). Given the diverse races gathered on colonial port cities in the archipelago, many non-European inhabitants might well have been identified by the early nineteenth-century colonial authority as "Malay." I can only speculate on what form of colonial scholarship or travel writing De Quincey drew on for his figure of the Malay. In his eyes the Malay may even have stood for the "horrid intercourse" peculiar, in his view, to those hybrid Asiatic societies, neither Chinese nor Indian, produced by the global upheavals of colonial capitalism. In this case, the Malay would signify the proper name of the "Asiatic" inhabitants of a specific region but would also stand as a general figure for an irreducible racial mixing:

> In 1826, or seven years after the British occupation of Singapore, the population of the island, in round numbers, had already amounted to 13,000. In 1850 it had risen to nearly 60,000. . . . The ingredients of this population were very heterogeneous, and composed of no fewer than fifteen nationalities. The most numerous were the Chinese, forming fifty-three parts out of a hundred, or better than half of the whole. Then followed the Malays, or proper natives of the country, forming twenty-three parts, or less than a fourth; natives of the continent of India, chiefly of Bengal and the Coromandel coasts, forming fourteen parts, natives of Celebes four parts, and Javanese three parts. The coloured descendants of the Europeans amounted to no more than 922, and the Europeans themselves, the rulers, only to 360. The languages spoken are, at least, as numerous as the nationalities. The Chinese speak three different tongues, the people of Continental India four, and those of Celebes and Java two each. Then come English, Arabic, and Persian. But the common medium of intercommunication, the language which unites all classes of inhabitants, and prevents such a variety of tongues from making a Babel of the place, is the liquid, easily-acquired Malay, of which all strangers acquire at least an useful smattering.
>
> (Crawfurd, *Descriptive Dictionary*, 400)

What matters from this perspective, more than visible markers, is that the Malay is marked by the fact that he speaks the Malay language. For my purposes, the Malay is best identified as an effect of the language, not in terms of a racial or ethnic category, which turn out in the colonial archive to be vanishing terms.[28] As recently as the early twentieth century, an eminent scholar-official offered this description of the internal heterogeneity and plurality of "Malay," undermining somewhat the reified logic of racial enumeration initiated by the colonial institution and mythologized by the postcolonial Malaysian state:

> In recent historical times the mixture of Malay races has proceeded rapidly in British Malaya.... Old Malay [precolonial] Malacca was full of thousands of Javanese and many Muslim Gujeratis and Tamils, and these aliens must have left their mark on a population that was a collection of strangers from the beginning. Selangor may have traces of old Malacca suzerainty, but the modern nobility are Bugis and there have been numbers of recent Sumatran immigrants. Negri Sembilan has been Minangkabau almost from the first. In Kedah and the Northern States there has been an infusion of Siamese blood. Again, in every State in the past there has been intercourse with the aborigines, and aboriginal women have borne children to Malay fathers. Wavy or curly hair, dark complexions and other evidence of Semang blood distinguish the Malay of Upper Perak. South of that is the lank-haired Indo-Chinese Malay type, whose ancestry is Sakai on the distaff side.[29]

As it is used by De Quincey, the word "Malay," like the archipelago from which he comes, is viewed as an effect of a global commodity regime; the self-identity of "Malay" as a univocal term has more to do with the phantasms of the global as perspective than with the historical complexities of the region. "Malay," like "opium," serves in different ways to secure the "identity" of a global civil society founded on commodity exchange. Out of this global mode of seeing is carved a presumption of equivalence or commensuration through which the opium eater presumes to identify the Malay as a "fellow":

> My knowledge of the Oriental tongues is not remarkably extensive, being indeed confined to two words—the Arabic word for barley, and the Turkish for opium (*madjoon*), which I have learnt from Anastasius. And, as I had neither a Malay dictionary, nor even Adelung's *Mithridates*, which might have helped me to a few words, I addressed him in some lines from the *Iliad*; considering that, of such languages as I possessed, Greek, in point of longitude, came geographically nearest to an Oriental one. He worshipped me in a most devout manner, and replied in what I suppose was Malay. In this way I saved my reputation with my neighbours: for the Malay had no means of betraying the secret.
>
> (*Confessions*, 56–57)

For all the humor and lighthearted irony, the Malay is produced—becomes visible and is cognized—exclusively within the terms of an ongoing project of a disciplinary mapping of the world: a common pattern is revealed among taxonomies relating to the cultivation of cash crops, philology, lexicography, and geography.[30] If nothing else, this helps induct De Quincey's reader (or "neighbors") into the lines of correct perception, a mode of thematizing the world that is passed off as natural and true. Just as the Malay's identity is viewed in terms of this frame, the issue of perspective itself does not become a consideration, for everything is a matter of accurate information and finely calibrated techniques to discern and tabulate the differences by which "identities" are produced. It is no surprise that the absence of the "Malay dictionary" appears to be all that stands in the way of responsible intercourse between the Malay and his European interlocutor.

The perceptual horizon that I discuss above is now insensibly concatenated with a scholarly and discursive apparatus that conceives of translation as a rendering common of heterogeneous and distinct languages on the order of currency exchange, with the imperial metropolis serving as the point to which all languages refer: Arabic, Turkish, Malay. The disparity of being in the world is made legible within a mode of thematization that is "remarkably extensive." This global style of seeing and speaking is displayed in the opium eater's attempt, tongue only half in cheek, to address the Malay in Greek since this language's home is, "in point of longitude," nearest the Malay Archipelago. It is a minor point, but De Quincey shows himself aware of the influential speculations on the common origin of the "Indo-European" languages whereby ancient Indian languages and customs could be subsumed, by a curious public, into a Eurocentric frame.[31] Whereas such groups often regarded themselves as noncoercive, open-minded, and attentive to difference, their modes of thematization already exemplify the practices of the common metric of enabling a purely quantitative measure, in which difference is underwritten by a deep if unacknowledged identity.

V. THE "MALAY DICTIONARY"

The commodity regime makes available a style or code of valuation in which De Quincey posits a social bond between himself and the Malay. As the Malay prepares to leave, De Quincey offers him "a piece of opium," inferring that "to him, as an Orientalist, I concluded that opium must be familiar" (*Confessions*, 57). De Quincey is aware that when country traders began flooding Asian markets with opium, local elites were quick to grasp the lucrative power of the commodity, which they used to shore up different power bases in their several struggles against one another in the context of widening British and Dutch interference in local politics and culture. Opium brought new technologies of weaponry and intensified rivalries between local elite groups, contributing to the further destabilization of the societies of the archipelago.[32]

Opium would have been familiar to the Malay, but this familiarity would be more likely owing to the ruinous effects of Indian opium in the archipelago. It is impossible to reconstruct the perspective of the Malay, or his context as it might be elaborated from this perspective, if only because he is invoked in De Quincey's text as a foil for the European subject's self-consolidation. De Quincey says that the Malay accepts the opium and swallows at one mouthful "the quantity [that was] enough to kill three dragoons and their horses" (57). It is never revealed why he ingests the opium or if he survives the overdose. Soon afterward the Malay appears in the opium eater's dreams as a vengeful and violent figure.

But it is precisely from this confined view that a shift occurs: opium as narcotic enables the figure of the Malay to be grafted onto the hallucinations of the opium eater. The Malay appears in these visions as a historical agent; he interferes with the value system set in place by the system of commodity exchange. It begins when De Quincey, despite his claim that he knows no Malay, utters a Malay word:

> This incident I have digressed to mention, because this Malay (partly from the picturesque exhibition he assisted to frame, partly from the anxiety I connected with his image for some days) fastened afterwards upon my dreams, and brought other Malays with him worse than himself, that ran 'a-muck' at me, and led me into a world of troubles.

> (*Confessions*, 57–58)

The Malay word is, of course, "a-muck." The quotation marks draw attention to the fact that it is not an English word and give it the appearance of a scientific or objective term. An authoritative footnote is also appended: "See the common accounts in any Eastern traveler or voyage of the frantic excesses committed by Malays who have taken opium or are reduced to desperation by ill-luck at gambling" (58). The entry for *amuk* in the *Oxford English Dictionary* suggests that by the time of the publication of the *Confessions* in 1821 the word had found enduring form as the indiscriminate and brutelike violence that inexplicably overcomes the lesser races. The current *OED* definition has "amuk" as "a violent Malay." However, a less clear picture of "a-muck" develops in a Malay-English dictionary that was compiled by the eminent linguist and historian William Marsden, who served as an East India Company official in West Sumatra in the 1770s:

> **Amuk**: engaging furiously in battle; attacking with desperate resolution; rushing, in a state of frenzy, to the commission of indiscriminate murder; running a-muck. It is applied to any animal in a state of vicious rage. *Segala pahlawan datanglah mengamuk mengikut rajania* (all the warriors rushed on to the attack in imitation of their chiefs). *Segralah iya tampik kaduania sama mengamuk* (immediately both parties shouted and rushed on to battle). *Lalu bertikam-tikaman dan beramuk-amukan* (then was there mutual stabbing and mutual slaughter). *Mengamuk kadalam rayat* (to rush with fury into the ranks). *Pada sangkania orang mengamuk juga rupania* (they were thought to have the appearance of persons running a-muck). *Orang iang mengamuk nakhodania* (persons—belonging to ships—who murder the masters of them).[33]

It is remarkable that all six sentences offered as examples of the word's usage, which Marsden drew from Malay manuscripts and letters, suggest something akin to calculated and purposeful violence. This is best conveyed by Marsden's invocation of the "desperate resolution" of those who go into battle. Far from solely indicating the indiscriminate or mindless bloodletting associated with "running a-muck" (the idiomatic phrase in English that both De Quincey and Marsden use), *amuk* seems to also have been a term used by locals to describe military combat and other forms of premeditated violence.[34] There is also no mention of opium in either Marsden's definition or in the Malay-language examples he provides.

Marsden made his dictionary at the end of several centuries during which the Portuguese, Dutch, French, and British wrestled for control over key positions and territories in Asia.[35] More immediately, the dictionary's publication coincided with the British invasion of Java in 1811, the first full-fledged attempt by the British to become a territorial power in the Malay Archipelago as they were in the Indian subcontinent. However, as a disappointed De Quincey notes in a passage I have quoted, Java would be returned to the Dutch in 1816. We know that Marsden's dictionary was of great use to the occupying forces. It was acclaimed throughout Europe and was regarded by colonial scholar-officials in Southeast Asia as the most formidable work of its kind.[36] It is, however, worth musing over the apparent disjunction between Marsden's definition of *amuk* and the Malay usages he quotes. There is no way to tell if the violence through which Europe established its dominance in the region played any part in the accretion of new connotations to *amuk*, not least those having to do with mindless violence or "indiscriminate murder."[37] An instance, perhaps, of the "lost" perspective I discuss in my introduction, the word was also used to describe the trancelike rage drawn on to fight against overwhelming odds. The word *amuk* may combine both the crazed aspect that De Quincey discerns in the imaginary Malay *and* the desperate courage of those natives who fought a powerful foreign aggressor in the face of certain death.[38] Such acts may well have appeared crazed to European soldiers and impartial spectators alike. But the view that phrases like "state of frenzy" and "vicious rage" describe actions that have a historical cause finds support in a history written by a colonial official, Stamford Raffles, an architect of the British invasion of Java in 1811. In his *History of Java* (1817), he wrote: "Those acts of vengeance, proceeding from an indiscriminate phrenzy, called *mucks*, where the unhappy sufferer aims at indiscriminate destruction, till he himself is killed like a wild beast, whom it is impossible to take alive."[39] Even though Raffles's account tacitly places such "vengeance" in the context European military aggression, it is worth pointing out that what was in Malay usage a verb—*mengamuk*—is here transformed into a noun—"mucks."[40]

By means of such lexical transvaluation, the *OED* now defines *amuk* as "a frenzied Malay." By reading *amuk* in the manner of a Quinceyan "palimpsest" (*Suspiria de Profundis*, in *Confessions*, 139–43)—that is, as a word informed by and acting upon history—I wish to suggest how the perspective in which such a definition is produced may be troubled. Translation serves to highlight how the univocity of the global perspective is inscribed by a prior context—language here indexes the uneven manner in which meaning passes from one regime of value to another. By way of a consideration of the relation between the English "amuck" and the Malay "*amuk*," we see the heterogeneous valuations that are brought into view, as the dominant mode of sense making comes into contact with others.

In an important dictionary compiled by R. J. Wilkinson more than a century after the publication of Marsden's pioneering work, an interesting twist appears in the *amuk* entry: "*Colloquially and in modern times* of 'running amuck', ie. indiscriminate murder by a desperate man who neither expects nor desires mercy. Laksamana **mengamok**."[41] Of interest is the conjunction "and" in the italicized phrase; the "colloquial" Malay usage seems to have been affected by the uncomplicated official use—in the sense of mindless or frenzied violence—to which the word had been put by the modern colonial state. By Wilkinson's day the colloquial Malay use corresponded to a definition foreign to Marsden's dictionary. What was disjunction between English definition and Malay usage in Marsden is a century later deemed perfect correspondence: "*amuk*" is now synonymous with "amuck."[42]

Colonial scholarship—aptly dubbed "the prose of counter-insurgency" by one historian—is of little direct help in this regard; one must approach the historical transvaluation of *amuk* with a different imagination.[43] In a discussion of the difficulty of accounting for the opaque and uneven periods between a definitive change in the meanings and values attached to words, Gayatri Spivak reflects on the Sanskrit word *lāsya* in the context of female temple dancers in ancient India. Referred to in fourth or fifth century A.D. texts as a dance that "enhances the auspiciousness" of social gatherings, according to Spivak by the twelfth century the word came to describe the "art of lust," the "stylization of seduction" performed by young female temple dancers (*devadasis*):

> Who knows exactly how *lāsya* changes into the art of lust? . . . Words change meaning bit by bit, here excess, there lack. We find fossils of 'earliest use' and strain this intimate mystery of linguistic change at ease from the incomprehensible social field of manifestation and concealment and sublate it into one line of a dictionary. Any history that tries to imagine a narrative of the subaltern woman's oppression must imagine that familiar lexicographic space, that line in the dictionary, into the uncanny; the strange in the familiar. That space is the mute signature of the process by which the woman becomes a ventriloquist, beginning to act as an 'agent' for *lāsya*. If this painful invitation to the imagination does not produce the disciplinary writing of history, then, as an apologetic outsider, I would submit that it might strengthen the discipline to recognize it as a limit.[44]

The relation of concealment and disclosure suggested in the relation between "*amuk*" and "amuck" enables such a turning, such an attempt to "imagine that familiar lexicographic space, that line in the dictionary, into the uncanny." Just as Spivak reflects on the opacities of linguistic change to propose imagining the subaltern woman as "a ventriloquist, beginning to act as an 'agent' for *lāsya*," my interest might be described as an attempt to learn how to turn the figuration of *amuk* in an unfamiliar direction; it is in this sense that I read the Malay as an agent of *amuk*. "Agent" is in both instances used in the sense that De Quincey describes himself as an agent *of* opium.

In what follows, I draw on lexical definitions to roughly outline three distinct valences of *amuk* as it corresponds to the precolonial, colonial, and nationalist periods. I then propose that these different meanings effect a displacement of De Quincey's perspective. This is the peculiar "agency" of *amuk* as activated through the figure of opium. I will argue that it brings about a reversal, whereby the text invites reading of De Quincey as he is thematized by the Malay. This makes imaginable the effaced perspective of the Malay without its being reduced to the order of equivalence that the narrator elsewhere takes for the basis of all relation.

Given the contexts in which the word was deployed, part of the interest of "amuck" is that in the disjunction between its definition and its varying usages, a trace remains of a movement or impulse that cannot be fully made to fit the terms of the colonial archive. Generally, from the fifteenth to the eighteenth centuries the European conceptions of "*amuk*" seem to have been derived largely from the way the word was used in Malay. As cited in Marsden's dictionary, the word referred to premeditated or military violence; broadly speaking, this local usage appears to have set the limits to how Europeans (Portuguese, Dutch, Spanish, and English) used the word.[45] The entries for "amuck" in *Hobson-Jobson: A Dictionary of Anglo-Indian Terms* run to four pages, but here are some examples of how *amuk* was accordingly adopted in these European languages. My aim here is to draw on these usages to imagine the uneven texture inhabited by diverse value-producing agents:[46]

> After the **Zamorin** had reigned 12 years, a great assembly was held at Tirunavayi, when that Prince took his seat surrounded by his dependants, fully armed. Any one might then attack him, and the assailant, if successful in killing the Zamorin, got the throne. This had often happened. [For a full discussion of this custom, see Frazer, *Golden Bough*].
>
> (1566) "The King of Cochin ... hath a great number of gentlemen which he calleth **Amocchi**, and some are called *Nairi*: these two sorts of men esteem not their lives anything, so that it may be for the honour of their kings.—*M. Caesar Frederike in Purchas, Pilgrimes*, ii. 1708.
>
> (1624) "Though two kings may be at war, either enemy takes great heed not to kill the King of the opposite faction, nor yet to strike his umbrella, wherever it may go ... for the whole kingdom of the slain or wounded king would be bound to avenge him with the complete destruction of the enemy, or all, if needful, to

perish in the attempt. The greater the king's dignity among these people, the longer period lasts this obligation to furious revenge ... this period or method of revenge is termed **Amoco**, and so they say that the **Amoco** of the Samori lasts one day; the **Amoco** of the king of Cochin lasts a lifetime; and so of others."—*P. della Valle*, ii. 745 [Hakluyt Society, ii. 380].

(1672) Every community (of the Malabar Christians), every church has its own **Amouchi**, which ... are people who take an oath to protect with their own lives the persons and places put under their safeguard, from all and every harm."—*P. Vincenzo Maria, Ill Viaggio all' Indie orientalí del P ... Procuratore Generale dè Carmelitani Scalzi, 1672.*

(1783) At Bencoolen in this year (1760)—"the Count (d'Estaing) afraid of an insurrection among the Buggesses ... invited several to the Fort, and when they had entered the Wicket was shut upon them; in attempting to disarm them, they *mangamoed*, that is **ran a muck**; they drew their cresses, killed one or two Frenchmen, wounded others, and at last suffered themselves, for supporting this point of honour."—*Forrest's Voyage to Mergui*, 77.

The word is sometimes used to refer to "gentlemen," possibly feudal lords or retainers sworn to protect the king.[47] At the other extreme, it describes a practice of ritual violence that is part of kingly succession. The other entries refer variously to mercenaries, local heroes, or sworn protectors of the community. One entry suggests a comparison with the Amerindian tribes and the final entry I include below refers to a political assassination carried out by Malay rulers in the face of growing British interference:

(1798) "At Batavia, if an officer take one of these **amoks**, or **mohawks**, as they have been called by an easy corruption, his reward is very considerable; but if he kills them, nothing is added to his usual pay.—*Stavorinus, Voyage to the East Indies (1798)*, i. 294.

(1803) "We cannot help thinking, that one day or another, when they are more full of opium than usual, they (the Malays) will run **a muck** from Cape Comorin to the Caspian."—*Sydney Smith*, Works 3rd ed., iii 6.

(1875) "On being struck the Malay at once stabbed Arshad with a *kriss*; the blood of the people who had witnessed the deed was aroused, they ran **amok**, attacked Mr. Birch, who was bathing in a floating bath close to the shore, stabbed and killed him.—*Sir W. D. Jervois to Earl of Carnarvon*, Nov. 16, 1875.

What begins in the sixteenth century with attempts to understand how the word was used by locals or to describe practices associated with the word, turns by the nineteenth century into Sydney Smith's "run a muck," also used in Marsden and De Quincey.[48] It may be significant that this use of amuck to denote mindless violence begins a few decades after the East India Company and English country traders began flooding the archipelago with the profitable drug in the 1770s.[49] After Smith in 1803, it is striking that virtually all (English-language) uses of the word in the nineteenth century presume irrationality on the part of the agent of *amuk*. In the last entry included above, Sir William Jervois in 1875 describes the native plot to assassinate a British resident as the result of unmasterable impulse: "the blood of the people who witnessed the deed was aroused."[50]

The passages quoted above go some way to pointing out the shifting ideological charge attending the word's deployment over time. As is clear in Wilkinson's 1932 dictionary, the irrationality associated with "amuck" by the nineteenth century comes to inform colloquial use and the definitions in Malay dictionaries compiled in the modern era. What is common, however, to the passages quoted, and here I include Marsden, is that they are all exclusively concerned with physical violence. In the Malay dictionary compiled under the auspices of the national academy of language established by the government of independent Malaysia, the following is offered as an example of correct usage: "*Maka segala hulubalang Melayu tampil pula amuk dengan feringgi* [all the Malay warriors clashed with the Europeans]." The script of violence is retained but cast in the language of a concerted and unified anticolonial struggle, indicative perhaps of one more epochal transvaluation.[51] Whereas the Malay *amuk* was subsumed under the figure of the insane or the irrational by nineteenth-century colonial lexicography, twentieth-century nationalist discourse neatly reverses this valuation by according it the full weight of a modern political struggle.

VI. OPIUM AND THE GLOBAL

De Quincey's overt reliance on a vision of the global imposed by colonial capitalism is an affirmation of both nationalist sentiments and civilizational hierarchy, but his writings have a tendency to undermine the triumphal or complacent strains that accompany such an attitude. Here the figure of opium troubles the postulation of a hygienic division between self and other, inside and outside. Even as opium as commodity serves as an allegory for the virtues of free trade—national sovereignty guaranteed by drawing more foreign spaces into the orbit of the market system—the narcotic agency of opium pulls in a different direction, attentive to possibilities that are not comprehended by the single measure of the global as an effect of the universal market system. It is according to this protocol of De Quincey's text that a link is intimated between the "a-muck"—itself a word derived from a linguistically heterogeneous and discontinuous archive—and De Quincey's own relationship to the exteriority that is his memory:

> What else than a natural and mighty palimpsest is the human brain? Such a palimpsest is my brain; such a palimpsest O reader, is yours. Everlasting layers of ideas, images, feelings have fallen upon your brain softly as light. Each succession has seemed to bury all that went before. And yet in reality not one has been extinguished. And if, in the vellum palimpsest, lying among the other *diplomata* of human archives or libraries there is any thing fantastic or which moves to laughter, as oftentimes there is in the grotesque collisions of those successive themes, having no natural connexion, which by pure accident have consecutively occupied the roll, yet in our own heaven-created palimpsest, the deep memorial palimpsest of the brain, there are not and cannot be such incoherencies.
>
> (*Confessions*, 144)

As so often happens in De Quincey, the attempt at the end of the passage to reclaim some unified identity compares unfavorably with the contrasting images of centrifugal play that are so powerfully evoked. Subjectivity is imagined by analogy with external forces and historical chanciness. On the next page, once more, the image of memory as a sheet written upon from the outside is evoked once more: "the mysterious handwritings of grief or joy which have inscribed themselves successively upon the palimpsest of your brain; and like the annual leaves of aboriginal forests, or the undissolving snows on the Himalaya, or light falling upon light, the endless strata have covered up each other in forgetfulness" (*Confessions*, 145). Memory is analogized with the inscriptions of external forces, taken in without being a function of "interiorization." And at the moment of death or in the opium experience, De Quincey suggests, all these memories take on a simultaneous existence: life itself appears as a palimpsest, in which "every act—every design of her past life lived again—arraying themselves not as succession, but as parts of a coexistence" (*Confessions*, 145).

De Quincey's insights into the nature of memory have some relation to the way in which we might read the different dictionary meanings and usages of "amuck." The palimpsest of individual memory "inscribed" upon by the force of dreams or events begins to resemble the palimpsest upon which different meanings and uses of "*amuk*" and "amuck" are given density, both in succession and in simultaneity. Like individual memory, the various dictionaries can be imagined along the lines of such a "vellum palimpsest," the general form upon which words are rewritten according to their changing usage. With these different meanings gathering around the constellation *amuk* and amuck the Malay is given a reality effect in a manner not unrelated to De Quincey: whereas the former is a virtual effect of lexicography, the latter is the displaced or externalized enactment of opium's being. Like the individual memory described by De Quincey, the discontinuous entries in the various dictionaries and glossaries substantialize a "character" for the amuck. Like the opium eater whose life gains meaning and density in the context of opium, the Malay's identity is produced as an effect of the canonical revaluations of *amuk*. Speaking of individual memory in the *Suspiria*, De Quincey claims that, "Each succession has seemed to bury all that went before. And yet in reality not one has been extinguished" (*Confessions*, 144). In this light the Malay who runs amuck can be newly conceived as a subject who is comported in some manner to De Quincey—albeit one whose "character" is operated by an archive in a manner analogous to the complex relation that obtains between the opium and its eater.

We are obliged to imagine the Malay through the resonances that accrue to the word *amuk* since this is the only word associated with the single act that he autonomously undertakes in relation to De Quincey; the "character" of the Malay I am trying to configure otherwise becomes more complex if we have recourse to postcolonial Malay dictionaries compiled for local use. Published in postcolonial Malaysia and Indonesia, these works indicate that the word can be used to evoke a state of anxiety, mental agitation, alienation (*berkecamuk, kacau fikiran, bergelora*). It can also denote unbearable longing, as for a loved one; being head over heels in love; being overwhelmed by the smell of mouthwatering food; the confusion wrought by the claims of reason and passion; the play of conflicting emotions; the raging of winds; and being swept over, as by an earthquake.[52] The common thread linking the many uses of *amuk* is not violence but the feeling of being overwhelmed, physically, sensorially, emotionally. Acts of violence could be part of such overwhelming, but they are not its sole expression. In a Malay dictionary compiled after Indonesian political independence from Dutch rule, there are more hints of this other trajectory, inasmuch as definitions are not merely confined to the language of vicious rage and determined fighting or the instrumentalities of colonial and the postcolonial states:

> **Amuk**: to go berserk, to run amuck. 2. rage violently: *diamuk lindu*. To suffer the violence of an earthquake. *Pikiranku diamuk kehabisan bensin*. My thoughts turned inside out because we had run out of gas. *Aku amuk memukul siapa saja yang mendekat*. I went wild, striking at whoever came near. A literary use appears with *Mengamukkan*: 'to incite to violence' *Mengamukkan anak buahnya*. He incited his men to violence. *Berkelahi amukan*: to have a knock down, drag-out fight. 2. uncontrolled raging *amukan kerinduan*. *Amukan angin topan*: raging of the typhoon winds.[53]

In a continuum with the Malay examples Marsden draws upon, and the rationalization of *amuk* as alienation or deliberate violence signaled in the Malaysian *Kamus Dewan*, the definitions suggested here, particularly the latter examples of violent passion or raging winds, suggest a strange kinship with De Quincey's own image of inspiration as visiting him, as it were, from the "outside" (*Confessions*, 91). *Amuk* in these instances suggests being overthrown by an external force (from which the "self" may not be fully distinguished) to which an easy or familiar relation cannot be claimed.

The uncanny interface between the effects of opium and *amuk* enables me to propose a distinct approach to the encounter between the two. The dense significations of *amuk* allow something like a figure of the Malay's desire as it brushes against the vector in which De Quincey claims him as a kindred spirit. The opium eater's complacent appeal to the "familiarity" of opium was the means of claiming fellowship with the Malay stranger who appears at his door: "[The Malay] lay down upon the floor for about an hour, and then pursued his journey. On his departure, I presented him with a piece of opium. To him, as an Orientalist, I concluded that opium must be familiar: and the expression of his face convinced me that it was" (*Confessions*, 56–57). For De Quincey, opium serves as an unambiguous token of goodwill. For reasons already noted, it is reasonable to suppose that the Malay does not contemplate the commodity with the same serenity as De Quincey. Indeed, to many Malays of the time, no commodity could have served as a more pernicious symbol of how social structures were undermined for the sake of profit.[54]

The broader perspective governing the "gift" of opium to the Malay is hinted at in an essay De Quincey published two decades later on the occasion of the annexation of a key region of Ceylon. The gift is revealed here to be a euphemism for unequal exchange:

> Is cotton a British gift? Is sugar? Is coffee? We are not the men lazily and avariciously to anchor our hopes on a pearl fishery; we rouse the natives to cultivate their salt fish and shark fisheries. Tea will soon be cultivated more hopefully than in Assam. Sugar, coffee, cinnamon, pepper, are all cultivated already. Silk worms and mulberry-trees were tried with success, and opium with *virtual* success.[55]

Writing in *Blackwood's Magazine* in 1843, the opium eater addresses an implied audience for whom the roll call of commodities serve as metonymic substitutes for the names of peoples and places around the world. This mode of naming reflects a sensibility (on the part of writer and perhaps the audience) already disciplined to reduce social actions with distinct values to the homogenous and uniform register of modern commodity exchange. In this light the native's satisfaction with a mere "pearl fishery" may well seem a failing of both the economic and moral imagination. For this reason, perhaps, arguments for the violent incorporation of non-European peoples into the capitalist networks of exchange could in good faith be viewed as an expression of global sympathy, carried out, as it were, for the sake of the natives—in short, "a British gift." What, then, is one to make of the Malay's reaction to the opium?

> Nevertheless, I was struck with some little consternation when I saw [the Malay] suddenly raise his hand to his mouth, and (in the school-boy phrase) bolt the whole, divided into three pieces, at one mouthful. The quantity was enough to kill three dragoons and their horses: and I felt some alarm for the poor creature: but what could be done? I had given him the opium in compassion for his solitary life, on recollecting that if he had traveled on foot from London, it must be nearly three weeks since he could have exchanged a thought with any human being. I could not think of violating the laws of hospitality, by having him seized and drenched with an emetic, and thus frightening him into a notion that we were going to sacrifice him to some English idol.
>
> (*Confessions*, 56–57)

The Malay's action puts an immediate stop to the opium eater's claims of fellowship and sympathy. Whatever his motives, his act interrupts the dream of harmonious exchange. Following this mysterious act, De Quincey says:

The Malay has been a fearful enemy for months. I have been every night, through his means, transported into Asiatic scenes. I know not whether others share in my feelings on this point; but I have often thought that if I were compelled to forego England, and to live in China, and among Chinese manners and modes of life and scenery, I should go mad. The causes of my horror lie deep; and some of them must be common to others.

(72)

Even as the narcotic dream draws on the meaning of *amuk* laid down by the colonial lexicon, it seems evident that, contrary to De Quincey's claim that the Malay is murderous, he only seeks to "transport [De Quincey] into Asiatic scenes" (72). These journeys also appear to be made possible by the Malay, for it is "through his means" that the opium eater finds himself physically confronted by "Chinese manners and modes of life and scenery."

What is the outcome of this encounter? A clue is lodged in "transport": the word evokes at once opium consignments moving with indifferent regularity between the isomorphous terms "Calcutta," "Singapore," and "Canton" and the narcotized movement open to distinct notions of exchange. Through the figure of *amuk*, the narcotic insinuates a skeptical evaluation of the commodity dream. Although the opium eater invites the reader to participate in the comforting thought that opium appears in the same light to him and the Malay—the gift is, after all, made with the harmonious ideals of global civil society in view—the tragic consequences of the Malay's action suggest that something is out of joint. The Malay's bolting "in one mouthful" of the commodity reveals more than a lack of good manners; it amounts to a rejection of civil society. The Malay's dissimulation of his relation to the commodity turns him, in De Quincey's eyes, into "an enemy." Not only has the opium eater been spurned, he has also been duped, and he turns against the Malay when the latter returns. A complex interplay of perspectives forms in De Quincey's claim to be "transported" by the Malay:

No man can pretend that the wild, barbarous, and capricious superstitions of Africa, or of savage tribes elsewhere, affect him in the way that he is affected by the ancient, monumental, cruel, and elaborate religions of Indostan, &c. The mere antiquity of Asiatic things, of their institutions, histories, modes of faith, &c. is so impressive, that to me the vast age of the race and name overpowers the sense of youth in the individual. A young Chinese seems to me an antediluvian

man renewed. Even Englishmen, though not bred in any knowledge of such institutions, cannot but shudder at the mystic sublimity of castes that have flowed
apart, and refused to mix, through such immemorial tracts of time; nor can any
man fail to be awed by the names of the Ganges, or the Euphrates. It contributes much to these feelings, that southern Asia is, and has been, for thousands
of years, the part of the earth most swarming with human life: the great *officina
gentium*. Man is a weed in those regions. The vast empires also, into which the
enormous population of Asia has always been cast, give a further sublimity to
the feelings associated with all oriental names or images.

(72–73)

This passage ironically embodies the insensible processes through which
the growing field of Orientalist scholarship, official colonial memoranda,
and international trading practice converge to produce an image of a premodernity that conforms to the European archive's taxonomic predisposi-
tions. The one-sidedness of De Quincey's gift is exposed by the rapidity
with which sympathy changes to procrustean objectivity. The terms "su-
perstition" and "religion," "tribes" and "castes" have since become staples of
social scientific vocabulary. And so even as the opium eater claims that the
sublime backwardness of Asia is wholly alien to Europe, he inadvertently
reveals the extent to which this insight into difference has been produced
and made possible within the discourse of the same, by an overriding
desire for equivalence. But what the opium dream stages is not so much
the other but the taxonomy that produces difference and its intensification through a refinement of its protocols of knowledge production. The
alterity produced is a phantasm that says more about the observer than
the thing observed. By the same token, what is to be feared by the opium
eater—who now places himself as the object of its gaze—is less the thing
described than the process that gave rise to a description and an imagination of such terrifying power.

And it is here that the narcotic dream puts the opium eater in a strangely
vulnerable position, where he construes himself as a victim of that form of
scrutiny that he had trained upon the other. He imagines himself being
objectified by the other, and he cannot see the other who observes him
as anything but an object to be loathed and feared. Here is the strangely
disorienting rhetoric of the erstwhile conqueror employed to describe his
subjugation:

In China, over and above what it has in common with the rest of southern Asia, I am terrified by the modes of life, by the manners, and the barrier of utter abhorrence, and want of sympathy, placed between us by feelings deeper than I can analyze. I could sooner live with lunatics, or brute animals. All this, and much more than I can say, or have time to say, the reader must enter into before he can comprehend the unimaginable horror which these dreams of oriental imagery, and mythological tortures, impressed upon me.

(Confessions, 72)

In speaking of the paraphernalia of the orient "impressed" upon him, the opium eater disorients the reader with a series of substitutions. The opium eater stages himself as being thematized by an "orient" that is an occidental projection. The aggressor puts himself in the place of the victim, with a strange awareness that this is what he is doing. In this way he foregrounds the extent to which this "China" and "southern Asia" are the products of an overheated discursive mechanism that is more fearsome than anything to be feared from that other. Although he is the putative victim, the opium eater identifies equally with the force that metes out the harshness and the "unimaginable horrors."

In a similar fashion the figure of an unimaginable and terrifying vastness, in which individuality and subjectivity are subsumed and destroyed, seems to come from a source much closer to home. If the vision of terrifying otherness is produced as an effect of equivalence, it is equally striking that allusions to "vast empires," "enormous populations," and the workshop of peoples that the opium eater calls *officina gentium* refer less to the unsteady reach of enfeebled Asian powers than to the nascent superpower in Europe. What the imperial historian C. A. Bayly has called "proconsular despotisms" is embodied in the absolute power wielded by Warren Hastings in Bengal or Stamford Raffles in Java.[56] Similarly, the ambitious transplantation of crops and human labor undertaken by the colonial order, the radical transformation of landscapes, the destruction of customs and practices that followed the institution of a global market system evoke with far greater force the *officina gentium*—a workshop where people are manufactured—than anything dreamed up by the Asian regimes of the day.

Opium as narcotic shows up the alien as an effect internal to the modalities of the commodity regime. Heterogeneity is not in this case in "excess" of the comprehensible or thematizable in the manner of the sublime object; rather, it gnaws at the system from within. And there is a stirring of resistance within the world that is newly "assembled" and "brought together" by the opium eater. The vision that follows is an artistic equivalent of Marsden's violent "a-muck":

> Under the connecting feeling of tropical heat and vertical sun-lights, I *brought together* all creatures, birds, beasts, reptiles, all trees and plants, usages and appearances, that are found in all tropical regions, *and assembled them together in China or Indostan.* From kindred feelings, *I soon brought Egypt and all her gods under the same law.* I was stared at, hooted at, grinned at, chattered at, by monkeys, by paroquets, by cockatoos. I ran into pagodas: and was fixed, for centuries, at the summit, or in secret rooms; I was the idol; I was the priest; I was worshipped; I was sacrificed. I fled from the wrath of Brama through all the forests of Asia: Vishnu hated me, Seeva laid wait for me. I came suddenly upon Isis and Osiris: I had done a deed, they said, which the ibis and the crocodile trembled at. I was buried, for a thousand years, in stone coffins, with mummies and sphynxes, in narrow chambers at the heart of eternal pyramids. I was kissed with cancerous kisses, by crocodiles; and laid, confounded with unutterable slimy things, amongst reeds and Nilotic mud.
>
> (*Confessions*, 73–74; emphasis added)

A strange confusion of substance takes place as a consequence of the dreamer's ambition to bring together planetary life "under the same law." The directing presence of the Malay "compels" him into forms of interaction and exchange over which he has no control. In a manner reminiscent of the misleading docility of the Malay in Dove Cottage, he finds his hopeful vision "hooted at, grinned at, chattered at" by animals that are ostensibly brought under control. Gods that have been reduced to museum exhibits show unexpected willfulness in seeking revenge for an unspeakable act: "I had done a deed, they said, which the ibis and the crocodile trembled at." Indeed the reaction of the gods does not so much offer a figuration of the sublime—as De Quincey would have us believe—as desperate resistance to the manner in which a narrow discourse of progress is used to transform reason into an oppressive myth. The "transport" of the opium-eater has less to do with the challenge of a premodern or non-European other than the interruption of the perspective of colonial capitalism and its forms of knowledge. The strange complicity of opium as narcotic with *amuk* enables this wayward rhetoric to be grafted onto the main narrative. What is significant then is that the opium eater's expression of horror at the Asiatic is double-edged, for it also serves as the means by which the dominant power is seen other-wise, or, put differently, has its way of seeing defamiliarized.

The narcotic vision reveals that the sources of sublime terror may lie much closer to home than expected, but it also abets, through the figure of *amuk*, new forms of complicity: the dreamer finds himself "*confounded with unutterably slimy things*" (*Confessions*, 74). Kissed by the crocodile and compelled to live with him for centuries, the opium eater awakens to see his children before him, linked in some way to the "unutterable monsters and abortions of [his] dreams" (*Confessions*, 74). The narcotic therefore produces a different kind of self-relation in the opium eater from that tacitly elabo-rated by the commodity regime, revealing once more the schizophrenic or agonistic character of the "hero" of this tale. A polyvalent description of this self-relation might be "*amuk*." Between the creation of difference by the dream of equivalency and the experience of difference through a self without self-relation, something like a heteronomous exchange comes into view.

The opium-eater is spoken for; the peculiar sympathy produced here is not that of the spectator who complacently defines the terms of his involve-ment with the other. Instead he finds himself possessed and transported by the Malay. It is within the loathing for an already infected self that a new kind of sympathy for the other is confusedly articulated. In this bizarre com-mingling, this "horrid inoculation upon each other of incompatible natures," the opium as narcotic enables the Malay to speak his torment through the opium eater and to register his "loathing and fascinat[ion]" (*Confessions*, 74) for the new Asia produced by a Europe rampant. As so often happens in the narcotic dream, the one who sees is not identical with the one who speaks; it is in this way that De Quincey is possessed by the Malay. If the living Malay paradoxically withholds something from the blandishments of the commodity by his silent acquiescence, the dead Malay who returns in De Quincey's dreams is a trace of the subaltern vector that survives at an angle to the dream of equivalence. To be "transported" by the ecstatic figure of the *amuk* may in this sense turn out to be the Malay's gift to De Quincey; an attempt to reciprocate the latter's gift of opium. The figure of *amuk* makes it impossible for the opium eater to secure the terms of this exchange: "I was the idol; I was the priest; I was worshipped; I was sacrificed" (*Confessions*, 74). Rising up within the sanguine vision sponsored by colonial capitalism, the narcotic points to the activation of ungovernable difference within a world that has ostensibly been made safe in being made same.

3

NATIVE AGENT

Abdullah bin Abdul Kadir's Global Perspective

I. A FRAME OF AGENCY

Adam Smith's and Thomas De Quincey's texts illustrate the diverse and sometimes contradictory ways in which the Malay Archipelago in particular and Asia in general were imagined as an effect of free trade and homogeneous exchange. Smith argues that the "native Indian" ought to be liberated from the excesses of monopolistic coercion and tutored by the improving agents of the British state, while the "Malay" in De Quincey's *Confessions* is the object of a sympathy made possible by the universalization of production and exchange for the market. Conceived within these modes of thematization, what rules of interpretation and analysis should be brought to bear on *Hikayat Abdullah* (1849) by Abdullah bin Abdul Kadir, a writer who lived in the nineteenth-century British trading settlements of the Malay Archipelago?[1]

Given the formidable explanatory power of colonial knowledge production, it would be unwise to read the historical and autobiographical Malay prose narratives by "native" subjects in the nineteenth century exclusively as cases of the authentic self-expression of a society resisting European domination in a manner that conveniently looks forward to the arguments of twentieth-century elite anticolonial nationalisms. On the other hand, it is equally inadvisable to assimilate them to universalist narratives of global modernization.[2] The latter tendency, which may unite elite metropolitan

ideology in the global North and South today, has as much to do with
the forms taken in such representations as it does with the way modern
subjects are trained to interpret texts. The defining feature of such training is systemic inattention to the matter of representation. In the humanities as much as the social sciences, where concepts and terminologies were
produced within the complex and changing structures and exigencies of
European imperialism, insufficient attention is paid to the mediated forms
through which reality effects are instituted.

Shuttling between the contesting claims of European and non-
European social attitudes and institutions in the context of colonial Melaka,
Abdullah's writing is imbricated with this prior web that its authorial per-
sona *purports* to thematize and describe in an objective fashion. Rather than
assimilating the *Hikayat Abdullah* into foregone narratives of modernization or nationalist "awakening," both of which typically direct discussions
of this work, I engage with how the rhetorical strategies of the text set to
work new and mixed ways of producing "value," understood in its broadest
sense as making the world available for action and intervention. In this
chapter, I concern myself with how Abdullah self-consciously tries to replicate the representational form of the global perspective, most notably as
it is conveyed to him through the conventions of realism and the frame of
intelligibility provided by colonial knowledge production. I argue that his
attempt to reproduce the conditions of truth production is itself generative
of historical effects.

Born in 1797 to a family of Arab-Tamil traders resident in Melaka[3]—itself an
ancient Malay port and seat of the Melaka Sultanate that had fallen to the
Portuguese in 1511 and subsequently to the Dutch in 1641—Abdullah was a
translator, language teacher, and scribe who worked for the British in nineteenth-century Melaka and Singapore. As an adult he moved to Singapore,
where he served as a language teacher to numerous European merchants
and travelers and as a go-between in transactions involving Europeans and
natives. Working with Christian missionaries, he also translated the New
Testament into Malay and operated a printing press in Melaka. Abdullah
was at other times employed as a small trader who, despite his close connections with the British colonial power, never sought to turn his capital to very
great profit. He was neither a member of the native elite, nor did he appear

to have had any substantial knowledge of the Malayan hinterland and its peoples. He lived and died in the polyglot and creolized colonial ports in which Chinese, Arabs, Malays, and Indians were familiar presences.

When the Netherlands fell to Napoleon's forces, Britain preemptively seized control of Dutch Melaka in 1795 in order to prevent the French from establishing a foothold in the Malay Archipelago. Dutch imperial ambitions also had to be checked because the India-China trade (upon which the British East India Company had grown so dependent) and the security of the Coromandel coast of India all hinged on control over the Melaka Straits.[4] The ascendancy of European power in the Malay Archipelago was a final nail in the coffin for the precolonial trading networks going back to the thirteenth century that had brought traders from the Arab world, China, India, and the archipelago to ports such as Melaka and Batavia. As a result of the changed historical conditions, once-prosperous native-run ports such as Aceh and Riau were reduced to "outposts of progress" by the middle of the nineteenth century.[5]

Britain's victory over France in 1815 led to intensified activity in the Malay Archipelago, dominated by the search for a naval base and port of reshipment to service ships on the India-China route and a center of distribution for the valuable goods and markets of the East Indian archipelago.[6] These objectives were complicated by London's desire to use the Dutch (a weakened imperial power that no longer posed a threat to the British) in the region as a buffer against any reassertion of French interests. The Anglo-Dutch treaty of 1824 would divide the Malay Archipelago into "spheres" of Dutch and British influence, barbarously transforming at one stroke the culture and history of the region and paving the way, in the period of decolonization that followed the Second World War, for the creation of separate successor states such as Malaysia, Singapore, and Indonesia.

Abdullah's own background testifies to the complex history of the archipelago well before the arrival of the British. His great-grandfather was a Yemeni trader and religious teacher who traveled to Mysore in South India, where he married and settled down with a local woman. The four sons born to the couple all moved to various parts of the Malay Archipelago in the course of the eighteenth century. Abdullah's father, Abdul Kadir, was thus the son of a trader who had worked for the Dutch in Melaka. Abdul Kadir rose to the rank of a middling official in the Melaka port, and he also served as an emissary for the Dutch in their dealings with local rulers. Although this meant that Abdul Kadir was proficient in the courtly Malay required for correspondence with the native powers, Abdullah also says that his father's native tongue was Tamil, not Malay or Arabic. Abdullah himself grew up speaking Tamil to his mother and grandmother, both of whom were of Indian extraction.

The *Hikayat Abdullah* is a classic of Malay literature. Virtually every history of modern Malay letters begins with a reference to Abdullah's achievement, even if debates continue over whether he was "Malay."[7] This raises an apparent paradox, that the "father" of modern Malay letters was perhaps not Malay, at least in the ethnic and racial senses that determine usage in the postcolonial period.[8] As a prose narrative, therefore, the *Hikayat* simultaneously puts vernacular Malay writing on a new footing and draws attention to the author's peculiar "identity" in the Malay-speaking world. As I argue in this chapter, the two dimensions are related, but in the unexpected sense that acts of literature undermine the fictions of identity.

The *Hikayat* combines aspects of autobiography, history, journalism, spiritual reflection and advice, and ethnography.[9] Much of the work is an oblique reflection on the undoing of the Malay polity and, conversely, the rise of the British, who trick and outgun the Malay elite at each turn as they bend the trading and agricultural networks of the archipelago to serve the needs of a global capitalist economy. Abdullah's book is written to teach the natives of the archipelago how to emulate Europe's success by adopting the modes of perspectivization necessary to become historical agents. In retrospect, Abdullah's influence in the Malay-speaking world has been greatest in this regard. Even where they have condemned Abdullah's uncritical support for British rule, modern Malaysian and Indonesian nationalists have echoed Abdullah's emphasis on changing the mindset of Malay readers in order to make them better able to negotiate the terms of the new, abstract, and complex political and economic order that has been imposed on them.[10]

Some critics have downplayed the significance of Abdullah's works on the grounds that he had no empirical audience.[11] I contend, however, that Abdullah's work ought to be read less as sociological artifact than as an attempt to constitute the audience or implied reader its author deems normative. The *Hikayat Abdullah* stages the perspective and representational frames that the native reader must learn to occupy as "natural." Abdullah seeks to wean the natives from older ways of sense making and being in the world in order to describe the conditions by which they can become agents in the new historical regime.[12]

In his narrative Abdullah puts forth a new mode of perspectivizing as a way of making sense of a deeper epistemic shift. This shift exceeds the forms taken by colonial capitalist exploitation and oppression; therefore, the everyday humiliation suffered by the natives should not blind them to the steps necessary for a more far-reaching empowerment. This perspective manifests itself in the way Abdullah communicates to his readers the existence of a wider world. At one point the narrative recounts how a younger Abdullah was taught the attitudes and values that accompany such a mode of thematization: the colonial official Stamford Raffles shows him a friendly letter from the king of Siam to the British colonial authority in the Malayan Peninsula. One of the edges of the page on which the letter is written, however, appears to be "deliberately torn." Raffles construes this as a calculated insult. Abdullah reports Raffles's words: "In his pride and arrogance and stupidity the King of Siam thinks that his own kingdom is the whole world and that other countries are merely as the small piece of paper he has torn off" (*Hikayat*, 185; 236). The king of Siam, Raffles says, is like the boy who turned blind shortly after seeing only one thing in his life, a cockerel. When told of anything new, he insists on comparing it to the cockerel:

> "If the King of Siam had regarded other matters [*memandang perkara lain*] he could have compared them to himself [*bolehlah dibandingkannja dengan dia*]. That is the way of the King of Siam, because he has never regarded [*memandang*] other countries and other kingdoms and their huge fighting forces he thinks that his country is the only country and his kingdom the only kingdom in the world [*disangkannja negerinja itulah sahadja dunia ini dan keradjaannja itulah sahadja dalam dunia ini*], like the blind person who had seen [*lihat*] only a cockerel. If he were to see countries as large as England and other great powers and realize how enormous they are, how wealthy, how populous, how powerful their armies, then at last he would understand that his own country is a small spot on the roundness of the world [*baharulah ia mengetahui negerinja itu seperti suatu noktah djuga dalam bulat dunia ini*]."[13]
>
> (186; 238)

Abdullah has not himself "seen other countries and other kingdoms," but he offers Raffles's mode of perspectivizing as the preferred alternative to that of the Siamese king, who is unable to comprehend his country as one among many equivalent countries that can be compared as objects. This is indicated by Abdullah's use of different words—*lihat* (to see) and *pandang* (to regard or view)—in the passage above. Abdullah uses the first word to suggest a literal seeing (the cockerel is seen [*dilihat*] by the boy before he goes blind) and the second to suggest an abstract sort of sight, as in the king of Siam's failure to take into consideration, or bring into view [*dipandang-nnja*] the situation in other countries. The movement from a literal to abstract seeing (*lihat* to *pandang*) is Abdullah's way of enacting the recoding of value that he seeks to communicate, naturalizing an alien way of seeing by coding it as "the seen." Through language we see the slow process by which an epistemic remaking is put to work; that is to say, the language aims to gives a new way of seeing and saying that helps constitute "reality." Abdullah's words—I make no claim for his "intentions"—reproduce the terms in which a adequate analysis can emerge. In this light it is a secondary concern that Raffles's enthusiasm for territorial expansion in the archipelago may trouble other regional powers or that the tensions may result from Siam's traditional claim of suzerainty over the Northern Malay state of Kedah, in which the British too have an interest.

II. EXPANDING DEFINITIONS OF "SURPLUS"

In the following passage, Raffles draws on sound economic arguments to justify his decision to ignore the commands of his superiors in founding the free port of Singapore and to explain why the company cannot afford to give in to the demands of the angry Dutch, who want the British out of what they consider their "sphere of influence":

> By a statement I forwarded to the Court of Directors in February [1821] it was shown that during the first two years and a half of this establishment no less than two thousand eight hundred and eighty-nine vessels entered and cleared from the Port. . . . It appeared also that the value of merchandise in native vessels arrived and cleared amounted about five millions of dollars during the same period and in ships not less than three millions, giving a total amount of about eight millions as the capital payment.[14]

In everything Raffles wrote the language of abstract reasoning and objectivity served the instrumental needs of commercial and imperial strategy. Modeling his writing on the representational modalities of a colonial order intent on establishing a global civil society founded in imperial trade and commerce, Abdullah's narrative repeatedly implies that such seeing ought to be internalized and reproduced because it has the power to bring about great practical changes in the real world. Practically speaking, this desire is expressed in terms of Abdullah's desire to reproduce in the domain of representation what Karl Marx calls a "general equivalent," which is a metric by which the objects of the world can be described and compared within a single frame, just as material exchange in advanced societies takes place through a universal measure known as the money form:[15]

> The specific kind of commodity with whose natural form the equivalent form is socially interwoven now becomes the money commodity, or serves as money. It becomes in its specific social function, and consequently its social monopoly, to play the part of the universal equivalent within the world of commodities.[16]

The *Hikayat Abdullah* aims at a systematic account of the Malay language and a narrative of history whose representational structure is informed a mode of seeing and saying that reflexively operates within the universal value form. Abdullah's work attempts to outline for his readers this manner of making visible and legible entities as well as the condition of truth-production. At the request of an English missionary and his wife in Melaka who are bemused by their Chinese servant's claim that her son was attacked by a demon, Abdullah produces a long list of spirits, demons and ghosts, having declared such notions falsehoods (*bohong*) passed from generation to generation that reflect the ignorance and gullibility (*bodoh dan sia2*) of the common people. When Abdullah tells his reader that he chuckled and "explained clearly" (*ku-artikanlah...dengan terangnja akan segala nama2 hantu* [134]) to the Milnes the meaning of words like *djinn* and *afrit*, he performs a distinct function for his implied audience. He suggests that a native can become the figure to whom Europeans turn to for enlightenment because he has mastered this mode of representation, not because he is a mere native informant.

But even as he lists the different types of demons and spirits, it is significant that his description shifts from the form of universal equivalence in terms of which he claims to name and classify these objects. The metropolitan reader, much like the missionary Milne, is unable to grasp the principle by which he classifies and describes. Milne seems as astonished by this as he is by the diverse names of ghosts and spirits that Abdullah carefully lists:[17]

> Their number I am unable to say. Their full nature I cannot explain. But I will mention them briefly: devils (*hantu shaitan*), familiar spirits (*penanggalan*), vampires, birthspirits (*pelesit*), jinns, ghost-crickets, were-tigers, mummies (*hantu bungkus*), spirit birds, ogres and giants, the rice planting old lady (*nenek kebayan*),

apparitions, jumping fiends, ghosts of the murdered, birds of ill-omen, elemen-
tals, disease-bringing ghosts, scavenging ghosts, *afrit*, imps. . . . There are also
many occult arts the details of which I cannot remember, such as magic formu-
lae to bring courage and subdue enemies, love philters, invulnerability, divina-
tion, sorcery, rendering a person invisible, for blunting the weapons of one's
enemies, or for casting spells on them. . . . Then I drew a picture of a woman,
only her head and neck with entrails trailing behind. . . . I said, "Sir, listen to the
story of the birth-spirit."

(134–35; 115–16)

Abdullah's list extends over several pages: he digresses into stories of how
spirits are trapped for daily use, how the spirits who possess individuals can
be made to confess to who they were sent by, and even details about how
long it can take a person to die who has been possessed (136; 117).

It is less significant that Abdullah declares all this to be falsehoods
propagated by ignorant or backward people, for his substantive claims are
undermined by his reversion to an older type of presentation. What matters
for my discussion is that unlike the universal equivalent represented by the
money form, Abdullah's style of description begins to resemble that realm
of "constant connections" to which Marx gives the name "total or expanded
form of value." Here commensuration is endlessly repeated without a uni-
fying metric or center: "The value of a commodity, the linen for example,
is now expressed in terms of innumerable other members of the world of
commodities. Every other physical commodity now becomes a mirror of
the linen's value."[18] Value is coded so as to appear as "a particular equivalent
form alongside many others" whose series is by definition incomplete because it "never comes to an end." The form of value that obtains before the
institutionalization of the capitalist mode of production can be expressed
as, "z commodity A = u commodity B or v commodity C = w commodity
D or x commodity E = etc."[19]

The formal inconsistency or contradiction in Abdullah's text offers insights into a distinct but sympathetic way of reading the global. In light
of the effects produced by Abdullah's text, I wish to argue that to study
the global is to see how the universal equivalent and the total or expanded
form of value at once interfere with and supplement each other, challeng-
ing us to evolve new styles of reading. In Marx's language, value is differently coded in the total or expanded form and the universal equivalent. In
the context of colonial capitalism these two ways of coding value are in an

overlapping and interruptive relationship. In both forms, value can serve as a general name for the variable "currency" that establishes the possibility of "exchange, communication, sociality itself."[20] In the colony, as elsewhere, value coding names the different ways in which such sociality finds expression as colonial capitalism comes into contact with native institutions. Read alongside Heidegger, Marx's account enables us to see how Abdullah's work brings this contested terrain into view in an uneven manner. The colonial space is viewed less as an empirical object in this reading than as a patchwork of uneven value codings. Even as they overlap with one another, these codings make it possible to see how value is produced but also lends itself to being interrupted and channeled in new ways. At the same time, Abdullah's text is a kind of palimpsest that registers how the imperial institution pulls into its orbit the material relations of the less advanced society even as it relies upon tribute and other forms of extra-economic coercion, often drawn from "local" practices, to achieve its modernizing ends.[21] In the colonial capitalist economy, these two heterogeneous planes are in a mutually constituting and interruptive relation with each other; empirically, the total or expanded and universal equivalent forms inhere to both the "local" and the "global." It is therefore essential to learn to read the global in terms of this interaction between the two expressions of value coding (always already in overlap and interference), where the "money-form of value is letting in the total or expanded form of value surreptitiously."[22]

This mutually interruptive coding of value is at work in the scene where Abdullah speaks of all the hard work he has undertaken to educate himself. Education is something that is "more" (*lebih*), in that it raises him above the ordinary, but it is also in excess of itself because it expresses the creation of more value (*kelebihan*). What is striking here is that this notion of "moreness," or a value-creating value, is coded through the idioms of the everyday Malay. Abdullah implies that the difficult religious and moral education that he underwent in childhood accounts for his receptivity to the utilitarian and pragmatic values disseminated by the colonial institution:

> But I will not elaborate further the things that I suffered on account of my studies, like an *aur* stem rubbed the wrong way. My body became thin, my face sunken with the strain of thinking. I was anxious because I had not yet succeeded, I was ashamed at the prospect of being scolded. But I realize now that however high the price I paid for my knowledge, at that price I can sell it [*Adapun sebab itulah bagaimana kubeli mahal demikianlah hendak kudjual pun mahal*]. If I had

picked up my knowledge as I went along, merely copying and listening, so far from people wishing to buy it I would be quite prepared to give it away free for the asking. It is well known to you, honored sirs who are reading this *hikayat*, that anything cheap must be faulty: and anything expensive must be in some way in be greater than itself [*Dan tiap2 benda jang mahal itu dapat-tiada adalah djuga sesuatu kelebihannja*]. Is not the precious diamond but a stone? Why is it held in such high regard by everyone? Is it not because of its light?

(Hikayat, 32; 49)

The surplus made available through the concept of *kelebihan* (moreness) is itself derived from the practices, idioms, and schemata made available within an education coded by *agama*, a word that is translated as "religion." The teachings of his grandmother, his father and uncles, and itinerant religious teachers enable Abdullah to gain this "surplus." It is in this context that the relation with the modern conceptions of economic profit introduced by the colonial capitalist order is engaged in *Hikayat*. The texture of Abdullah's thought is such that he broaches the universal equivalent through the total or expanded form of value.[23] This notion of something that is greater than itself, produces an excess, or gives more value—"*adalah djuga sesuatu kelebihannja*" carries these connotations—unexpectedly resonates with Marx's own definition of labor power as exceptional because it is the only commodity capable of creating "more value [*Mehrwert*]." *Mehrwert* is usually translated as "surplus value," the excess produced by the worker that is withheld by the capitalist in the interests of capital accumulation. If Marx studies *Mehrwert* on the rational and abstract register of the economic, Abdullah's use of *kelebihan* inadvertently partakes of the endless connections in which the "cultural" overlaps with the "economic."[24] Abdullah shows that these forms are "motley," they do not cohere to produce a single or unified, that is, global perspective on the world: the total or expanded form of value is a disparate and heterogeneous chain of equivalents. The *kelebihan* or "surplus" is juxtaposed with and interferes with the *Mehrwert* by which Marx sought to denote the "surplus value" of colonial capitalist extraction.[25]

This *kelebihan*, or moreness, is described through a labor embedded within the context of Abdullah's childhood; it emerges from *agama*, the values and faith that his father is concerned to defend. It is this native education that enables him to gain this "surplus," this *kelebihan*, the more with which one can do more: the ability to make more. This mixed coding of value is not simply directed at the impositions of the colonial order. For one thing, it allows us to imagine the internal heterogeneity of the native's "home." Abdullah's father's first wife was a Malay woman from a village in the interior of the Malay Peninsula called Lubuk Keping. Abdul Kadir had settled there and had two children from his first marriage. However, Abdul Kadir was persuaded by his Tamil-speaking relatives to divorce his first wife, who remains nameless, and return to Melaka, where they arranged to have him married to a recently converted woman from Kedah named Selamah. This woman is Abdullah's mother, and it is from her that Abdullah learns Tamil as his mother tongue. In the context of the colonial regime's preoccupation with "ethnicity" from the end of the nineteenth century, it is worth noting the role assigned women in securing precolonial social-structure "identities" may indeed have informed how inhabitants of the Malay Peninsula in particular, and the archipelago in general, were classified through procrustean definitions of race and ethnicity.

Nonetheless, the fact that Abdullah has been described as "Tamil," whereas his half-brother and -sister are likely deemed "Malay," may not be assimilated to the terms in which ethnicity came to define political identity in the era of colonial and postcolonial Malaya.[26] There is difference, but not along the lines produced by the general equivalent "ethnicity" or "race" into which they will be subsumed by official discourse. Women were assigned by the patriarchal structure in these instances to arrest what appears to have been the internal heterogeneity of fluid social and cultural spaces of the Malay Archipelago that preceded the identitarian politics of the colonial and postcolonial eras. All the same, the critique of colonial and postcolonial reifications of race cannot be replaced by a celebration of precolonial creolity. How then to enter this text in such a manner that this practice comes to inform and interfere with the hygienic definition of *kelebihan* Abdullah provides? After all, he says that he learns of *agama* (moral and cultural norms coded through "religion"), much as he learns Tamil, from his grandmother and his mother. This opens a suppressed line of vision; whereas Abdullah discusses the travails of his education in terms of a struggle between his enlightened values and the blind traditionalism of people like his father, the figure of women educators points at once to an "internal" difference and to other ways of imagining the way value can be read. It shows how the tradition-modernity binary oppositions can be displaced through textured attention to the effaced assignation of women by which such binaries are either upheld or deemed superseded.

Although the global is conventionally analyzed as the subsuming of the total or expanded form of value to the general equivalent, most particularly in the rhetoric of a necessary transition to modernity, for the literary or cultural critic the two modes of valuation interrupt or interfere with each other.[27] What I suggest, therefore, curiously parallels Abdullah's effort: if he writes the *Hikayat* to induct himself and his benighted readers into a new and superior style or reflex of being in the world, my task is to see what in that text enables a vision of the other perspectives—invoked by Abdullah as the "value chain" with which he is most familiar—that are nonetheless effaced in the very process of producing the "correct" narrative of transition to modernity. Abdullah's attempt to replicate the global perspective gives way to other tendencies that cast a distinct light on the very form of historical agency that he endorses. These tendencies appear as an effect of the text; they interrupt Abdullah's laudable aims of empowering his native readers by teaching them the language and modalities of the correct way of thematizing the world.

The replication of the global perspective is again put to the test in an incident of "*amuk*" narrated in the *Hikayat Abdullah*. The incident centers on the stabbing of the British resident, Colonel William Farquhar, by a merchant from Pahang named Sayid Yasin. It occurs in 1823, four years after the establishment of a trading post on the island, at a time of especially tense relations between the Malay rulers and the British.[28] What is interesting about Abdullah's presentation of the story is his attempt, first, to imply a connection between an isolated case of assault to the broader political struggles between the British and the Malays, and, second, to turn the overreaction of the British into an instance of colonial pedagogy. In this episode, the interaction between the universal equivalent and the total or expanded forms of value can be studied by way of the different charges that accrue around the translation of a Malay word: *amuk*. Abdullah tells how, in his capacity as magistrate, the British resident, Colonel Farquhar, jails one Sayid Yasin, a respectable and well-known trader from the northern Malay state of Pahang, for his failure to provide a guarantor who will stand surety for his debt of four hundred dollars to one Pangeran Sharif. (The details of the case are hazy, but here is a brief outline: the Pangeran may have been a personal friend of Colonel Farquhar; Pangeran Sharif and Sayid Yasin appear to have known each other. Abdullah himself tells the reader later that he knew Sayid Yasin and had on several occasions discussed the lawsuit with the latter.)[29] Later that same day, Sayid Yasin gets permission from Mr. Bernard, the court clerk, to leave the jailhouse on the pretext of appealing to the Pangeran, his creditor, to allow payment to be delayed. But his intention, so Abdullah tells us in his retrospective account, is to murder the Pangeran. When the Pangeran sees the Sayid approaching his house bearing a knife, he slips out the back and runs to Farquhar's residence for help. Presumably a friend of the man in whose favor he had ruled earlier that day, Farquhar takes two Indian sepoys and a young lieutenant named Davies with him and heads for the Pangeran's house with the intention of apprehending Sayid Yasin. Abdullah's "eyewitness" account of this story starts here. When Abdullah runs into Farquhar, the colonel tells Abdullah to stay with him because the streets are unsafe.

In Hill's translation of *Hikayat Abdullah*, Farquhar speaks of "someone who has run *amok* in Pengeran Sharif's house." However, Abdullah's Malay text asserts only that someone is being violent in Pangeran Sharif's house: "*ada orang mengamuk dirumah Pangeran Sjarif*" (214; 170).[30] Whereas in Malay the word "*amuk*" refers to a planned attack or violent behavior, "*amuck*" conforms to that word's transvaluation through the prose of colonial counterinsurgency.[31] The strongest evidence of this transvaluation is that *amuk* is not so much translated as replaced by an English phrase "run amuck." The Malay word is already brought into view through the lens of the colonial state apparatus; it *appears* in the transcoded form of "amuck," appearing within the forms of native violence coded by the colonial institution (the naturalization of this history of violence conditions the *Oxford English Dictionary*'s definition of *amuk*: "a violent Malay").

I follow Hill's scrupulous translation here because he offers an insight into the way other ways of seeing can be inadvertently suppressed or occluded, despite best intentions. My argument will be that literary or cultural study in the age of globalization must attend to this tendency within itself, not least because the language of general equivalence is an indispensable condition of agency. We are operated by or spoken (for) through language in ways that fall before or beneath what we intend to say. The representation of truth as adequation is itself produced by and generative of "truth effects" that are not true or false in any obvious sense. For it is in his *inaccuracy* that the translator Hill, not the "original" Abdullah, catches at the "truth" of the event: what is at stake in Abdullah's account—his definition of truth—is how it is necessarily perceived within the colonial frame of reference. But whereas Abdullah reveals his imperfect fluency in this mode of thematization—he only knows *amuk*, and cannot do amuck—his readers, naturalized as subjects of the global perspective, may find in such lapses a way to defamiliarize "plain sight."

In the context of colonial aggrandizement in the Malay Archipelago, there are good historical reasons that a term the natives use to denote violence is appropriated in the master's voice. It is Hill, who, mistranslating, catches at the transvaluations involved in colonial rule and thereby "corrects" Abdullah. The error upraises the original, drawing it away from the diverse and confused meanings of the Malay word to organize a frame for the global as perspective, in which "amuck" refers to frenzied violence often directed against the ruling authority. Even if Farquhar had used the *Malay* word in his exchange with Abdullah, the transcoding is underway, for such an utterance was necessarily produced within the discursive attempt to render native violence legible to the colonial state. Abdullah's repetition of the same word, drawn as it is from a different historical texture that does not frame *amuk* from the perspective of native revolts or violence in the context of colonial expansion and conquest, necessarily fails to grasp the terms of this shift. Insignificant as the case may seem, it hints at similar forms of displacement and reconstellation in the colonial context through which the native is coaxed into new ways of thinking and being in the world.

Here my aim is to slow down the drive toward meaning and explanation, which is the dominant impulse in discussions of globalization, but not for the sake of a celebration of the "local." Rather, I want to attend to the limits or failures of the global perspective in order to facilitate the process of connecting with elements that are already imbricated with the terms of the general equivalent. If Abdullah's perspective is the one effaced in translation, I want now to point to how this effacement cannot be separated from his attempts at producing the global perspective in his own right. When Farquhar arrives at the Pangeran's house and searches its surroundings, he discovers Sayid Yasin, who suddenly stabs him. As he tries to get away, the Sayid is cut down by the young lieutenant Davies and the two sepoys. News of the attack on Farquhar spreads, and "all the white men came and stabbed and hacked [*menikam dan mentjentjang*] at the corpse of Sayid Yasin until it was so mutilated as to be unrecognizable [*sehingga hantjurlah, tiada berketahuan rupa lagi*]" (216; 172). Raffles rushes to the scene, thinking that a native has attempted to assassinate a colonial official.[32] The extent of the corpse's mutilation makes it impossible to ascertain the identity of Farquhar's attacker. Given the tense relations between the British and Malay authorities and the impossibility of identifying the assailant, the Europeans begin to wonder if it could have been an attack orchestrated by the Malay elite. Abdullah reports that suspicion falls on the Temenggong Abdul Rahman, who resides in Singapore. There is now an extraordinary turn of events as the Indian sepoys are instructed to aim their guns and cannons on the Malay ruler's residence. Captain Davies repeatedly requests permission from Stamford Raffles to bombard the residence of the Temenggong. Raffles hesitates; eventually the corpse is identified and the mystery cleared up. The lives of the Temenggong's family and his followers are spared.

Despite the fact that there is no evidence of a conspiracy, the British are both terrified and infuriated by Farquhar's stabbing. Raffles treats the stabbing as a political crime. He persuades himself that Sayid Yasin's actions are connected to the sultan, who has been causing the company much trouble. Raffles decides to make an example of Sayid Yasin by having his corpse publicly displayed. A frame is built that night and four Indian "slaves [*hamba*] of the [East India] Company came carrying ropes with which they tied up Sayid Yasin's body by the legs. They dragged it to the middle of the open space in the town where there was a guard posted, and hurled it on the ground [*ditjampakkannja ditanah*]" (*Hikayat*, 173; 219). Abdullah does not speculate over whether Raffles's decision to display the dead man's body was an attempt to cow the native population or to indirectly warn the Malay leaders against testing the company's strength. He makes no mention of the shock and outrage felt by ordinary Malays at the treatment of this respectable trader whose body is subjected to further indignity. In the words of a Dutchman who was in Singapore at the time, "all the natives adopted a threatening attitude [towards Europeans] . . . settlers and traders, as well as the Chinese who took the side of the Europeans were night and day under arms . . . since this upset there has been no very great sense of security amongst the merchants of Singapore."[33] Moreover, Abdullah does not describe the gruesome spectacle of a mutilated corpse at the center of the Singapore Padang, rotting slowly in the tropical sun, guarded by armed Indian sepoys. He barely hints at the symbolic gains the Johor rulers made from the widespread perception of British injustice, or that the sultan could claim a moral victory and increase his prestige amongst the locals by retrieving the Sayid's corpse and burying it with great ceremony. Abdullah deliberately suppresses the details of the ensuing tension between the British and the Malays, just as he leaves out the diverse codings of value by which the mutilated and gibbeted corpse of the Sayid is turned into a shrine and place of pilgrimage for the inhabitants of the island and, it would appear, the archipelago.[34] This lacuna is made up for in the reassuringly smug record of the incident kept by a British expatriate, who further codes the event as an expression of racial and religious hatred on the part of resentful Malays: "[Sayid Yassin's] body was then buried at Tanjong Pagar, where the results of the proceedings was (which Sir Stamford [Raffles] did not anticipate) that it became a place of pilgrimage, and Syed Yassin was considered a great saint, because the holy Syed had only killed a Fakir [an Indian sepoy] and wounded a Nazarene [Colonel Farquhar]."[35]

Believing perhaps that such codings of value (on both sides) are either irrelevant to or incommensurate with the mode of thematization requisite for empowerment, Abdullah moves toward the broader lessons that the native rulers must draw from this episode. Abdullah's discourse is not that of the oppressed victim but that of the subject who turns his masters into an object of knowledge and who turns the master's style of thinking and modalization of power into a reflex of his own. Writing as and for the common reader of Malay, Abdullah translates the perspective of the colonizer for the benefit of the natives: he seeks to induct them into a successful way of thematizing reality. We catch the at once historical and rhetorical character of this double or simultaneous transvaluation. Even as the British transcode Malay "*adat*"—this is the precursor of the anthropologist's "custom" or "culture"—into the terms of colonial law, Abdullah recommends that the Malay reader see how this transvaluation offers cues to positioning oneself as a proper subject of modern value coding. The ideological issue—support for or opposition to British rule—is a secondary concern. Decades after Abdullah's death, even as Malaysian nationalists became adept at deploying such critiques of colonial domination, the terms of valuation and the mode of perspectivization must take on the lineaments proposed by Abdullah.[36]

Abdullah foreshadows the pragmatic language of a particular nationalist imagination in Malaya, as well as a global capitalist imagination, for there is about him an urgency, a desire to have the benighted masses grasp that they too must internalize the values of the British if they are to have any chance of success in the new world order. For all his alleged lack of sympathy for the historical plight of the Malays, nationalists are quick to note that Abdullah aimed at empowering them by interpellating them into the symbolic order of colonialism, the alternative to which, Abdullah correctly believed, would be a disenfranchised state, one characterized by subalternity. In the process, what his text intuits is the figure of the colonial subject emancipated by education as historical sub-oppressor.

I am considering how rhetoricity, understood in this broader, "performative" sense, produces historical effects. It raises the question of how literary or cultural study in a globalizing age can attune itself to institutionalized coding in criticism and pedagogy. This takes us beyond the realm of intention. Abdullah necessarily ignores the complexity of the uneven social terrain upon which the Sayid's death is read: it is, after all, irrelevant to the production of a truth that will have purchase in the culture of imperialism. This is also the culture that the postcolonial subject will be trained to internalize as the language of his or her "arrival." In this light, Abdullah is producing neither history nor propaganda, only an effective way of seeing. In his account, the colonial master's disastrous handling of the Sayid Yasin case is turned into a lesson in (or at least coded as) "justice." When the Europeans and Malay rulers are assembled the day after the assault on Sayid Yasin, Abdullah stages this public exchange for the benefit of his readers. Although the passage tacitly exposes the cynicism of Raffles's attempt to use the dead Sayid as an excuse to illegally proclaim the East India Company the rightful authority in Singapore, this is not what exercises Abdullah:

> When they were assembled Mr. Raffles took the chair and said, "Your Highness the Sultan and Tengku Temenggong, what is the practice [*adat*] under the laws of the Malay peoples [*undang2 orang Melaju*] if a commoner [*seorang ra'yat*] thus commits treason [*mendurhaka*] against his ruler [*radjanja*] in this manner?"[37] The Sultan replied, "Sir, Malay custom [*adat Melaju*] would require that he and his family and relations all be killed, the pillars and roof of his house overturned and thrown into the sea." When he heard the sultan's words Mr. Raffles replied, "Such punishment is not just [*Itu hukum bukannja adil*]. Whosoever commits an offence deserves to be punished [*dihukumkan*]. But why should his wife and children, who are entirely innocent, also be put to death? . . . That is the custom of the white man [*Demikianlah adat orang putih*]."
>
> (219; 174)

Raffles is made the mouthpiece for a way of producing justice that is at once new and based upon a recoding of familiar, everyday Malay terms. What began as a crisis of colonial authority and then turned to British advantage is now transformed into a lesson on proportionate and just punishment: imperialism as civilizing mission and Raffles as company functionary turned ruler (*raja*) tasked with establishing civil society in another benighted corner of the globe.[38]

Abdullah does not fully grasp the justification for or basis of such "enlightened" thought. Instead, he offers an insight into how the colonial legal order was being translated for the natives. It is a moment of "iteration"— where under the pretence of adequation to a liberal or enlightened system of justice, the British draw on the Malay terms *rakyat, derhaka, adil, adat* (the people, treason, justice, custom) and recode them into the universal equivalent language of a new "despotic" order, cast as "improvement." Abdullah's role in this as an artist is not a small one; the postcolonial state will rely on much of this legacy for its right to speak in the name of the people, just as in the era of globalization the same language will inform the consensus for "governance." The relay of the general equivalent is passed on and reworked accordingly.

But a different "translation" was itself taking place beneath and around the colonial lines of power. I track this other movement not to celebrate it but to ask what lessons it might hold for a cultural studies that seeks to interruptive this dominant style of coding value. Unmarked by Abdullah's text, an "*amuk*" had been recoded by the local Malays as a "*keramat*" (or saint). (Abdullah is evidently aware of this recoding by the natives—since he notes that the sultan pays for the dead Sayid's funeral—but it is left out of his account.) The British seek to institute "rule of law" by using the Sayid's body as an example of what happens to traitors and evildoers. Here the imposition from above of a general equivalent by a civil—lawful—society forms the basis of the *kelebihan* that Abdullah (from below) says awaits those who educate themselves. But a different, if defective, excess is generated by the figure of the Sayid's corpse. A rival coding takes place here. The colonial authority's attempt to introduce civil society through "rule of law" is recoded as "martyrdom" by the enraged populace.[39] And because the supernatural power generated by such an act remains in force, the death of the Sayid produces a shrine which is daily visited by supplicants. The Sayid as *keramat* is absorbed into the supernatural world of *djinn* and *afrit* that seems so much a part of the everyday native world that Abdullah, perhaps under the guidance of Alfred North's letter (see p. 119), so categorically dismisses in a passage I discuss above. The spirits and supernatural effects banished earlier in Abdullah's account now return to trouble the terms in which the objective representation takes place. This is a perspective foreclosed in Abdullah's historical account. Nonetheless, what is exposed are the overlapping forms of "surplus" generated by this crossing of the "general equivalent" with the "defective" forms of value coding; they trouble the distinction between the "economic" and the "cultural." It is worth remarking here that Abdullah speaks of "*kelebihan*" (32; 49)—moreness—which comes with being educated. In Abdullah's reckoning, such "*kelebihan*" is a surplus or bonus that makes for better ethical subjects. Given Abdullah's intentions, however, it is not possible to elaborate upon how the *keramat* may have served also suggested other ways of revaluing the global equivalence by which it was activated.

The political significance of the *keramat* was also seized by the sultan, who sought to capitalize on this popular valorization of the dead Sayid's treatment by taking charge of the latter's funeral. The native elite were, like the colonial authorities, quick to seize the initiative to serve their ends, and once more the perspective of the lower orders of society—the heterogeneous and diverse groups Abdullah calls the *rakyat*—is effaced by such mobilizations. To an extent, the prize was as much control of the city as the new port that was read, by elite Malays, as a latter version of the Riau destroyed by the Dutch in 1784.[40] What remains to be read is how the Sayid who is made into a "*keramat*" is an instance of such an alternative, in Marx's words, a "defective" way of coding value. While such moments do not displace the narrative that Abdullah seeks to establish in the name of a general equivalent, they nonetheless yield other "connections" that contaminate the main narrative thread. By attending to such tangled encounters, I suggest an approach that reconnects with the general equivalent in ways that remain open to other forms of ethical desire and historical possibility, precisely as such forms can only intuited as an effect of the archive. These subaltern codings have to be imagined; they cannot be computed within the logic of the global as perspective. Inasmuch as the general and the "defective" forms of value coding interpenetrate one another, the one can as little be thought of as true as the other, false; the issue is what kinds of critical functions are enabled by an engagement with the truth effects produced in their interaction. This may yet yield a more nuanced conception of the global than has been presumed possible.

III. QUESTIONING IDENTITY

But it is Abdullah's stated aim that the colonizer's mode of thematization be communicated far and wide, for it is the condition of native empowerment. The connection is never directly made, but the emancipated "I" who exults in his newfound powers of independent analysis and objective evaluation is, in Abdullah's account, repeatedly linked to the native who has grasped the forms of valuation enabled by the military, technological, and economic prowess of the colonizing power. The word Abdullah repeats in this regard is "*heran*" (wonder, amazement, astonishment).[41] The prodigious power of colonial knowledge production to predict and manipulate reality impresses Abdullah. Without denying the importance of these insights, what has to be noted is the manner in which this mode of global thematization becomes something like an absolute horizon in which meaning is established. Abdullah repeatedly laments the foolishness of the natives who fail to grasp the extraordinary material advances made possible by the colonial forces.[42] They remain insensible to the great material changes that are made possible by British organizational and technical expertise.

Glimpses of this lack of commensuration are found in an argument that breaks out between Abdullah and his father, Abdul Kadir. Just after he has been trying, without much success, to persuade his Malay friends to send their children to study in the missionary-run Anglo-Chinese School of Melaka, Abdullah's father tells him to stop working with the British:

> My father was angry and stopped me saying, "I don't like you going to study English and its letters, for there isn't a single Muslim who does so. Besides, many people say that such work is not right: it will destroy your values [*merusakkan agama adanja*]. . . . Many people have told me that you will certainly be spoiled by learning English and following the white man's teaching [*menurut pengadjaran orang putih*]." I replied, "Is it not right that we should adopt good customs and renounce bad ones [*menurut adat jang baik dan membuang jang djahat*]? If a man passes from ignorance to knowledge is his reputation damaged [*Kalau dari pada bodoh mendjadi pandai rusakkah namanja*]?"[43]
>
> (126–27; 149–50)

The phrases Abdullah's father uses to assert the dangers of colonial education are coded in the language of the loss of one's bearings or values: "*dimasukkan Inggeris*" (149; literally, "to enter Englishness"), which signifies being converted to Christianity; "*merusakkan agama*" (149), or destroying (one's) beliefs or values. The idea of "*masuk Inggeris*," like the opposite, "*masuk Melayu*" (370), refers to the transformation of a way of life or ethos. Hence Abdul Kadir says, "For many people have told me that you will become spoiled as a result of studying English and following the teachings of the white man [*Karena banjak orang2 kata sama aku bahwa engkau nanti rusak sebab beladjar Inggeris dan menurut pengadjaran orang putih*]" (126; 150). The ambiguous word "*rusak*," which refers to breakdown or spoiling (of character, customs, values), is used by Abdul Kadir to mean being deranged from the modes of making sense of the world in the normative terms defined by the native patriarchal elite.[44] To be *rusak* is to be deranged or cut off from existing modes of making sense of the world.

Even as the British, with the help of locals like Abdullah, are busy translating the social codes and idioms of the native society into a representational structure given coherence by the universal claims of the "general equivalent," native subjects like Abdullah's father retranslate in "defective" ways this powerful new perspective. Abdul Kadir's intransigence is interesting since he had worked as an envoy for the Dutch merchants and spoke their language, albeit in a different historical dispensation where the rhetoric of universalism and improvement of nineteenth-century liberals were not yet prevalent. There is the hint of a distinct force here, in which the exposure to the values of the cosmopolitan West leads to a continuing negotiation with colonial power, not an acceptance of a superior or objective set of values. The native translates the colonial order into versions of the "total or expanded form of value," much as the colonizer is busy sublating the native world into the terms of the general equivalent. It is useful to keep this other perspective in mind, especially since colonialism is so often regarded by historians as the placeholder for an inevitable or necessary "modernization."

Whereas Abdullah's father frames his fears in the terms of a way of life, a mode of making sense of the world that will be deranged, Abdullah demands to know how the increase of knowledge—which is surely intrinsically valuable—can cause one's name or reputation to be spoiled (*rusak namanja*). Whereas Abdul Kadir conceives of learning as it is encompassed by the values of Muslim society in Melaka, Abdullah refuses to believe that knowledge production or acquisition have anything to do with the realm of social mores. Abdul Kadir speaks of the spoiling of "*agama*" ("belief," in the deeper sense of a space of precomprehended actions), but Abdullah refuses this connection and interprets (only to dismiss) the possibility that one's reputation or good name (*nama*) may be spoiled by learning. Western science and knowledge are, in his view, good in and of themselves. This exchange need not, however, be framed in terms of the usual "tradition" versus "modernity" polarity, in which difference is tacitly subsumed within the necessitarian or normative perspective defined by "the modern." Instead, it can be read as a historical negotiation, in which attempts at recoding take place in both directions, both "universal" and "defective."

Such an approach would be salutary not least because of Abdullah's commitment to the univocal discourse of "modernity." This reflex is active in Abdullah's attempt to communicate a form of rational organization of which the Malays are unaware. Abdullah speaks most forcefully of the need to reform the Malay language, to codify and systematize the grammatical rules in order to halt the heterogeneous ways in which the language is spoken across the archipelago. He calls for a standardization:

> You must know that from the past right up to the present time the English have been improving their language day by day. They have simplified its structure, cut away its accretions, and discarded its useless forms. Its pathways have been made clear and the words classified each with its appropriate rule for use. English is like Malay in having borrowed words from other languages and incorporated them in itself. Therefore it is in my opinion a very easy language to understand; so easy that a carriage could be driven along its paths in midnight darkness because they are all so carefully marked out. But this Malay language of ours is surely like a large forest full of thick undergrowth, prickly thorns, tangled roots and matted brushwood strewn in the way, its paths tortuous, its ground hilly. The further one goes the muddier becomes the way because the rain, beating down on the ground, has sloughed it up. For ages past has any living person tried to put in order or to map out its roads and their boundaries? The majority even of the people born in this forest are caught by the thorns and stumble hither and thither falling head over heels in the mud.
>
> (227; 302–3)

The comparison between the Malay and English languages, like that between the Malay and English peoples, is construed in terms of Enlightenment "stadial" theory.[45] In the postcolonial era such comparisons are no longer made, but the peculiar instrumental character of the template remains very much in place. Abdullah sees in the power conferred by colonial classificatory mechanisms a link with the forms of modern bureaucratic and military discipline and organization: the colonial power distinguishes itself from the colonized subjects in the way it manages the movement and mobilization of bodies. Early in the *Hikayat*, Abdullah describes his astonishment at the organization, coordination, and discipline peculiar to modern European armies; he watches the newly arrived Anglo-Indian cavalry conduct their maneuvers and exercises in Melaka before their invasion of Java in 1811. He sees enough to know that this army can be deployed to devastating ends and that there is no force on the archipelago that is able to withstand it. A detailed description of the heart-stopping feats of the British army culminates in the wonder at seeing animals trained with such a degree of discipline. Their every movement seems predicted and regulated:

> By their natural skill the [Indian soldiers on horseback] rode the galloping horses, looking as if they were flying through the air. So far from falling off, they did not even shift their positions as they fired and reloaded their rifles and stuck out their swords. The officer instructing spoke no words of command but had a bugle in his hand. To give an order he blew the bugle and all the horses galloped off at once as quickly as lightning. On the bugle being sounded again they halted simultaneously, not one after the other, all their legs in line. Again, and the horses would break rank to form four sides of a square like a fort. Yet again, and all the soldiers fired their rifles at the same instant. The noise was like a single shot. Again, and rifles were reloaded. Again, and rifles were slung back across the shoulder and swords were drawn. Once more the bugle sounded, and at once the men ran up the hill, forming a circle around it like a stockade. Then suddenly lascars came up, that is, people who cut down the bushes. They carried lengths of cord round their waists with which they kept tying the undergrowth into bundle after bundle while they slashed it down, one man to each sheaf. In a moment the stockade was exposed to view. Then the bugle sounded again and they ran down the slopes with a noise like thunder, and formed up in order before their officer.
>
> (86–87 [Hill trans.]; 92)

The soldiers, horses, and lascars act as a fearsomely well-coordinated unit. It is significant that Abdullah stages his astonishment (*heran*) at this alien sight within a description that is admirably detailed and precise. Because the terrifying organization and power of the East India Company's army is being unleashed on wretches across the water in Java, rather than on the people of Melaka, Abdullah's description dwells on the regular and controlled nature of the display, rather than the devastation and death it will wreak in a few weeks. Abdullah has no idea what technique could produce such feats, which are obviously the product of methods aimed at "a meticulous control of the operations of the body."[46] He does not even use the metaphor of machinery to describe the behavior the men and animals. He can only affirm that the animals somehow "understood [*mengerti*] the language of the bugle [*perkataan terompet*]," and is surprised at "the intelligence [*kepandaian*] of the horse, which resembled the actions of human beings [*kelakuan manusia*]" (93; 87).

Abdullah intuits a relation between the rules and techniques underlying this newfound capacity—a capacity founded in discipline and training that are recast as "understanding"—and the overwhelming military and economic triumph of the British in Asia. His own imagination of reform and material advancement is accordingly produced within this vein, as a discourse of material and technological emulation that will also be the basis of how anticolonial discourse imagines the empowerment of the native world. Native elites long after Abdullah also inducted themselves into the colonizers' terms and demanded that the non-elite do the same if there was to be the possibility of *politically* emancipating themselves from Western domination.[47]

But in his day Abdullah writes for an audience that does not exist; the *Hikayat Abdullah* does not therefore assume the existence of an implied reader but outlines such a figure by laying out the protocols of a correct or adequate reading. As Abdullah is obviously aware, such a task cannot be achieved overnight; indeed, the sense of failure and despair at the obstreperousness of the natives pervades the entire text. The superiority of the British in every department of cultural and economic life is as blindingly obvious as the Malays' failure to recognize or appreciate this superiority. This non-comprehension, or failed interpellation, can be described as a form of a generalized "subalternity" that Abdullah believes must be overcome. But that will be no easy task. Even in the awesome display of British military power, Abdullah aptly registers a dissonant note. He overhears someone near him say, "These English are truly demons [*djinn*]" (87; 93). Rhetorically, this has the effect of casting the colonizers as altogether alien, even repugnant figures; their abilities do not make them objects worthy of emulation in the eyes of the untutored native bystanders.

Abdullah makes his way of *perspectivizing* his life a model on which the new Malay might begin to conceive of a qualitatively distinct kind of relation to self and world. He does so by teaching a mode of thematization designed to awaken a sense of astonishment at the wonders of modern knowledge. The "autobiography" is less the story of an individual's life written by himself than a misnomer for the generalized and disparate set of techniques intended to induce this sight and an appropriate response to that which is seen. Returning to my discussion of the disagreement Abdullah has with

his father, it is clear that the use of "I" (*sahaja/saya*) in *Hikayat* implies commensuration with this new training of the self to see and act in conformity
with the colonial episteme. The "I" is defined as an effect of the ability to
thematize objects and to evaluate them in a manner commensurate with
the colonial episteme.[48] Needless to say, such conformism is not peculiar to
collaborators such as Abdullah but shared by anticolonial nationalists and
modernizers of different stripes. The remarks of the American missionary
Alfred North are significant here. Abdullah confirms the fact that North
had urged him to write "a little memoir of himself." But Abdullah is not
sent on his way after being asked to write his life story; there is, after all,
nothing to suggest that the autobiography genre is a natural or universal
form of "self-" expression. North appears to Abdullah with a set of exercises
and techniques by which to flesh out the self as an effect of the mode of perspectivization. The capacity to enunciate an "I"—posing as interiorized—is
not just a formal perspective; it represents the attempt to naturalize a novel
and higher system of values:

> I suggested to [Abdullah] that he might compose a work of deep interest, such
> as had never been thought of by any Malay. . . . I told him that I had never found
> any thing in the Malay language except silly tales, useful indeed as showing how
> words are used, but containing nothing calculated to improve the minds of the
> people; and it was a sad error into which they had fallen in supposing every day
> occurrences, and all manner of things about them, too vulgar to be subjects of
> grave composition; nay, that unless they could be convinced of their error, they
> could never go forward a single step in civilization. I then gave him a list of top-
> ics on which it would be proper to enlarge a little, in writing a memoir of him-
> self, such as the character of his father, his opinions, treatment of his children,
> and the like; then the circumstances of his own early education, and whatever
> of interest he could recollect of his whole life; with these things should be in-
> terspersed remarks on the character of the eminent men he had taught, Raffles,
> Dr. Milne, Crawfurd, and others; on Malay superstitions, schools, domestic life;
> their rajas, customs, laws and whatever Europeans would like to be informed of,
> which would naturally be concealed from their observation. From these general
> hints, he has composed a work of singular interest, in beautiful Malay, and in all
> respects a new thing in the language.[49]

Read alongside Alfred North's "list of topics" and "interspersed remarks,"
the *Hikayat*, now recast as a memoir or autobiography, becomes an instrument or a technology "producing" selfhood in the sense that it is designed

to invoke an "I" as the means to an objective and adequate sight. Abdullah does not merely recount incidents; the perspective produced by his autobiographical "I" is actively involved, at the level of presentation, in shaping the correct way of bringing the world into view, the proper responses to events by imitating, that is, instituting, a new mode of perspectivization.[50] For this there is no need for a historical account or for an inquiry into "principles" underlying "free trade" or "rule of law." There is only an attempt to communicate the new rules of the game through the always already charged process of description and evaluation. Abdullah's "I" produces the global viewpoint of the British: quite literally, it teaches the natives how to see. Abdullah's *Hikayat* is an attempt to communicate this mode through a technology of representation; he also seeks in this way to produce a normative idea of the "I" that thematizes not so much as an interiorized subject but rather as the refracting lens that makes visible that perspective that distinguishes Europeans from the non-Europeans.

To write an autobiography is in some sense to produce an adequate "I," that is an "I" commensurate with the terms of the general equivalent. But in Abdullah's telling of his story, this "I" is set to work in a number of ways that suggest something of a relation with the terms of *kelebihan* (defective value codings), rather than simply *Mehrwert* (general equivalence), at least in the received understandings of both terms. A different way of looking at it would be to say that a different "I"—one infected by context—comes into view if the terms of *Mehrwert* are crossed with the *kelebihan* that various figures, such as Abdullah's father, are made to represent. In reading Abdullah in this way, I am obviously not seeking to valorize a reified "tradition" at the expense of "modernity," but to see how their interanimation in the colonial context can allow us to imagine the global differently.

This other "I" is an effect of the diverse spaces in which Abdullah is educated: by his Tamil-speaking grandmother, the Arabic teachers who pass through to Melaka on their way to Java, and the Malay teachers in Melaka that he seeks out on his own. Abdullah shows that these forms are "motley"; they do not cohere to produce a single or unified, that is, global perspective on the world. The total or expanded form of value is a disparate chain, plural and heterogeneous. At the same time, however, these forms of education highlight the internal heterogeneity of the "Malay" world to which Abdullah, as an Arab-Tamil living in a European-run port city, is native. The *kelebihan* or "surplus" hinted at here cannot be subsumed into the more general figure of *Mehrwert* by which Marx sought to denote the "surplus value" of colonial capitalist extraction. It is plausible to argue that the value form of general equivalence, deployed as an absolutist horizon of meaning that sees itself as an "advance" on all that came before colonial capitalism, reduces the wealth, or "surplus," as it might be imagined through the realm of social texture. In this light, Abdullah's father's protest need not be read condescendingly—as an older way of life that must be overcome—and is instead activated in an interruptive and supplementary relation to the dominant colonial order.

From the incidental details of Abdullah's early life and education, it would appear that trade practices in the Malay world are caught within a broader weave of sociality and "civil" affiliations that shape the "choices" made by the individual. (Although I lack the space to elaborate on it here, a different picture emerges of the Sayid Yasin case if we draw upon Abdullah's own background to interpret the natives' reaction to this incident.) These choices and loyalties are not necessarily opposed or competing but are instead mixed in with or interruptive of one another. If examined from outside the normative Eurocentric framework—in which the socioeconomic relations of the native world are recast in a "transition" narrative to the uniformity of capitalist exchange—a related but distinct vector emerges in Abdullah's account that does not reduce the Malay practices to a triumphalist vision of colonialism as the story of capitalism's progress. Instead, these heterogeneous forms can be read as active cultural-historical media that interrupt even as they are woven into the fabric of capitalist exchange.

Market forms of exchange, which existed before the colonial transformation of native society, often came mixed in with peculiar social obligations.[51] According to Renfrew's typology, Abdullah's father engaged in different forms of exchange: he traded with upriver folk in Sungei Baru and became a religious official who fathered two children, Mohamed Ali and Sharifah, and lived there for several years. His work or vocation—*pekerdjaan* is ambiguous—involved trading and giving moral and religious guidance at the same time.[52] Indeed, Abdul Kadir is embraced (*kasihlah*) by the local Malays, marries, and assumes the position of *khatib* in the mosque in Lubuk Keping. This highlights the fact that the profit motive is imbricated within a web of sociality. It also recalls the story of Abdullah's great-grandfather, a "teacher of religion and language [*pekerdjaannja itu mendjadi guru dari pada agama dan bahasa*]" (31; 5). In the early decades of the eighteenth century, Sheikh Abdul Kadir, who was an Arab trader from Yemen, married and settled in Nagore, in southern India. His relocation unfolded over a period in which the medieval networks of "indigenous" trade were starting to unravel. This process was hastened by civil war in Yemen, the collapse of the Mughal Empire on the Indian subcontinent, as well as the collapse of the Safavids in Persia and the Ottomans' loss of control over the Red Sea trade.[53] In a period thus marked by the decline of Indian trading activity with Southeast Asia, S. Arasaratnam includes Nagore in a short list of the South Indian ports whose Hindu and Muslim merchants continued a brisk trade, well into the eighteenth century, with Malay ports such as Aceh, Kedah, Melaka, and Johor.[54] It is likely that Abdullah's forebears were small, independent traders who participated in the complex "peddling" trade in different parts of the wider region that encompassed the Arab, Indian, Malay, and Chinese worlds (as described by J. C. Van Leur in *Indonesian Trade and Society*). Against this broad, precolonial canvas, traders from South Indian ports sojourned or settled in Malay ports such as Melaka and Kedah. Over the centuries, enduring social and cultural links were established between different parts of this trading world.[55]

Abdullah makes no mention of the potential conflict between the dispersed activations of the "I," particularly the one he seeks to activate as the medium of correct representation and the one supposed by relations and contextual assignments within which it is embedded. He does not suggest that the one supersedes the other, as in a "transition" narrative from premodern community to modern society. In practice, therefore, Abdullah's "I" is already attuned and responsive to the terms of *kelebihan*; it is folded into conceptions of *faedah* (benefit) and *agama* (belief) that his father had unsuccessfully sought to point out earlier. Abdullah's attempt to depict a disembodied or objective "I" as the condition of political agency should not be rejected—his impulse is a valuable one—but it needs to be read alongside this other movement. A failure to heed such an engagement simply results in conformist narratives of "progress" and "transition" that return us to the thematics of the text at the expense of its texture.

Social and commercial exchange appear to have coexisted in informal ways. Conceptions of civility, with transactions linked to forms of obligation, appear to have been a feature of much commerce before the epoch of European armed trade. In historical scholarship on the Cairo Genizah collection, which is drawn from documents belonging to Jewish traders who traded in North Africa, the Mediterranean, the Red Sea, and the Indian Ocean in the early modern era, K.N. Chaudhuri observes of one trader:

The author was a traveling merchant as well as a user of the consignment system. He and his business partners were held together in a mutual bond of personal friendship, complete trust, and financial interest. In a community of such close-knit ties, the sanction against a defaulting member was the loss of his credit and reputation; a man who was not worthy of trust would quickly exhaust his fund of goodwill. There were certainly well-established conventions in commercial contracts in all the trading cities of the Mediterranean and the Indian Ocean. The legal corpus protected merchants when the contracts were concluded between inter-communal members, and the reputation of the port of trade turned on the fairness of its legal traditions.[56]

Abdullah's father, Abdul Kadir, spoke Tamil well and "he used to write and keep accounts in it" (31; 6). Also skilled in court Malay, Abdul Kadir taught the language to the illustrious scholar-official William Marsden, to whom I referred in the previous chapter. Abdul Kadir's links with the wealthy Tamil traders of Melaka may well have opened up opportunities that were distinct from the kind of relationship he formed with the Malays of Sungei Baru. Abdullah's formal study of Tamil is, in turn, informed by this double connection between knowing a useful language—since so many wealthy traders were Tamil—and learning the requisite skills of financial accounting that seemed to accompany the study of the language. Although Abdullah grew up speaking Tamil to his mother and grandmother, he notes that his formal study of the language begins only after he is circumcised, suggesting perhaps a link between this ritual and his initiation into a community of men who are identified as traders:

> About a month after I was well my father sent me to a teacher to learn Tamil, the Indian language [*bahasa Keling, iaitu bahasa Hindu*], because it was the custom from the time of our forefathers [*dari pada zaman nenek-mojang semuanja*] in Malacca for all the children of good and well-to-do families to learn it. It was useful for doing computations and accounts, and for purposes of conversation because at that time Malacca was crowded with Indian merchants. Many were the men who had become rich by trading in Malacca. As a result the names of Tamil traders became famous in Malacca. That is why the people made their children learn Tamil.
>
> (45–46; 29)

The "I" is situated or given its place as an effect of prior relations and contextual claims. The very significance of language learning and use seems to derive from such constitutive claims. Abdullah's "identity" is obviously shaped by these assignments in a manner that is not readily codable in the hygienic terms of market relations that his mode of representation elsewhere suggests.

Curiously, Abdullah's fails or refuses to note the fact that he was taught to read and write by his grandmother and mother—which is most likely to have taken place in Tamil. He becomes nostalgic at various points about his love for his mother and the central role she played in his education—his father was often away—but the language in which they are likely to have communicated from his infancy is given a solely utilitarian connotation in his *Hikayat*. Abdullah's discussion of the knowledge of Tamil is connected to a set of merely practical issues, even though elsewhere he indicates that it is also the language of home and familial intimacy: it is the language in which Abdullah communicates with his mother and grandmother in childhood and with his wife, as an adult.

His failure or refusal to countenance this space of sexual difference simultaneously triggered by the Tamil language forecloses an opportunity to engage the realm of "defective" value codings as internally heterogeneous. This line of difference within the "native" culture would have expanded the terms in which unevenness might be imagined. Indeed, that domestic space is suppressed as Tamil is assimilated to a narrative of Abdullah's entrance into the public world of traders on the threshold of manhood (as marked by the circumcision ritual). The occlusion of this gendered space suggests that Abdullah discusses language (whether Tamil or Malay) chiefly as a correlate of the exchange economy. The relationship between language learning and the skills of a trader and the social networks within which commercial exchange takes place are not elaborated; they are taken for granted.[57] Language played an obvious role in facilitating these homosocial bonds. In this context, the nature of Abdullah's language learning takes on a different significance when seen through the fact that he is instructed by his father to worship at the local mosque five times a day—despite his arduous Tamil lessons—and the fact that he is told to allow his spelling of Malay names and words to be corrected by his elders and social betters in such "public" spaces. In a related way, the study of Tamil takes place in the context of a community of local- and foreign-born male Tamil speakers in Melaka. Trade and commercial relations appears to have been enmeshed within this set of social relations.

A similar relation between trade and civil associations of an "Indian Ocean" trading world that predates the arrival of European armed trade in the sixteenth century offers an older context for Abdullah's desire to learn Hindustani and Arabic. However, it is not simply that Abdullah learns many languages but that his relationship to each language, as well as the context in which he learns them and the purposes they serve, are located within heterogeneous contexts, all of which are framed by different motivations of profit. It produces in Abdullah a number of identifications and affiliations around which the "I" is produced.

> After some eight or nine months of painstaking recitation and writing of the Koran my learning had reached a high standard and the road to serious study was increasingly opened to me. . . . After that my father ordered me "Every day you must go to the evening prayer and recite the Koran in the mosque. For in the mosque there are hundreds of people going in and out, and if they hear you make a mistake they will certainly point it out."
>
> (44; 27)

> One day my father said to me "you must no longer spend time doing nothing. I have brought some paper. Sit down and write the Koran at home." And he showed me how to follow on paper the lines on a tablet. So I sat down and wrote. . . . This went on for six or seven months, my mistakes being pointed out to me. By the end I could correctly transcribe the Koran and Arabic manuscripts. When my father saw that I could write the Koran, he said: "Here is a manuscript written in Malay and Arabic, a very fine one. Make a copy of it." So I copied it and after some time it was finished.
>
> (48; 33)

When the Indian sepoys arrive in Melaka and Abdullah copies Koran texts for their use:

> A difficulty arose for me because I did not understand Hindustani and when I wished to converse with the soldiers we could only gesticulate like dumb people. Moreover at that time people who knew the language were very hard to find. Therefore I was very keen to learn it myself. I told one of the officers how anxious I was to learn Hindustani. He replied "Come to my house in the Fort and I can provide you with food and tell my teacher to give you lessons. You can become teacher to all of us [of Arabic] and write Koran texts which our men will buy."
>
> (49; 34)

Abdullah refers to the Malay language as his (*bahasa diriku*), even in the sense of a collective "we" (*bahasa kita* 40; 53), even as he sometimes distinguishes himself from the Malays (ironically enough, for not taking the study of "their" language seriously). The confusions multiply: who constitutes the "we" in the phrase "our language" (*bahasa kita*)? Here the autobiographical self appears as the dispersed effect of relations and assignments that suppose and shape the perception and will of the "I," a self that is an effect of a sociality that preexists the arrival of a colonial capitalist order. This is quite unlike the self associated with the objectifying, impersonal "I," which largely functions as the index of an episteme defined by the mastery of the world as picture.[58]

It is in the displaced or split "I" that Abdullah enunciates a different conception of progress. The global imagination that Abdullah so painstakingly articulates for the benefit of his readers undergoes a confusing displacement. The thematic aim of the *Hikayat* is to imagine (and thereby induct) the native world as ready to imbibe the rules of the new regime of colonial capitalism and to imagine "difference" within the terms of this plane of homogeneous being. But this task becomes diverted as a strange pluralization of identity repeatedly shows itself. The vision or theme of the *Hikayat* can be read differently in this context.

Abdullah's study of languages effects a textual "I" that is at odds with his narrative claims; it activates identities and identifications on his part that cannot always be squared with the authorial agenda of teaching the natives how to imagine themselves into the "universal equivalent." When he travels to the east coast of the Malay Peninsula, he predictably expresses shock at the absence in Kelantan of a marketplace of the kind found in every British-controlled settlement. But it is in this very space of nonmarket relations that Abdullah discovers other conceptions of exchange that supplement the conception of selfhood and identity that he justifiably declares to be the condition of political agency within colonial capitalism. It centers on an encounter with non-Malays who are native speakers of the Malay language. He meets the "old wife of the head of the Chinese community [*bini Kapitan Cina*]" in Terengganu. I include the original Malay passage in full because the translation does not capture the evocative power of the original:

> That old lady had very fine manners and was eloquent. She did not mispronounce her words, as the Chinese usually do, but spoke like a Malay person. After we had sat for a moment, she had tea and local oranges served, which she

invited us to consume. Then the young women of the house emerged. I saw that
their behaviour, dress and manners were all like that of the Malays; and with
great courtesy one said, "Please remain seated for a moment sir, I will instruct
someone to fetch you a young coconut."

Maka adalah orang tua itu terlalu baik budi bahasanja, lagi dengan manis per-
kataannya. Maka sakali-kali tiada telornya saperti China melainkan saperti
orang Melayu adanya. Maka sebentar dudok, maka dikeluarkannya ayer teh dan
limau manis, disurohnya makan. Maka keluarlah segala anak buahnya perem-
puan-perempuan. Maka sahaya lihat kelakuan mereka itu dan pakaian mereka
itu dan perkataan mereka it dan tabiatnya, semuanya seperti Melayu, serta dengan baik budi bahasanya, serta katanya, "Dudoklah tuan sebentar, nanti sahaya
suroh ambilkan kepala muda."[59]

(25; 55–56)

Language and etiquette establish a bond between the Indian traveler and
the local Chinese family in this Malay state.[60] Abdullah is charmed by and
attracted to the Chinese here most of all by their refined and cultivated
Malay speech, which serves not simply as a lingua franca for Abdullah and
the family elder, neither of whom is Malay, but as a source of expression by
which an affiliation is tacitly affirmed. Malay is a language that is neither
alien to nor the mother tongue of either Abdullah or the Chinese family.
Such people have been called "creolized" Chinese.[61] It is reasonable to suppose that not only would Abdullah have been amenable to including such
groups as part of a conception of "*orang Melayu*," defined here as Malay-
speaking peoples, he would also have been struck by the comparability of his
own history and genealogy with theirs. Abdullah's identification takes place
through an emotional attachment to the Malay language and its idioms. It
is this sensitivity to the language that affords a more capacious and diverse
sense of "identity." Abdullah and the Chinese family he meets are (differently) "mixed" and Malay in the diverse sense precipitated by this mixture:
the old "Chinese" lady speaks Malay well and the "Tamil-Arab" Abdullah
takes pride in the language spoken thus. Language, not an essentialist conception of ethnic or religious Malay identity, enables this sense of plurality
and internally heterogeneous difference. At the same time, language affords
the possibility of identity (and identifications) taking place not as an effect of sameness but difference; the Malay identity might well be imagined
through such differences. Differently mixed individuals (Abdullah and the

Kapitan Cina's wife) unite themselves through a common language and manners that are, as historical artifacts, always already hybrid. Abdullah's insight is literary in the robust sense; it teaches how to loosen the Malay language from its definition as the expression of a single or monolithic identity. In this light, each community Abdullah encounters in Terengganu, not least the group classified "Malay" by official censuses in postcolonial Malaysia, may become open to imagining itself as plural.

In Abdullah's text the global perspective is displaced by the various contexts in which it is activated. I read this as an interruptive embrace of the global that allows for the discovery of the possibility of new affiliations and forms of identification. This displacement takes place as a result of his attempt to embrace the representational framework of the global. Abdullah's "I" is dispersed in a variety of ways. I have already discussed how Abdullah calls Malay his language (*bahasa diriku*, 159) and speaks admiringly of Malay teachers like Dato Sulaiman, who explains the subtleties of the Malay language to him. He arranges for his deceased daughter and his wife to be buried in a Tamil Muslim cemetery (*dimasdjid Keling*, 365, 395). He feels a secret pride when he sees the cavalrymen from Delhi, whom he believes to be of Arab descent. He is attracted to the Chinese in Kelantan because they speak Malay with eloquence and behave like Malays, perhaps seeing in them something of himself. Conversely, at one point he refers to Abdulkadir, the Tamil Muslim interloper in the Sultan's court, as "*anak Keling*," distancing himself from that group with which he is "objectively" defined.

In its performance, the "I" of the *Hikayat* resembles less the self whose global perspective frames objects from a distance than an entity embedded within the "chain" of endless connections implied by the "defective" figure of the total or expanded form of value. The global perspective is at once reproduced and interrupted from such a multiplicity of sometimes conflicting perspectives. The mutations of Abdullah's "identity" resemble the metonymic relations that hold in place the different *djinns* that he named for the edification of the missionary and his wife, which I quote earlier in the chapter. The "I" draws on the *kelebihan* produced by this complex and uneven social fabric. The normative identity of the autobiographical or autonomous "I" commensurate with the global as perspective is displaced through a series of lateral identifications, which do not repudiate the colonial capitalist episteme so much as displace it. The *Hikayat* invites us to imagine that even as we find the idea of trade and travel pointing to economic relations to be caught up in webs of sociality, globality itself comes to be bound up with a tacit acknowledgment of the heterogeneous constitution of various indigenous groups whose claims are both overlapping and mutually interruptive.

In this way the "I" that Abdullah seeks to present as the refracting lens of a univocal global perspective is repeatedly confounded in its imbrication with the entities described. The "I" is not separable from the entities it claims to thematize, and the global perspective is made attentive to forms of difference that it does not seem equipped to comprehend. North tells Abdullah what sorts of themes and issues Europeans dealt with in their travelogues, and although Abdullah goes on to lament the putative absence of markets in the states ruled by native princes, he notes with some surprise that people in Pahang seem fairly well accommodated—exports from this state include gold, tin, woven-silk products, kemuning wood, and rattans. Imports include opium, silk, salt, rice, and European cloth. The aboriginal population nearby also supplies forest produce such as eagle-wood, benzoin, resin, and rattan. The aborigines work for the Chinese in the goldmines, and "they had plantations of their own and brought in all kinds of fruit which they exchanged with the merchants for tobacco and salt."[62] It appears likely that the money form is not established as the universal medium of exchange. He finds evidence of the total or expanded form of value, with its "motley mosaic of unconnected or disparate expressions of value" (Marx) mixed in with the more "advanced" money or general value form. From this we may infer what Abdullah fails to remark, that the lack of shops or markets is not necessarily a symptom of deficiency; it may indicate a different mode of organization of social and productive relations. And even as Abdullah attempts to name this deficiency on the part of native society, he is drawn into a narration of its texture from a viewpoint that is aware of but not reducible to the global as perspective. *Hikayat Abdullah* serves not as the model for a self-consolidating identity but as a text through which can be imagined other forms of belonging that at once inform and interrupt the global as perspective. What begins as the induction of the native into the colonial episteme opens into an exploration of the heterogeneous constitution of the indigene. The attempt to deploy the global perspective leads first to its being supplemented by relationships and assignments that serve to keep in play an imaginative template that is not simply directed by Eurocentric notions of progress. Second, it opens up a relationship to truth that is caught within the interruptive web of the things it thematizes. Abdullah's text can show that what is called "diversity" can exceed the epistemic frame within which

it is presented: *kelebihan* brushes against *Mehrwert*. A reading attentive to
the interruption of the global perspective can serve to expand its horizons:
not by making the global more comprehensive but by asking of the different
ways it can be waylaid by and responsive to texture.

Despite his intentions, Abdullah's encounter with the British enables
him to express an effort to imagine the global differently. This does not
involve counterposing a local to a global—the local is after all produced as
an effect of the global as perspective, and the local deploys the global as the
condition of agency—but rather showing how the global, interrupted by
texture, opens the local up to internally unequal and heterogeneous vectors
through which solidarities might be imagined.

Here a contrast can be offered with the topic of my next chapter. Abdullah's "I," as I showed, is produced as an effect of the representational frame
that the native must learn. The putative reader accedes to historical and
ethical subjectivity by learning how to produce an "I" of the kind commensurate with modern knowledge production. The discourses known as "literature" and "history" are part of this general configuration in which the world
is made visible and legible. In Joseph Conrad's *Lord Jim* this deployment
of the global perspective is the precomprehended point of departure in his
searching study of ethical subjectivity. The normative understanding of the
self there is the solitary individual, an interiorized, ethical subject. In a manner akin to Abdullah's encounter with the Chinese *Kapitan*'s wife in Terengganu, Jim benefits from the hospitality of Doramin and his wife, leaders of
the Bugis in Patusan; we shall have occasion to reflect upon the differences
and similarities between Jim's and Abdullah's responses to the possibility
of a conception of collectivity—set in motion against a backdrop of global
imperialism—in which identification does not presuppose identity.

To turn from Abdullah to Jim is to see the distance between the native
who has yet to become fully savvy to the terms of the global perspective and
the imperial metropolis where it is produced. Abdullah's peripheral status is
marked in this way: whereas the "I" in both the *Hikayat Abdullah* and *Lord
Jim* signifies a self responsible for its actions, it is only in the latter work that
this "I" is evaluated in terms of actions and standards that are precomprehended as universal. What is in Abdullah chiefly an attempt to see correctly
is in Jim the need to *repair* the severed link between adequate sight—which
he takes for granted—and ethical obligation. Through the distinct deploy-
ments of the global perspective that separates Jim from Abdullah, the terms
of responsibility shift from instrumentality to sacrifice.

The "I" of Conrad's *Lord Jim* takes on a different shade than the subject in the *Hikayat*, but the two make for an interesting comparison in this regard. If I have sought to read Abdullah's "I" in relation to the context by which he is necessarily supposed, I am interested to read Jim's ordeals back into the native world in whose context his own struggles unfold. In this regard, the interruption of Abdullah's "I" can provide a clue to my own strategy of reading in the next chapter. It will be my aim to see how the global as perspective reveals itself otherwise as Jim is himself read back into the native context from which his ethical struggle is so strenuously distinguished by the narrator. Against the grain, I read Jim's struggle not as a medium for the glorification of the heroic (if flawed) individual, but rather as a prism of sorts that enables us to bring into play the native world that appears a passive, undifferentiated foil to his inner struggles. Once again, Abdullah's own attempts to produce correct sight are instructive inasmuch as they show how such moves are waylaid by the formal conduct of the text. They reconstellate the global by training us to read otherwise.

It is also worth noting that whereas the first two chapters of this study relate to the global imagined as an effect of "free trade" and the configuration of a transnational "civil" society centered upon production and exchange for the imperial market, this and the next chapter deal with the question of individual agency as it engages the global episteme through the figure of the "I" conceived as ethical subject. In the informal division structuring this study, the first and last two chapters respectively map onto (quantitative) economic with (qualitative) individual progress. If in Abdullah's tale the complex relationship between the autobiographical "I" and the community by which the former is supposed is imagined in the native's attempt to deploy the global perspective, then in Conrad's *Lord Jim* the metropolitan depiction of the European as exclusive subject of ethics and history turns into a searching exploration of the native community operating on the edges of the global capitalist system. Whereas Abdullah writes as the native who seeks to gain entry into the terms of political and historical agency, Conrad broaches the nature of subaltern agency through the fall from grace of the privileged European subject who is, in Marlow's words, "one of us."

4

ANIMALITY AND THE GLOBAL

SUBJECT IN CONRAD'S LORD JIM

The theme that *Hikayat Abdullah* attempts to elaborate is the point of departure of Joseph Conrad's *Lord Jim*. For Abdullah, those who can produce the global perspective are ethical and historical agents, whereas those incapable of doing so are doomed to subalternity. Thus the way in which the natives are described in Conrad's novel seems uncannily to fulfill an apparently unheeded warning made in Abdullah's text: unless the natives learn to make the terms of their seeing and saying compute with that of the colonial institution, they risk having themselves excluded from being considered historical, that is to say, properly human, agents.

In *Lord Jim* the global perspective names that way of seeing and saying that constitutes the everyday. The global mode of perspectivizing—which is to Abdullah characterized by its adequacy and comprehensiveness—is reconstituted in Marlow's narrative as ordinary, normal. By extension, the global is now linked in representation to a particular kind of subject, defined primarily by a highly developed sense of self-awareness and moral duty. The global subject is in this context conceived not just as the one who has an adequate way of grasping the world but also as the one whose attempt to act and transform the world is the expression of "inner worth."[1] The tacit assumptions evinced by Marlow and the anonymous narrator of *Lord Jim* do not simply mobilize the global perspective as an objective description of the world; they also show how that capacity to describe the world is inextricably linked to subjective interiority. It is in this sense that the global as a mode of thematization encompasses in Conrad's novel a set of beliefs about the world as well as the kind of subject who seeks to comprehend that perspective—at once to confirm and improve upon it—most obviously by acting upon a non-European world ignorant of the need for improvement or transformation. Far from being exceptional, Jim's fantasies of heroism are typical of the ethical imperialist subject, who is nothing if not good. Whereas Abdullah sought, with uneven success, to insert himself into that script, growing up within the imperial core, Jim need imagine nothing other than his own condition as the basis of ethical and historical agency.

Marlow portentously claims that Jim's ethical dilemma solicits "mankind's conception of itself." I take this ethical configuration as it elaborates the global perspective at an advanced and stable moment of colonial capitalist rule in Asia. I argue that the novel's central figure, Jim, can be read differently, not just as the all-consuming concern of the novel but as a means to engage the figure of the native communities that appear as *pre-texts*, which is to say, that provoke a moral dilemma without themselves figuring as ethical or historical agents in their own right. Notwithstanding Conrad's use of the Malays as a foil in a searching exploration of ethical responsibility that is exclusive to the interiorized European subject, I explore the ways in which the occluded figure of the natives can be activated by reading the text against the grain. My approach defamiliarizes the global perspective as it is complacently enunciated in the metropolitan core, and it enriches and expands the ethical parameters by which interpretations of the modern novel have been traditionally defined.

I. NATIVE BLANKNESS

A bizarre episode early in the novel points to the heart of the problem. A leak is discovered in the *Patna*, and the ship seems certain to sink at any moment, carrying to their deaths the eight hundred Malay Muslim pilgrims sleeping on board. On deck, the suspense is heightened by the contrasting reactions of the other European officers, who unhesitatingly prepare their own escape, and the chief mate, Jim, who is overcome by panic and concern for the sleeping pilgrims. While the reader's attention is directed to the unfolding drama, something inexplicable takes place at the margin of this tableau: two Malays remain motionless at the helm of the ship. As the

Europeans struggle with quiet frenzy to prepare a lifeboat for escape, the two Malays stare blankly:

> Jim stood on the starboard side of the bridge, as far as he could get from the struggle of the boat, which went on with the agitation of madness and the stealthiness of a conspiracy. The Malays had meantime remained holding on to the wheel. Just picture to yourself the actors in that, thank God! unique episode of the sea, four beside themselves with fierce and secret exertions, and three looking on in complete immobility, above the awning covering the profound ignorance of hundreds of human beings, with their weariness, with their dreams, with their hopes, arrested, held by an invisible hand on the brink of annihilation. These beggars by the boat had every reason to go distracted with funk. Frankly, had I been there I would not have given as much as a counterfeit farthing for the ship's chance to float.
>
> (Conrad, *Lord Jim*, 60)

The helmsmen continue holding on to the wheel of a ship that has lost its steerage way. They do not try to stop or join the Europeans in their escape; they do not try to alert the hundreds of sleeping Malay men, women, and children to the emergency. How to account for such impenetrable behavior in a novel that is otherwise concerned with delineating the subtlest shades of individual responsibility and motivation?[2]

To my knowledge, no critic of *Lord Jim* has pointed out an obvious if inconvenient fact: human beings do not behave in this way.[3] It is inconceivable, for instance, that two English steersmen would have stared passively while their fellows made their escape. If the two Malays evidently possess the technical skill and practical judgment needed to steer a ship, why do they not react to the fact that the ship *can no longer be steered*? What category of sentient or mechanical being are we invited to think in terms of here? In light of their "immobility" (60), do they partake of certain attributes of the human without entirely belonging to the category? Here is the anonymous narrator on the native helmsmen after the discovery of the leak: "The eyes of the Malays glittered towards the white men, but their dark hands remained closed on the spokes" (17): the inanimate "glittered" and the limited consciousness of "closed" hands hint at a more profound existential privation.[4]

Their eccentric and unpredictable bearing at the official inquiry into the *Patna* incident some weeks later makes it unlikely that Malay helmsmen are automatons. Nonetheless, their weird reactions suggest a fundamental

limitation or flaw in their makeup. What the Malays say at the trial shockingly reveals their *continued* inability to grasp the significance of the events
on the *Patna*. Asked why he stayed put at the helm of a sinking ship that
could no longer be steered, the old Malay's answer is reported by Marlow as
follows: "There had been no order . . . why should he leave the helm?" (60).[5]
Since the officers authorized to give such an order were openly making their
escape at that very time, this reply obviously makes no sense. It would seem
that the Malay can make choices but is not altogether capable of rational
deliberation, which is to say that the nature of his relation to the everyday
world is circumscribed in some nebulous but absolute way. This peculiar
combination of capacity and incapacity puts one in mind of conventional
characterizations of an animal's relation to the world. According to this
view, although an animal may powerfully negotiate with or manipulate its
relation to its immediate surroundings, it is barred from access to many
aspects of the world. Put differently, the nature of the animal's involvement
in the world is inherently impoverished.[6] Because I want to track at some
length the peculiarity of the native who possesses consciousness but not
reason, it may help to note at the outset that I am not exercised primarily
by metaphors or similes involving animals. Instead I follow the figure of the
animal as it marks some undefined opacity or lack of full access to reason
as a trait of the native world. I take up this question by first examining how
the animal serves Marlow's narrative agenda of highlighting the capacities
he considers proper to human being: reason, interiority, and history.

Marlow's narrative alternately presupposes a hierarchy *and* an absolute
gulf that separates European from native consciousness in the novel. Even
the least sympathetic or thoughtful Europeans, such as the German captain
or the second engineer of the *Patna*, possess the capacity to evaluate and to
judge. The same cannot be said of the Malay helmsmen. Marlow's audience
is expected to share this attitude; this is why his listeners do not balk or
express incredulity at hearing the younger helmsmen imply that he felt no
anxiety or fear during his two days aboard an abandoned ship that was likely to go down at any moment. Whereas all the Europeans on the ominously
still *Patna* reveal "their aversion to dying" (63) by panicking—following a
conventional view, the anticipation of (one's) death is a capacity unique to
humans—the young Malay is unable to foresee or imagine such a prospect.
If what he says is true, and Marlow gives no reason to think otherwise,
the inference is that the young Malay is unable to comprehend any event
that is not immediately in view, evoking yet again the figure of an animal

circumscribed in its access to the world. Like the animal, the Malay lacks
the faculty of imagination.[7] How else to judge the young Malay's assertion
that, adrift at sea for several days with little hope of rescue, "he thought
nothing" (60)?

The older helmsman's testimony is equally stunning:

> He jerked back his spare shoulders, and declared it never came into his mind
> then that the white men were about to leave the ship through fear of death. He
> did not believe it now. There might have been secret reasons. He wagged his old
> chin knowingly. Aha! secret reasons. He was a man of great experience, and he
> wanted that white Tuan to know—he turned toward Brierly, who didn't raise his
> head—that he had acquired a knowledge of many things by serving white men
> on the sea for a great number of years—and, suddenly, with shaky excitement
> he poured upon our spellbound attention a lot of queer sounding names, names
> of dead-and-gone skippers, names of forgotten country ships, names of familiar
> and distorted sound, as if the hand of dumb time had been at work on them for
> ages. They stopped him at last.

(61)

Nothing the old Malay says helps the judges make sense of the events on
the *Patna*. Marlow underscores the essential poverty of both Malays with
this surreal image of the ship after it had been abandoned by its European
officers and crew: "So these two lascars stuck to the helm of that ship without steerage-way, where death would have found them if such had been
their destiny" (61). Marlow would have the reader believe that is where they
remained—eyes "glittering" blankly, hands still "closed over the wheel"—
until the French gunboat chanced upon the *Patna* some days later.

Given the Malays' ontologically stupefied relation to the world, one
would have thought them hardly worthy of representation. But Marlow's
decision to give them such prominence begins to make sense if situated
within a more general thesis about the relation between existential vacuity
and historical backwardness. It makes sense if seen in terms of the connection Marlow makes between the senseless "immobility" (60) of the steersmen on the *Patna* and the historical "immobility" (151) of the inhabitants of
Patusan in the later parts of the novel. Immobility in the first case refers to
an incapacity for autonomous reflection and in the second to the absence
of progressive temporal development.[8] Defined thus, this combination of
individual and collective shortcoming bars the native world from proper
access to the terms of narrative. When the old Malay helmsman pours forth

without self-consciousness the names of many dead seamen and ships, Marlow dismisses this prodigious feat of memory as an expression of "dumb time" (61)—as distinct, presumably, from *historical* time.

Although the Malays' actions are inexplicable, one thing is clear: like the animal, they could not have autonomously decided to remain on the ship because they do not possess reason or imagination. And because this in turn indicates the absence of an inner life—where interiority is depicted in Marlow's account of Jim as the incalculable bonus of the interplay between reason and imagination—the Malays also cannot properly be considered human or historical beings. In this connection Stein, the European revolutionary turned middleman, hints at why Jim's life is more valuable than that of the natives: "'Evident! What is it that by inward pain makes him know himself? What is it that for you and me makes him—exist?'" (132). It is Jim's "inward pain" that makes his life narratable and, conversely, the natives' not narratable in Marlow's eyes. If interiority is indissolubly linked to historical being, it is the sine qua non of narrative value. Thus Marlow tells his listeners that before those "dark-faced men . . . [Jim] appeared like a creature not only of another kind but of another essence" (140).

Marlow's picture of the stultifying immobility of the native community in Patusan illustrates the nature of this deeper poverty. Untouched by the faculties of reason and imagination that distinguish the historical civilization of Europe—that "world where events move, men change, light flickers" (200)—the passions and actions of the natives of Patusan are surreptitiously likened to those of animals, whose struggles and aspirations cannot by definition effect a qualitative change in their relation to the environment:

> But next morning, at the first bend of the river shutting off the houses of Patusan, all this dropped out of my sight bodily, with its color, its design, and its meaning, like a picture created by fancy on a canvas, upon which, after long contemplation, you turn your back for the last time. It remains in the memory motionless, unfaded, *with its life arrested, in an unchanging light.* There are the ambitions, the fears, the hate, the hopes, and they remain in my mind as I had seen them—intense and as if for ever suspended in their expression. *I had turned away from the picture and was going back to the world where events move, men change, light flickers, life flows in a clear stream,* no matter whether over mud or stones. . . . [All the natives of Patusan] exist as if under an enchanter's wand. But the figure around which all these are grouped—*that one lives,* and

I am not certain of him. *No magician's wand can immobilize him under my eyes. He is one of us.*

(200–201; emphases added)

I have noted that the global as perspective finds substantive expression in a narrative of ethical responsibility in Conrad. My aim in this chapter is to pursue how a distinct conception of ethical possibility is elaborated in the novel in this peripheral strand of Marlow's story. I will show how it offers an insight into the limitations of Marlow's attempt to rehabilitate Jim, which progresses by way of a concealed relation with the ontological stupefaction of the natives. At the same time, I want to show how the hierarchical relationship that Marlow takes for granted in his vision of the global perspective as ethical project activates quite distinct movements.

For want of a more precise way to define this ontological difference, the figure of the animal serves as a placeholder for the line that separates European from native, historical from nonhistorical societies. It would appear that even if the native can learn to manipulate modern technology—and the Malay steersmen mark this empirical possibility—it is impossible to imagine this transition being fully effected, that is, at the level of subjectivity.[9] It is not that the animal bears no connection to the world of ethical or historical action; it is simply such a relationship can never be full or adequate in the manner presumed of human beings. The animal does not work, which is the minimal condition of effecting, in a self-conscious manner, a qualitative change in the relationship to one's environment. In turn, it is this qualitative change that produces something like interiority and depth in the working subject. Only Europeans are capable of work in the exalted sense of producing a meaning and value commensurate with the global as perspective.[10] Placed in this comparative light, Marlow's obsession with the psychological and moral implications of Jim's actions and the individual and collective ideals implied by such words as "work" and "solidarity" becomes clear.

But Marlow's conception of work can be profitably linked to the material dimensions of British dominance in Southeast Asia. This link will help illuminate the broader webs in which Marlow's conception of individual responsibility and ethical autonomy is implicated. I begin by noting that imperialism was in part a result of expanding needs of capital accumulation in eighteenth- and nineteenth-century Britain. It led to the search for new markets, raw materials, and cheap labor from Asia.[11] Conrad spent his formative years as a sailor in the Malay world, and his early works—from

Almayer's Folly (1895), *An Outcast of the Islands* (1896), *Tales of Unrest* (1898), and *Lord Jim* (1900)—bear ample testimony to the fact that he took for granted this conception of an "informal empire" geared toward profits and based on flexible relations between the Europeans and the native states guided by pragmatic mechanisms of negotiation and manipulation.[12]

In this domain of commercial imperialism, contact between the native and European worlds took place primarily through the merchant ships that sold and exchanged goods even in remote parts of the archipelago.[13] The expansion of the nineteenth-century British economy was enhanced by merchant ships that carried cheap cloth, iron, machinery, and coal to Asia, whence they obtained essential imports of basic food and raw material. This exchange of goods and services was carried out by Conradian figures like Marlow, MacWhirr, Lingard, and Whalley during the period of the Southeast Asian export boom, which lasted for several decades beginning in the 1870s.[14] Men like Marlow were the hired hands of the multinational peddling trade of Southeast Asia.[15] The tedious round of buying cheap from small cultivators in the "outer islands" and selling dear in urban centers within the region casts Marlow's professional ethic of "fixed standards" in an unflattering light.[16] These are the sordid material circumstances that cling incongruously to the high-minded Marlow as well as the philosophical Stein, the revolutionary turned middleman, "known by name to some few, very few, in the mercantile world" (133) who once lived in remote Patusan in Borneo. The legal historian G.J. Resink evokes something of the uneven relations of production and exchange in Patusan and other such effectively autonomous coastal areas of the Malay world during the 1880s, leaving to the imagination the kind of work done by the merchant seaman who was employed by a local trader or a European firm:

> Only after one has been to the Batak country, the Lesser Sunda Islands, or the hinterlands of Macassar will one really begins to grasp the fact that in Conrad's years an international, ephemeral, peripheral, and heterogeneous shipping and trade economy of "white and brown" obtained along the shores of Indonesia's islands, giving way just a few miles inland to what were in more than one way dark, homogeneous micro-economies of Indonesian realms and lands.[17]

One wonders how effectively even the nostalgic evocation of the days of sail before the seaman's craft was ruined by steam could have deflected the high-minded captain's attention from the nature of this exchange. Indeed, it is hard to imagine a time when the marine service did anything but serve middlemen and merchants and, beyond that, a colonial capitalist structure intent on the extraction of tribute and trade. This is not to mock Marlow's values; it is to point out that perhaps nostalgia and noble affirmations of rectitude may not offer the best approach to the interplay between personal fate and historical forces in the archipelago at the time.

It is also difficult to see the occluded historical conditions out of which the global as perspective is shaped. But in this way an economic relation is suggested between Marlow's idealized "work" and the solidarity with which it keeps faith, on the one hand, and the native world, on the other. The Malay Muslim pilgrims sleep as they are transported to Mecca. But ships such as these also carried other "native" passengers, who, although kept distinct from "Malays" in the eyes of the colonizer, belonged to the same class and were put to work in a different "sector" of the colonial dual economy: "The short metallic clangs bursting out suddenly in the depths of the ship, the harsh scrape of a shovel, the violent slam of a furnace door, exploded brutally, as if the men handling the mysterious things below had their breasts full of fierce anger" (12). Juxtaposed with the image of the sleeping Muslim pilgrims, one level below them in the spatial ordering of the tableau, is another, invisible native world of labor that had itself been transported from other parts of Asia in the very ships upon which its "unskilled" work was done. The vision of a different kind of "work" suggests itself here: the merchant ships transported native labor, the most precious commodity of any modern economy, for work in the colonies that were rapidly if unevenly transformed in the interests of global capitalism:

> Most of the [Indian and Chinese] immigrants came as simple laborers, packed in the steerage of "coolie" ships, owing passage money to those for whom they first worked. They came to work on the plantations of Malaya and Sumatra's East Coast Residency, to build railways in British Burma and Siam, to mine tin in Malaya and silver in Burma and to labor on docks, hand sawmills, rice mills, and building sites of port cities throughout Southeast Asia.[18]

These are the figures of displaced labor from other parts of Southeast Asia, India, and China that Jim will encounter in Patusan in the second half of *Lord Jim*. It is, after all, the merchant ship that holds together the plot of the two halves of the novel, just as it links the "formal" crown colony of Singapore to the "informally" manipulated areas like Patusan, that merely come within its sphere of influence. The merchant ship—and the broader meanings of "work" it now holds in place—brings together, in one constellation, the pilgrims on the *Patna* as they arrive from the agricultural hinterlands; the invisible forces of subaltern and "immigrant" labor that work the ship from below; and the aboriginal communities in Patusan, who do not necessarily conform to the received vision of colonial "plural society."[19]

To read against the grain of the native world's occlusion by means of its "articulation" into the global perspective is to interrupt the conformist attitudes to history that are presupposed by much literary and cultural criticism produced in the metropolis. My aim is not to recover a past that was destroyed by colonial capitalism so much as to interrupt the conformism of metropolitan perspectivizing. I read *Lord Jim* to see how an activation of the native—articulated through erasure for the sake of an ethics supposed to be global—can help make other connections for the present. I will first elaborate how to bring the natives into view and then, in the latter half of the chapter, elaborate on the way the native world affords a unfamiliar way of seeing the global perspective.

Marlow's evaluation of Jim according to the values of work can be perspectivized differently through the figure of the animal. If animality is most obviously used to enforce a hygienic division between European and native, this division also serves as a means to connect the two intertwined worlds. Such a strategy of reading would elaborate the interplay between the European and the native worlds in ways that raise ethical and historical concerns of a kind unfamiliar to Marlow, opening the global perspective to being activated in a distinct way. Returning to the thematic vector as it is set up by Marlow, I can now offer a rationale for the otherwise inexplicably gratuitous appearance of the Malay helmsmen on the *Patna* and in the courtroom: it is the benumbed native that best shows off by contrast the depth and complexity of Jim's emotions. Only the native, lacking the capacity to reflect, can perform the function of enriching or enhancing Jim's "inward" being in this qualitatively distinct way. (For this very reason, the sight of any European—the German captain, say—in the witness stand capable of reflecting on his actions would have, by contrast, detracted from the presentation of Jim's singular and unique "inward pain.")

This exclusion can be read "economically," not simply as an expression of racial or civilizational prejudice. The subtle denigration of the Malays is necessary if they are to serve as the raw material against or upon which the human condition may be illuminated. This is an important point to note given that *Lord Jim* is so ostentatiously concerned with ethical responsibility. A narrative economy is established in that the native's poverty of being throws into relief Jim's (and Marlow's) existential wealth. The same point can be made with another example: the case for Jim's exceptional status would be impossible to sustain had it been eight hundred *European* passengers on board the *Patna*. Quite the contrary, the struggles of one individual could not plausibly have been made the exclusive concern of the novel because Marlow would in that case have been compelled to entertain the hopes and fears of other subjects who (ontologically) qualify for narrative significance. Thus the virtual deaths of the Malay pilgrims are necessary for the narrative to work: only the Malays provide the pretext for an ethical dilemma whose "lesson" can be directed elsewhere. Hence Marlow may with impunity deem the sinking of the *Patna* "as devoid of significance as the flooding of an ant-heap" (57) even as he relies on its lessons to affirm his belief in the "sovereign power enthroned in a fixed standard of conduct" (31).[20] In *Lord Jim* the exclusion of the native as animal enables us to appreciate the exalted locus of human and ethical possibility.

Given the historical setting of the native world in *Lord Jim*, the similarity of such a strategy of representation with that of British officials in late-nineteenth-century colonial Malaya is obvious. Although Marlow asserts that Jim's fate in Patusan was ignored by the European powers in Southeast Asia because the region was "not judged ripe for interference" (142), it is perhaps more accurate to say that *Lord Jim* is set in the 1880s, a decade marked by the intensification of the British "forward movement" in Malaya as a reaction to growing German, Dutch, and French interest in the lucrative commodities in the peninsula and Borneo.[21] Marlow is in no obvious sense an advocate of British expansion in the Malay world, but his view that the natives lack full access to reason strikes a chord with a prevalent official view that, in the words of a British governor in Singapore, "Asiatics will [n]ever learn to govern themselves; it is contrary to the genius of their race, of their history, of their religious system, that they should. Their desire is a mild, just and firm despotism."[22] Marlow's distinction between the human and the animal reinforces the exclusions of an imperialist ideology; his deployment of the animal echoes the premises (if not the conclusions) of a viewpoint associated with the expansion of colonial rule in the interests of those who were thought constitutively incapable of representing themselves. In Marlow's artistic *production* of the native world that he claims merely to describe, there is an echo of the official language deployed to justify the political transformation of "terrain" into "territory"; in both cases the rhetoric of just and universal representation serves to conceal the material and existential enrichment of the few at the expense of the many.

The European and native worlds of *Lord Jim* are not separated by an absolute gulf but locked into an economic relation in which the native—ontologically distinct yet structurally necessary—serves as raw material for the refinement of narrative and subjective value. It is also worth noting that Marlow's narrative *demands* to be read and evaluated by a community of readers that views subjective interiority as the condition of historical civilization. Failure to comply with these protocols will necessarily result in an incompetent reading of the novel, that is to say, one insensible to the complex inner struggles of its titular character. Marlow's representation of the native as animal in the context of nineteenth-century Malaya therefore has as much to do with his assumptions about who qualifies for literary subjectivity as it does with the framing suppositions of the historical archive.

The native is described as an animal within a mode of perspectivizing whose agents (artistic and political) take technological superiority and material domination to be justification of their belief in an essential difference between white and nonwhite; here the chromatic term serves as a placeholder of qualitative temporal difference.[23] The implicit view here is that to be a subject—and therefore responsible—one has to be modern. If this goes some way toward describing the underpinnings of racism in the colonial period, it is equally possible to note in hindsight that the discourse of modern subjectivity appears, in the context of a more recent "globalization," *not* to be the sole preserve of the white European. If the term "white"—which connotes the valorization of subjective interiority as the mark of historical arrival—is the placeholder for a *temporal* category, Marlow's point of view may be affirmed in practice, even if disavowed in principle, by the formerly colonized (non-European) subject who has—as a result of modern education—become the "inward" subject that makes his or her way up in the era of global capitalism. Today it is possible for a certain kind of native to be viewed (in Marlow's phrase) as "one of us" and, more insidiously, for this to be taken—by imperialists and certain anticolonial nationalists alike—as a sign of progress or emancipation.[24] This is, after all, what makes it possible for the former colonial subject to be(come) the felicitously modern reader of *Lord Jim*, that is, one who secretly glorifies the exclusive valorization of interiority even as he or she self-righteously condemns the negative portrayal of the natives.

The link between interiority (in narrative) and progress (in history) as it informs representation is not as easily loosened as the empirical oppressor can be denounced. In light of these deeper continuities, charging Joseph Conrad with racism may be a necessary but insufficient condition for a "postcolonial studies" attentive to the problem of difference as it is thematized within the modern. At the obvious risk of simplifying an enormously complicated problem, I want to suggest that certain modes of perspectivizing inaugurated during colonial rule today find hegemonic expression through models of "economic growth" (overproduction and overconsumption) prescribed by the West.[25] Notwithstanding the fact that in the era of global capitalism the instruments of neo-imperialist coercion cloak themselves in the disingenuous rhetoric of "free choice,"[26] the modernizing postcolonial state's necessitarian and uncritical submission to "that world where events move" (Conrad, *Lord Jim*, 200) amounts to a failure to evaluate the presuppositions of a global order in which "animality" is a structural feature.[27] Thus in both the colonial and the postcolonial epochs the term "progress" operates, albeit in different ways, as a myth in the sense described by Roland Barthes, that is to say, a globally sponsored program whose ends are treated as necessary or self-evidently just. Progress in this narrow sense defines what *counts* as thought in *Lord Jim* (remember the helmsmen) just as it exists as the absolute if unacknowledged horizon within which *we* are trained to read and interpret texts in and of the West. It is in this sense that we might quite properly say of Marlow that he is "one of us." This is also why I believe that there can be no easy undoing of this fundamental prejudice, euphemistically called "common sense," only a slow undoing of what it is we accede to when we read.

For reasons of space I cannot elaborate further on the insidious and exclusionary power of *this* valorization of "interiority," which is corollary to the global perspective. Having suggested in outline the broader concerns that inform my reading, I confine myself here to the task at hand: to broach another way of evaluating the perspective assumed by Marlow's narrative. My aim is to ask whether it is possible to read the occluded natives as a means to imagine the global differently. To this end, I propose a radically different reading of the animal from the one with which I began. I want to argue that the animal does not serve solely to secure the hierarchy between European and native existence but that it also interrupts Marlow's narrative in quite extraordinary ways. To put it schematically, I show that the animal runs alongside and undermines the narrative belief in subjective interiority as the sole marker of historical being. In doing so, the animal brings the native world into view, obliquely suggesting a distinct perspective on historical becoming. Paying close attention to the interruptive effects of the animal, I suggest that it brings about a revaluation of the relation between narrative and colonial subjectivity in *Lord Jim*.

II. THE YELLOW DOG

Distractedly or fleetingly noted as it flashes up at the outer reaches of Marlow's eye or ear, the animal invites a distinct approach to the novel. It calls for a reading that cannot be squared with Marlow's exclusive valorization of interiority or with his correspondingly narrow views on historical civilization. Barely seen, the animal is evoked by Marlow as one of many apparently superfluous background details that cumulatively generate an effect of reality whose essence or truth is unfolding elsewhere. But this marginalization is precisely what makes possible a new configuration of the text. The animal interrupts Marlow's narrative vector through its association with movements or effects that cannot be ascribed to intentionality or conscious actions; it hints at how a different strategy of reading might allow the natives to be seen as individual and historical agents in a manner undreamt of in Marlow's philosophy. In my reading, the animal effects a revaluation of the narrative effacement of the native; it enables the reader to imagine the native in a manner that runs counter to Marlow's and colonial attitudes towards native subjectivity. In what follows I demonstrate this by way of an extended analysis of the "yellow dog" episode. This incident has implications for any interpretation of Jim's story and his relation to the native world.

As he makes his way out of the courtroom at the end of the second day of Jim's trial, Marlow notices from the corner of his eye a group of natives, probably Indian, who are accused of assaulting a moneylender. A native woman in this group, Marlow notes, "suddenly began to talk in a high-pitched, shrewish tone. The man with me instinctively looked up at her" (43). This man is a stranger who happens to be walking out at the same time as Marlow. Marlow continues:

> Whether those villagers had brought the yellow dog with them, I don't know. Anyhow, a dog was there, weaving himself in and out amongst people's legs in that mute stealthy way native dogs have and my companion stumbled over him.

The dog leaped away without a sound; the man, raising his voice a little, said with a slow laugh, "Look at that wretched cur," and directly afterwards we became separated by a lot of people pushing in. I stood back for a moment against the wall while the stranger managed to get down the steps and disappeared. I saw Jim spin round. He made a step forward and barred my way. We were alone; he glared at me with an air of stubborn resolution. I became aware I was being held up, so to speak, as if in a wood. The verandah was empty by then, the noise and movement in court had ceased: a great silence fell upon the building, in which, somewhere far within, an oriental voice began to whine abjectly. The dog in the very act of trying to sneak in at the door, sat down hurriedly to hunt for fleas.

"Did you speak to me?" asked Jim very low, and bending forward, not so much towards me but at me, if you know what I mean. I said, "No," at once.

(43)

Because Jim does not see the dog and because he cannot know that it was the now-disappeared "stranger" who uttered those words, he mistakes the word "cur" for a term of abuse directed at him by Marlow. And because Marlow barely notices the dog, he does not at first see what Jim is talking about. But when he realizes why Jim is so upset he points at the animal to clear up the misunderstanding. Marlow frames the "yellow dog" episode within *this* matrix of involvement to suggest how the circumstances of their first meeting lead him to take a deeper interest in Jim. Seen in terms of Marlow's interests, the yellow dog serves solely as a narrative conjunction; it is excluded from establishing a relation to the encounter between the two men.

But a different picture begins to emerge if Marlow's account is situated within its immediate context, if this encounter is read in relation to the events taking place around it.[28] From this perspective much that appears at first sight superfluous or marginal brings about a powerful revaluation of this initial encounter between Jim and Marlow. There is, first of all, the mix of half-comprehended sights and sounds concatenated around the dog. In the passage just quoted, the stranger stumbles over the yellow dog as a result of being distracted by the "high-pitched shrewish tone" of the native woman. This subtle association between native and animal is reinforced by the sound of an "oriental voice" within the courtroom that "whine[s] abjectly." This resonance offers the first indication of a world excluded from yet operating alongside Marlow's narrative agenda.

The separation of the two worlds is undermined in this episode, for the properly human engagement between Marlow and Jim is interrupted by a

senseless if insistent movement that originates from the other side. While
Marlow tries without success to converse with Jim, the native's whine inside the court possibly communicates something to the dog. It is not clear
why Marlow distractedly notes this oriental voice, but, as if in response to
it, the dog tries to enter the building housing the court. Here the opacity
of the animal's intent is registered by way of non sequitur in the passage
quoted above: "the dog, *in the very act of trying to sneak in* at the door, *sat
down hurriedly* to hunt for fleas" [emphases added]. This errant movement,
in which an extraneous force causes the dog to turn away from its intention, oddly finds a parallel in the Jim-Marlow encounter. In the process of
impressionistically conveying that Jim seems acted upon by occult forces
that render him insensible to reason, Marlow is himself diverted from his
narrative intent:

> It strikes me now I have never been in my life so near a beating—I mean it liter-
> ally; a beating with fists. I suppose I had some hazy prescience of that eventual-
> ity being in the air. Not that he was actively threatening me. On the contrary,
> *he was strangely passive*—don't you know?—*but he was lowering*, and though not
> exceptionally big, he looked generally fit to demolish a wall. The most reassuring
> symptom I noticed was a kind of slow and ponderous hesitation, which I took
> as a tribute to the evident sincerity of my manner and of my tone. We faced
> each other. In the court the assault case was proceeding. I caught the words:
> 'Well—buffalo—stick—in the greatness of my fear . . .'
>
> (44)

Jim is "strangely passive," "lowering," his movements marked by "a kind of
slow and ponderous hesitation." Marlow evokes here the implacable or un-
fathomable wrath of a beast, just as, in the preceding passage, Marlow describes him as "bending forward, not so much *towards* me, but *at* me, if you
know what I mean" [emphasis added].[29] It is in the very process of evoking
the animal that Marlow's narrative is, as noted, thrown off track. For the
odd syntax used earlier to describe the dog that sits down to hunt for fleas
"in the act" of entering the court can now be seen to infect how Marlow
proceeds at this point. With the dog in mind, one might paraphrase what
Marlow *does* in the narrative as follows: "In the very act of trying to gain
entry into Jim's mind Marlow refers to the goings-on in the courtroom,
where someone recounts a beating connected to a buffalo." Marlow further
enhances this weird resonance (between the human and the animal movements) by retrospectively claiming that he very nearly became a victim of

Jim's bovine fury. The associations that gather around "buffalo" momentarily turn Marlow's narration in an unfamiliar direction, much as the word "cur" disoriented Jim earlier. Like the dog that interrupts Marlow's narrative, the figure of the animal interferes to claim an active part in the staging of the scene. The two parallel worlds—European-human, native-animal—appear by this juxtaposition of sights and sounds to communicate or transmit something back and forth.

By such means Marlow's voice is interrupted and pluralized, for although he is the only one who speaks, we are not always obliged to see through his eyes. Other perspectives disrupt his authoritative interpretation: his discourse is at once deflected and animated by an unbidden resonance with the movements of the native-animal world. A different but related economy from the one described earlier—in which the human-animal distinction serves to mark the divide between modern and nonmodern—is brought into view here. In its confusion of the human plot with the animal movements that cut into and around it, this scene begins to resemble my discussion in the previous chapter of the way that the "general equivalent" or the universal money form becomes mixed in with and interrupted by the "total or expanded form of value." Just as the more advanced "money form" does not resonate with the variety of economic terrains that it nonetheless encompasses and "articulates" for the world market, the narrative of *Lord Jim* thus provides an intuition of the texture in which the univocal global perspective can be reconstellated for reading. Reading may then turn to consider what flexible historical or ethical imaginings are enabled by such textual interanimation, in which those perspectives that do not compute with the global as perspective can be activated for history. The global may have to be thought through the interruptions of its perspective, which is not the same as being romantically anticapitalist. The absolute distinctions between capitalism and precapitalism, history and nonhistory find themselves troubled by such wayward movements. Moreover, they invite us to rethink the global in the disorientation caused by such an experience of interruption and dispersal that lacks the commensurate character of an already domesticated "local." It is, after all, the figure of the animal that cuts into the narrative of the human.

Marlow does not accord such movements interpretive value since they do not originate in an interiorized subject. But the heterogeneously induced effects of a putatively inferior animality nonetheless "weave" (44) their claims into the narrative. Not only is this space not "immobile," it may even

be possible that it conceals possibilities of being human, as well as conceptions of development and value, that fall outside modern Europe's ken. In
short, it may be populated by agents whose codings of value cannot be validated by the mode of thematization relied on by Marlow. Reading against
the grain in this way also enables an activation of "context" that gives the lie
to Marlow's unstated assumption that the native world serves merely as an
inert backdrop to the unfolding of a dynamic European story:

> 'Stop!' I exclaimed. This checked [Jim] for a second. 'Before you tell me what
> you think of me, I went on quickly, 'will you kindly tell me what it is I've said or
> done?' During the pause that ensued he surveyed me with indignation, while I
> made supernatural efforts of memory, in which I was hindered by the oriental
> voice within the court-room expostulating with impassioned volubility against
> a charge of falsehood.
>
> (45)

Is it possible that the native thinks his story as interesting as Jim's? Or
does the native's "whine"—in which the animal is mimed—now parody
Marlow's bewildered protestations? More seriously, the "charge of falsehood" here echoes the accusations laid at Jim's door and therefore suggests
a parallel between the compromised moral or legal positions of the native
and Jim. Marlow works hard to establish an understanding with Jim that
is based on their common (European) rationality and their shared way of
perceiving the world. But it is now all the more striking that the native-
animal movement cuts across his declared intentions to forge a connection
involving *Jim, the native, and the animal,* just as, at the outset, a link was
made—also by means of a connection barely thematized by Marlow—between the dog and the native. Through these strange associations the recal-
citrant animal not only works itself into Marlow's narrative, it also opens
up a peculiar relation to Jim.

I began by noting that the yellow dog episode ingeniously brings Marlow and Jim together for the first time and that Marlow's gorgeously tac-
tile account of this episode is designed to make his audience richly aware
of Jim's frailties. Thus when Jim finally sees the dog and realizes his error
Marlow confidently draws a higher lesson from it: "There had never been a
man so mercilessly shown up by his own natural impulse. A single word had
stripped him of his discretion—of that discretion which is more necessary
to him than clothing is to the decorum of our body" (46). According to this
interpretation, Jim loses all dignity because his self-loathing now stands

revealed to the world. But Marlow may also suggest something more radical in the word "stripped": By exposing himself in this way, Jim degrades himself to the state of an animal that, lacking interiority, can neither dissimulate nor exercise a consonant responsibility in the higher name of "discretion." To be stripped of the inner is to cease being or to be made less than human. By this logic the terror that accompanies this realization is what draws Jim back into the community of right-minded Europeans. Marlow ends the theatrical presentation of his encounter with Jim on this triumphant note. In this vein the disclosure of the dog by Marlow's "pointing finger" symbolizes both an absolute separation between himself and the animal and a subtle reaffirmation of his narrative authority.

But Marlow's perspective fails to register the fact that Jim has been put on a different trail. The dog (like the buffalo) outlines a different movement and is not an empty placeholder, as Marlow supposes, for Jim's low estimation of himself. Jim "contemplated the wretched animal, that moved no more than an effigy: it sat with ears pricked and its sharp muzzle pointed into the doorway, and suddenly snapped at a fly like a piece of mechanism" (46). What Jim sees is *not* what Marlow tells us he sees. Jim sees that the animal has its muzzle actively "pointed" into the house of law. Unlike most readers of the novel, who have been content to follow Marlow's cue by thematizing the scene as a picture to be contemplated in a disinterested and objective manner, Jim cannot produce the representational frame that marks him out as a higher being. His disorientation marks his imbrication with the object; the signifying schemata he relies on are part of the context they presume to thematize as if from a distance. Jim resembles the animal—in the sense suggested by Marlow—in being stripped of the ability to produce an adequate, that is, objective description. His immobility allegorizes his inability, at this moment, to produce the global as perspective: "He appeared at first uncomprehending, then confounded, and at last amazed and scared as though a dog had been a monster and he had never seen a dog before" (46).[30]

This breakdown in Jim's capacity to signify correctly is accompanied by another sensation. This is the defamiliarizing shock of *seeing* the animal—existing and acting outside the framework of the Jim-Marlow encounter. Jim's astonishment seems informed by this realization when the animal becomes present to him in its sheer otherness. Needless to say, this sighting of the animal (as other) also takes place precisely when Jim is thrown off, dispossessed of the attributes of interiorization that Marlow rates so highly.

This small but crucial shift—which is hardly psychological—enables a separation of Jim's reaction from Marlow's grip so as to suggest that it has some affinity with the diffuse ensemble of perspectives produced by the natives and animals. These apparently meaningless sounds and sights that emanate from the impoverished native-animal world suddenly cut in to claim a conversation with Jim precisely when Marlow declares him "stripped." This word also recalls the fact that the dispossessed state in which Jim acknowledges the animal's presence is itself a putative instance of animality.

But could it also be that the interruptive flash of the animal communicates (with) the memory of another moment of exposure and humiliation? The clue here is that Jim's oblique riposte to Marlow's secure assessment of being "stripped" comes in an invocation of those final, agonizing moments he spent on the *Patna*:

> 'The cloud had raced ahead, and this first swell [of the storm] seemed to travel upon a sea of lead. There was no life in that stir. It managed, though, to knock over something in my head. What would you have done? You are sure of yourself—aren't you? What would you have done if you felt now—this minute—the house here move, just move a little under your chair? Leap! By heavens! You would take one spring from where you sit and land in that clump of bushes yonder.'

(65)

By invoking a fiction ("what ... if"), Jim appeals to Marlow's imagination to engage with a sight or evaluation caught up in and interrupted by the object thematized. It is a similar kind of seeing that the yellow dog opens up in Jim, for the shock and humiliation he feels when he finally sees the animal involuntarily activates the memory that *first* experience of being "stripped," when he jumped off the *Patna*. This association is what causes him to look "uncomprehending," then "amazed," and, finally, "scared" when he sees the dog.[31] It would seem that humiliation is here the source of an insight: it turns Jim away from Marlow's conception of responsibility, which is embedded in unwarranted claims about subjective autonomy and the superiority conferred by the capacity to produce the global as perspective. The perspective communicated—this is a catachresis—by the animal obliquely enables in Jim a turning away from Marlow toward a responsiveness to (the) otherness (of the self). It should therefore come as no surprise that Marlow mistakes Jim's recognition of the claims of the animal for a certain obtuseness on Jim's part ("Had he not understood its deplorable meaning?"). But this is precisely the point: Jim appears stupid because he is called by something unfamiliar. Momentarily dispossessed of his composure, forgetting himself, Jim *sees* the animal. The animal is not there to serve his needs. It is not there to consolidate his view of himself; it is turned elsewhere. The proliferation of sounds and sights that disrupt the univocity of Marlow's narration waywardly culminates with an externally induced shift in Jim's perspective.

III. JIM AND ANIMALITY

The yellow dog episode opens up new ways of interpreting the novel as a whole. It shows that the movements in the native world are not without meaning; they are not signs of existential or historical "immobility." These animal movements offer an insight into how a different conception of value can begin to emerge in the text, which is to also say that they suggest a different way to imagine "the human." Returning in this vein to those key moments on the *Patna*—and what constitutes *the* event of the novel—something shockingly new comes into view: the perspective opened up by the animal insinuates a *similarity* between Jim and the Malays in that, like the Malays, Jim is overcome by a blankness and immobility that is not amenable to the representation demanded of him later by the court. Marlow points out this similarity even if he makes nothing of it: "Just picture to yourself the actors in that, thank God! Unique episode of the sea, four beside themselves with fierce and secret exertions, *and three looking on in complete immobility*" (60). The "three" are, of course, Jim and the two native helmsmen, and this link is obliquely reinforced in Jim's court testimony:[32]

> The facts those men were so eager for had been visible, tangible, open to the senses, occupying their place in space and time, requiring for their existence a fourteen-hundred-ton steamer and twenty-seven minutes by the watch; they made a whole that had features, shades of expression, a complicated aspect that could be remembered by the eye, and something else besides, something invisible, a directing spirit of perdition that dwelt within, like a malevolent soul in a detestable body. He was anxious to make this clear. This had not been a common affair, everything in it had been of the utmost importance, and fortunately he remembered everything. He wanted to go on talking for truth's sake, perhaps for his own sake also; and while his utterance was deliberate, his mind positively flew round and round the serried circle of facts that had surged up all about

him *to cut him off from the rest of his kind: it was like a creature that, finding itself imprisoned within an enclosure of high stakes, dashes round and round, distracted in the night, trying to find a weak spot, a crevice, a place to scale, some opening through which it may squeeze itself and escape.*

(19; emphasis added)

Like the old Malay's testimony, a bizarre hybrid of human and animal is evoked here. The old Malay helmsman's sense of "something evil befalling the ship" (60) finds an echo in Jim's conviction that the "facts" on the *Patna* were acted upon by a "directing spirit of perdition." In this passage, what begins as Jim's earnest and deliberate invocation of facts disintegrates into the image of a consciousness that is likened to the desperate actions of a trapped beast. And just as the old Malay's outpourings have to be "stopped" (61), Jim is "cut short" (20). As in the instant when the dog became visible, the figure of the animal now induces an oblique insight into the forces that overcame Jim during those final moments on the ship. The description of his inability to organize his memory into a coherent narrative for the court seems to parallel his reaction on the *Patna* that fateful night, when it was impossible yet unbearable for him to decide on a course of action. The agony in which his mind had sought then (on the *Patna*) and seeks now (in the courtroom) "some opening through which [to] squeeze itself and escape" both describes and is an insight arrived at in a moment of animality, a moment heterogeneous to, and therefore not recuperable by, the language of reflection. This may also explain why at a crucial point in Jim's account to Marlow of his leap he switches abruptly from the simple past to the past perfect tense: "'I had jumped . . .' he checked himself, averted his gaze . . . 'it seems,' he added" (68)—the shift in tense limning an act taken in a moment emptied of "choice." What appears as a vacancy or a fundamental opacity in the narrative—the crucial moments leading up to and including Jim's leap are marked by blankness—is once again reproduced by way of the figure of the animal. Apart from its obvious importance to an evaluation of Jim's character, the animal perspectives I have explored may be taken to suggest a more general point about the possibilities opened up through a loosening of the exclusive claims of autonomous agency.

In the long passage just quoted it is "the circle of facts" demanded by the court that "cuts [Jim] off from the rest of his kind" (19). The ambiguous use of "kind"—it is not clear whether it indexes the race or species— alienates Jim from the Europeans to whom he seeks, like the similarly unsuccessful Malays, to be intelligible. Jim is cast outside the pale, but what is powerfully enabling about the display of Jim's moments of failure is that it simultaneously opens up a textual attunement to conceptions of belonging that exceed Marlow's representational abilities. It is when Jim is "stripped" of the coordinates of an autonomy-defining responsibility that it becomes possible to imagine how Jim's fall—or leap—opens up the apprehension of an other relation to the self, a relation posited on difference rather than the self-identity separating man from animal. This exteriority—produced in a moment internal yet irreducible to the language of interiority—affords a perspective different from the representational mindset that divides the world up between modern and premodern and that fails to see that the "sovereign individual" trained to construe his conditioning as freedom is not so far removed from the wayward animal that does not "have the right to make a promise."[33] The peculiar quality of (Jim's) experience here opens up a way of seeing in which interiority no longer appears as the exclusive sign of historical and narrative value but as an effect of the exteriority marked by the figure of the animal.

To identify with Jim in this light is to do more than bring into sympathetic view the occluded space of the natives, as if that world were merely the referent for "exteriority." The animal interruption of the main narrative serves as an experience of difference, experience *as* difference, a relation that folds, as it were, the closed space of interiority inside out, vouchsafing the possibility—which goes unelaborated because it is not "historically" realized—of as yet unimagined forms of individual and collective responsibility. We are called here *by the text* to imagine a relation that emerges in the shuttle between human and animal, reducible to neither term. Where the one is an effect of the other, this movement can suggest a different relation, directed in a new, if unverifiable, manner. In this also lies the possibility of a reading skeptical of the way "experience" has been mythically assimilated to a global perspective in which others become objects of sympathy only if they accede to the terms of "inward pain," that is to say, as "one of us." In short, this is to ask whether the protocols governing literary analysis and historical evaluation can productively move beyond Europe, where "Europe" is no longer the sign of a geographical space but an exclusive mode of temporalization.

In this sense the animal does more than just allow a reading of Jim's agency as linked to the trials and aspirations of the nameless many who endure on the far side of historical civilization, although this is doubtless one of its effects. For even as the animal interrupts Marlow's representation to remain within a representational discourse, it invites a reading attentive to how historical representation might respond to contextual unevenness in the manner I have discussed. The effects of Jim's own attunement to this other question is suggested in a passage where Marlow is startled into admitting that Jim does not feel accountable to him but to someone or something else:

> He was not speaking to me, he was only speaking before me, in a dispute with an invisible personality, an antagonistic and inseparable partner of his existence—another possessor of his soul. These were issues beyond the competency of a court of inquiry: it was a subtle and momentous quarrel as to the true essence of life, and did not want a judge. . . . I can't explain to you who haven't seen him and who hear his words only at second hand the mixed nature of my feelings.
>
> (57)

Whether or not the figure of the animal engages for Jim a secret interlocutor, its interruptive force enables Jim to see otherwise and to attune himself to human possibilities outside Marlow's grasp. Whereas Marlow worries over whether Jim is "one of us," the figure of the animal reveals the categories of "character" and "history" as the interanimation of differential forces opened toward other possibilities rather than as cultural or racial essences moving immutably through homogenous space and time. Jim's state is reconfigured by the "totally new set of conditions for his imaginative faculty to work on." These conditions are, by Marlow's own admission, "Entirely new, entirely remarkable" (133). The words "imaginative faculty" suggest about Jim a willingness for a time to engage differently with the possibilities opened up by new and unfamiliar relations.

It would for this reason be a mistake to think of Jim's life in Patusan as that of a white man who "goes native." Jim's vulnerability upon arrival there immediately puts him outside the pale of the racial and civilizational hierarchies subscribed to by votaries of the global perspective in the era of high European imperialism. He is first imprisoned and almost executed by the Malays, and he then seeks protection among the Bugis. At the time of Jim's arrival, Patusan is also overrun by anarchy and is inhabited by racially diverse merchants, laborers, and slaves. Although Patusan has not been annexed by the Europeans—Marlow describes it as being "of no earthly importance to anybody" (133)—it is articulated into the networks of trade and domination of a nineteenth-century global economy. In this connec-

tion Marlow succinctly notes how the insatiable European search for commodities has triggered violent struggles between local groups and caused
social upheavals across the region: "of course the quarrels were for trade"
(154).[34] Patusan is shaped by the flows of European capital and Asian labor,
and Jim's arrival—as agent of the middleman Stein—is part of a broader,
stratified process by which a motley of impoverished sojourners, migrants,
and refugees gather in the backwash of the European empires in late-
nineteenth-century Southeast Asia.[35] These include "foreign" and country-
born Malays, Bugis, aboriginals, Chinese, Arabs, and Eurasians.

Jim is as much an immigrant or sojourner as the Malay, Indian, Chinese,
and aboriginal peasants who find themselves in Patusan.[36] This is the difference between Jim and Kurtz of *Heart of Darkness*, whose pronouncements
are propped up by the military might of the East India Company. Kurtz is
invested with the power of a colonial official, whereas Jim is a refugee in
Patusan. Like the Malays (who could have killed him with impunity), the
Bugis do not accord Jim respect because he is white. Indeed, he first appears before them as a terrified fugitive, and the "motherly" (156) solicitude
of Doramin's wife is only one instance of the hospitality the Bugis show him
(a fact that is conveniently forgotten in Marlow's and Jim's accounts later,
where he is described as their protector). Jim's superiority does not therefore
lie in his whiteness; he earns the title "tuan" by distinguishing himself in the
battle with Sherif Ali. This is confirmed by the narrator's early observation:
"[The Bugis] called him Tuan Jim" (4). Given that all white men in the Malay
colonies were addressed as "tuan" (cf. "sahib" in Rudyard Kipling's *Kim*), this
observation would seem redundant *unless* we grasp the concealed point: that
in Jim's unique case the term functions as a mark of distinction *among* the
native immigrants. In naming him thus, they make him one of them.

To see Jim in this way is to also bring into view Patusan as a space in
which new affiliations can come into being, rather than yet another site in
which the simple oppositions of colonizer-colonized are replicated, or in
which is enacted the transition from a uniformly immobile "premodernity"
to a homogenously dynamic "modernity." This perspective is not fleshed
out in Marlow' narrative, but its availability is suggested in the kind of life
that Jim makes for himself in Patusan. In this regard, it is notable that
although Jim gets the weaponry and contrives to make the Bugis' victories possible, the knowledge he brings is never set apart—on the basis of a
spurious "modernity"—from its denizens. Because Jim lives as one of them
his knowledge is necessarily made accountable to the emergent social and

historical context, making it possible see how the inhabitants of Patusan shape their own ends. This two-way relationship is suggested several times, not least when Jim refers to some of the liberated aboriginal groups as "my own people" (207). Just as *Lord Jim* can be pried from its vaunted position in the English canon and resituated as a Malay novel (albeit one where "Malay" does not denote an exclusive racial or ethnic group), it is also clear how qualitatively distinct forms of individual and collective being—unfamiliar to Marlow as much as to the official historians upon whom Conrad relied—may be imagined to have found expression in this space.[37]

Jim's traits serve a prismatic function: they bring into view the different ways in which the pilgrims and the heterogeneous population of Patusan may, like the dog, be barred entry from the courthouse and negotiate with the dominant political and economic changes that have so profoundly affected their lives.[38] Jim is a European who undergoes a change of heart (although his reversion to assumptions of European superiority suggests the power of the template of the global as perspective), but his story also draws the reader toward the many other immigrants like Jim who find their way to Patusan. In light of the way the historical and ethical struggles in the novel have generally been read, this point is worth emphasizing: Jim is *not* the only agent or human being in Patusan.

In this sense Jim's traits have a diffusive effect: they make visible the different forces at play in the novel that cannot be comprehended in Marlow's account. One may extrapolate from this to say that the challenge lies precisely in not confining such possibilities within a tendentious discourse of "transition." This point is especially worth noting in light of the undiminished power of the historical script upon which Marlow draws, where narrow and homogenized conceptions of "progress" are foisted upon ostensibly benighted peoples in the form of a "free trade" regime.[39] Just as the animal opens up a new perspective on the human, the world of Patusan hints at the mere beginnings of a revaluation of "progress" and "diversity" in ways that may exceed the ken of a certain benevolent European imagination. The importance of this rescue work for the "imaginative faculty" is underscored by the fact that the fragile and heterogeneous unfolding of interests in Patusan is suddenly destroyed.

If in the first part of the novel this struggle and interanimation are expressed in the disruptive appearance of the animal, in the Patusan section the narrative strains to catch at a different rhythm of life, the peculiar possibilities opened up by this "impoverished" relationship to the environment. Marlow tacitly acknowledges the change in Jim:

> It was something to be proud of. I, too, was proud—for him, if not so certain of the fabulous value of the bargain. It was wonderful. It was not so much of his fearlessness that I thought. It is strange how little account I took of it: as if it had been something too conventional to be at the root of the matter. No, I was more struck by the other gifts he displayed. He had proved his grasp of the unfamiliar situation, his intellectual alertness in that field of thought. There was his readiness, too! Amazing. And all this had come to him in a manner like keen scent to a well-bred hound. . . . Now and then, though, a word, a sentence, would escape him that showed how deeply, how solemnly, he felt about that work which had given him the certitude of rehabilitation.
>
> (152)

This "rehabilitation" refers to Jim's absorption into a different mode of perspectivizing in regard to life at the margins of a colonial capitalist system. In opening Jim up to the heterogeneity of value creation, the animal arguably also enables the reader to see past the dominant historical script by which terms such as "progress" or "expression" are taken to mean one thing. This ought not to be taken for a "rejection" of modernity (as if such a choice were even available). Rather it amounts to a questioning of the terms of engagement between Europe and its other. Such questioning is imaginable in the case of Jim because, unlike Marlow, he learns to see with a different eye. I have argued why the "Lord" of the novel's title poorly translates an honorific (*tuan*) conferred on Jim by the inhabitants of Patusan on the strength of his conduct, not on the superiority of his race. Such a conferral indicates the agency of the nameless many in Patusan through the medium of Jim's story. Reading *Lord Jim* as an immigrant's story in this specific sense moves us away from the simple racial binaries of colonizer-colonized to speak of the particular circumstances by which this European subject learns, as it were, to heed difference, "within" and "without." It enables attentiveness to the absolute singularity of Jim's life without losing sight of the other lives and relations that so obviously sustain him.

This perspectival shift also shows that Patusan does not simply serve as evidence of the futility of all lives that seek direction outside the shelter of European civilization. Marlow himself very nearly admits this when he says that Jim's experience there leads him to "confess to a faith mightier than the laws of [Western] order and progress" (206). But this vision of a human progress at once more capacious and more humble than that asserted by modern Europe goes unelaborated. To give the narrative the benefit of the doubt, Marlow's rhetorical flourish betrays an awareness that perhaps something here escapes his grasp, but because he cannot evaluate his own values he necessarily turns away from the implications of this assertion. The narrative is to this extent constrained by its own "faith," aware of but unable to question its mode of perspectivizing. Rather, it is elaborated obliquely, by means of a secret resonance between Jim's story and the two modes in which the native world appears: as pilgrim and as immigrant. Following this strand, and in lieu of a conclusion, I explore the shape taken by this peculiar interanimation of "native" and "European" in order to activate Jim's story more fully within this other "context."

IV. PILGRIMS, IMMIGRANTS, AND OTHERS

The uncanny parallel with the Malay Muslim pilgrims is first suggested when Jim breaks with the script of his own initiatory rite of passage into a community of European merchant seamen by jumping from the *Patna*. Jim draws attention to its allegorical significance and Marlow repeats it shortly after: "[Jim] had indeed jumped into an everlasting deep hole" (68). Like the tormented pilgrim of Bunyan's allegorical *Pilgrim's Progress* (who finds his relation to a familiar historical script suddenly transformed), Jim undergoes a series of trials as part of a quest that none of his helpers can fully understand. From the moment of his leap, Jim is not at home in the familiar world. Following the humiliation of his trial in Bombay, he embarks on an animal-like meandering by taking jobs that drive him further east. It is a fitful and aimless movement that resembles and parodies the purposeful westward movement of the Malay pilgrims. In his quest Jim stops at various lesser shrines, represented first by Marlow's unnamed friend; then the ship chandlers Egström and Blake in Singapore; and the Yucker Brothers, who are teak merchants in Bangkok—before reaching Patusan in Northeast Borneo. The hostility he encounters upon arrival, not to mention its remoteness and poverty, makes Patusan an unlikely pilgrimage site.

In different ways Jim's presence in Patusan serves to undermine the stabilities of racial identification and the claims of indigenous priority. The following presentation of Jim's arrival in the Bugis' settlement not only troubles the fixed assumptions about racial loyalty held to by the "privileged man" of Europe (206), but is also ironically prescient about latter-day nationalist demands that autochthony (*bumiputera*) be the condition of full citizenship in the postcolonial state:[40]

> [Jim] reached and grabbed desperately with his hands, and only succeeded in gathering a horrible cold shiny heap of slime against his breast—up to his very chin. It seemed to him he was burying himself alive, and then he struck out madly scattering the mud with his fists. It fell on his head, on his face, over his eyes, into his mouth. . . . He made efforts, tremendous sobbing efforts, efforts that seemed to burst his eyeballs in their sockets and make him blind, and culminating into one mighty, supreme effort in the darkness to crack the earth asunder, to throw it off his limbs—and he felt himself creeping feebly up the bank. He lay full length on the firm ground and saw the light, the sky.
>
> (153)

Here is the European depicted as autochthon, born out of the mud of Patusan. Drawing on the images of both pilgrim and immigrant, Jim's ironic rebirth presages a new and unstable beginning. It is crucial to note that Jim's state upon arrival would apply equally to an unprotected Bugis or Dayak. A kind of anamorphosis takes place by this means, for in shedding its exclusivity Jim's condition is illuminated by the lesser lights of the other inhabitants of Patusan. As a consequence, his experience ceases to be altogether legible to Marlow.[41] Jim's victories are for this reason not those of a white man on a civilizing mission, drawing Patusan into the normative horizon of a foregone modernity.

To read contextually in this sense is to give texture to the different struggles in Patusan and not simplify a complex situation. It is to avoid thinking the Arab, Sherif Ali, an evil character, and Doramin, the Bugis, a good one, as one might in an adventure story. The alliance of the rebellious aboriginals with Sherif Ali, the Arab "wandering stranger" (157), may have to do with their exploitation and perhaps enslavement by the Bugis and the Malays, who seek labor to feed escalating European demands in the late nineteenth century for the forest products of the archipelago. The impersonal force of capitalism violently warps social space in intimate ways. A distinction is elsewhere made between "country-born Malays, who had been ground to a point of extinction" (138) by the foreign Malays (suggesting at once that the category of "Malay" is not a stable one and that many of the Malays are immigrants.) The latter Malays are ruled by Rajah Allang, and their conflict with the Bugis, "immigrants from Celebes" (157), emerges from competition over access to raw materials and labor. In this struggle between two powerful local factions for control over resources and labor, the terrorized small peasant cultivators and "fisher-folk" (148) are the ones who seek Jim's protection. Since Jim is also the agent of the middleman Stein, this double relationship indicates a possible conflict of interest since the "fisher-folk" and their like are turned into workers and slaves as a result of the insatiable European demand for primary commodities.

Jim cannot be seen in a romantic light; forgetting that it was the natives who saved his life by giving him shelter, he describes his relation to them in paternalistic tones (202–3). He does not acknowledge the extent to which he has been shaped by his new surroundings and companions. But because he lives among and is accountable to the inhabitants of Patusan, he ought to be distinguished from Conradian expatriates like Willems and Almayer. Instead, he resembles the outsider Tamb Itam, "a Malay from the north, a stranger who had wandered into Patusan, and had been forcibly detained by Rajah Allang" (165). Like Tamb Itam, Jim finds a "precarious refuge" (165) among the Bugis. When Jim is killed, Tamb Itam and Jewel both leave the settlement because their lives are no longer secure. Conversely, it is sometimes difficult to know what rule to apply—apart from variable political ones—to tell the native from the foreigner. Although Jewel is Eurasian she has lived all her life in Patusan; can she not claim to be more of a "native" than the Bugis Doramin or even the Malay Rajah Allang, who are both relatively recent immigrants? Without succumbing to the alternating rhetoric of nostalgia and hope in Marlow's narrative, it can be said that identities and filiations are negotiated anew in Patusan for a time. Historical possibility under these conditions can be read as a repeatedly interrupted stammer.

I conclude by pointing to the peculiar if unspoken reconstitution of the self that makes possible Jim's love for Jewel *and* by noting that even the historical daring presupposed by this relationship is open to being interrupted and pluralized by other forces. I will elaborate upon this point by way of noting that whereas neither Jim nor Jewel sees Patusan as fallen or impoverished in an unchanging sense, Marlow cannot see it without being tendentious. He sympathizes with Jewel only because he believes that she is in some way superior to the other natives. He believes her life to be wasted in Patusan, and he cannot express sorrow at her mother's death without disparaging the world of Patusan. It is in this sense that Marlow cannot hear or grasp what Jewel is trying to tell him when she recalls her mother's fate:

> [Jewel's tears] had the power to drive me out of my conception of existence, out of that shelter each of us makes for himself to creep under in moments of danger, as a tortoise withdraws within its shell. For a moment I had a view of a world that seemed to wear a vast and dismal aspect of disorder, while, in truth, thanks to our unwearied efforts, it is as sunny an arrangement of small conveniences as the mind of man can conceive. But still—it was only a moment: I went back into my shell directly. One *must*—don't you know?—though I seemed to have lost all my words in the chaos of dark thought I had contemplated for a second or two beyond the pale. These came back too, very soon, for words also belong to the sheltering conception of light and order which is our refuge.
>
> (190)

Despite the ambiguity of "a world," the squalor Marlow thinks he sees is not simply material but existential or ontological. But even as this conversation takes place in the darkness, with the misunderstanding between Marlow and Jewel taking up all our attention, something cuts in from elsewhere to put these concerns in their place:

> 'Why is [Jim] different? Is he better? Is he ...' 'Upon my word of honour,' I broke in, 'I believe he is.' We subdued our tones to a mysterious pitch. Amongst the huts of Jim's workmen (they were mostly liberated slaves from the Sherif's stockade) somebody started a shrill, drawling song. Across the river a big fire (at Doramin's, I think) made a glowing ball, completely isolated in the night.
>
> (191)

The sound is unpleasant not only to Marlow but in all likelihood also to Jewel (as well as the Bugis). All of them have had little contact with these indigenous people. It is perhaps significant that Jim's character is once again being scrutinized when this interruption takes place. For the "shrill, drawling song" recalls the "high-pitched" (43) native woman and the oriental "whine" (43) that interrupted Marlow's first encounter with Jim. Needless to say, the fate of these aboriginal folk is marginal to the relationship between Jewel and Jim just as, historically speaking, they are the invisible underclass forced into the service of the various groups vying for power in the region, whether Malay, Bugis, or European. These people are the lowest of the low, and although they are described as "liberated," their fate under

Bugis rule is uncertain. It is within this broader context that their "shrill, drawling song" breaks into the conversation between Marlow and Jewel. The indigenous people are barely mentioned again in the novel, but it may not be too much to say that the reader, like the Malay steersmen in reverse, stands in blank incomprehension before this song. It is an interruption that suggests yet another opening in the text.

CONCLUSION

I began the previous chapter by pointing out that a competent reading of the ethical crisis in *Lord Jim* requires that the bizarre behavior of the Malay helmsmen on the Patna not be recognized. Here literary competence—responding correctly to who qualifies as an ethical agent and historical subject—works to occlude what cannot be made to fit yet is somehow needed for the overarching narrative purpose. I read the scandalous fate of the helmsmen as an intuition of the workings of the global perspective, which represents by at once incorporating and effacing difference. Just as the subjectivity of the Malays, and the broader context of colonized subjects in the archipelago, can only be imagined (not retrieved) through the figure of animality, the encompassing claims of the global perspective call for a reading that brushes against the grain of this comprehensive perspective within whose terms truth is produced.

The central problem of today's global interactions is *not* the tension between cultural homogenization and cultural heterogenization.[1] It is rather that the global as perspective defines the terms in which historical narrative and political agency are shaped. Inasmuch as critics and boosters of globalization do not question the perspective in which the world is brought into view, they repeat the presuppositions by which are occluded perspectives that cannot find institutional validation. By definition a perspective that is adequate and comprehensive, the global is not the exclusive preserve of any one racial or cultural group. Where it raises agents in the South, as much as in the North, these agents may evaluate and analyze their own "local" liberation or emancipation in terms that oppose Eurocentric ideology while reproducing its ways of seeing and saying. What is at issue here is a trained reflex in which knowledge is produced and sight naturalized. But rather than pretend that the global can be rejected, or that it is not useful, I argue in this book that it is crucial to cultivate a form of analysis that makes the global accountable—in all its diverse empirical articulations—to the contextual unevenness it occludes. In this book I have argued that the matter of representation serves as an allegory of a historicity that situates or encompasses the mode of perspectivizing in which global histories are produced, and that it is precisely by means of representation's interruptive potential that it begins to acknowledge the complexity of the world in which we live. A historically informed study of literature that attends to the matter of representation can help train us as readers to imagine the global otherwise. Just as this act of reconstellating or displacing the global is not the same thing as its rejection, any engagement with the frame and matter of representation cannot be content to celebrate (or lament) empirical variations at the local level that support (or undermine) the view that globalization leads to a worldwide homogenization of cultural practices. It must instead draw on textured analysis to interrupt the naturalization of the global perspective in which such arguments take shape. Historical studies would then be read, in the robust sense, in order to enable ways of seeing and saying that are closed off in conventional social-scientific and literary analyses. It is in the displacements enabled here that the global can be made responsive to what had appeared simply a matter for thematization.

Through this engagement with literary analysis, empirical and social-scientific studies may yet evolve ways of attending to the limits of the perspectivizing that they take for granted, and experiment with ways in which the interruption of this perspective may enable a conception of the global that is more capacious—inasmuch as it is concerned less with being comprehensive than with how it needs to respond to difference it may not comprehend. Literary reading interrupts the historical or social-scientific lens through which the global appears because in literature language is supposed by and embedded in a context from which it cannot be fully extricated. An interruptive reading shows how the global is implicated within the web it presumes to configure, thus opening up a path for it to be read in new ways.

This is why a literary engagement with the global—literary criticism in the era of globalization—is not just about producing new or better explanations of globalization as condition or process. Because the issue is not a truth separable from its representation, the stakes of the game do not center solely on producing more (or different) truth claims. Rather, a step is taken toward elaborating the larger problematic of this critical practice by loosening the ways in which such a perspective is dissimulated as sight.

A reading attentive to the matter of representation can engage the ways in which the global is interrupted by perspectives from an already inducted periphery. In this book, I invent a conversation from such unequal encounters by exploring how the suppressed or disenfranchised valences of words such as "subsistence," "amuk," "I," and "animality" teach us to activate the global otherwise. In the process I show that the global perspective is irreducibly embedded with and ensnared by the objects and context that it purports to thematize, as it were, from an objective distance. Literary texture gives us a clue to the "historicity of history."[2] Through a reading that complicates the relationship between the mode of thematization and its object, I show how a more complex and uneven reading of history is put to work. Such attention to texture is historical in the sense that it shows how the text is an artifact (not simply "evidence") that intervenes in its time, charging that context in new ways and enabling it to be read with different eyes.

There is no question that the global is a perspective that is both powerful and useful. But if the global is to properly respond to the historical and contextual unevenness of the terrains it must represent, it must allow itself to be touched by difference. It is obvious that we ought to grasp this tension as something other than a contradiction and to see in it the possibility of thinking creatively about historical representation. Seen in this light, the task of knowledge production is to elaborate historically informed ways of inhabiting and interrupting the global perspective. It is in the creative displacement and reconstellation of the global through its relation to marginalized perspectives that the claims of the global may find fuller expression, where "full" no longer connotes a comprehensive grasp or the perfect power of prediction. In seeking to undo the univocal character of the global by attending to the uneven texture in representation, literary study contributes to our study of globalization through slow and patient attempts to change from within the way our reflexes have been shaped and conditioned in complicity with this dispensation.[3] By reflecting upon or catching ourselves at what we "naturally" do when we read—an instance of such conditioning being our necessary failure as competent readers of *Lord Jim* to see the Malay helmsmen or the aboriginal villagers in Patusan as ethical agents—we take the first step toward opening up the global to a vision that is at once more capacious and humble.

In elite anticolonial nationalist texts that point to the limitations of a Eurocentric perspective, such as the work of Pramoedya Ananta Toer and Jawaharlal Nehru, the global perspective is staged in ways that suggest the enduring relevance of the issues raised by Adam Smith. In this concluding section, I draw on these two twentieth-century writers, Pramoedya and Nehru, to reiterate the problems inhering in the global perspective as the means by which such difference is tacitly comprehended, even in non-European or putatively "local" sites. Given the straitened political and economic circumstances in which newly independent colonies found themselves, and given the habits of thinking into which nationalist artists and politicians are trained to re-present their order, developmentalist logic governs discussions of "progress" in the postcolony. Rather than question the worthiness of such presuppositions, I seek to supplement or interrupt them by drawing attention to the irreducibly "incomplete" nature of such global comprehension. To my discussion of the global as perspective and the relation of rhetoric to historical unevenness I append a sympathetic questioning of the global as it plays itself out in the representational modalities of the nationalist context.

With this in mind, one may ask, to what extent does a figure like Minke, the young hero of Pramoedya's novel, *Bumi Manusia* (*This Earth of Mankind*), question the global perspective in spite of his increasingly sophisticated awareness of the injustice of colonial rule? In Minke's monologue at the start of the novel, not only are the social applications of modern science and technology not subjected to questioning or reflection, they are celebrated as the framework through which human and social entities are interpreted:

> One of the products of science at which I never stopped marveling [*kukagumi*] was printing, especially zincography. Imagine, people can reproduce tens of thousands of copies of any photograph in just one day. Landscape pictures, big and important people, new machines, American skyscrapers, everything from all over the world—now I could see all this for myself on these printed sheets of paper. How deprived [*sungguh merugi*] had the generation before me been—a generation that had been satisfied with the accumulation of its own footsteps in the lanes of its villages [*sudah puas dengan banyaknya jejak-langkah sendiri di*

lorong-lorong kampungnya itu]. I was truly grateful to all those people who had worked so tirelessly to give birth to these new wonders [*keajaiban baru*]. . . .

   Reports from Europe and America were full of the newest discoveries [*penemuan-penemuan terbaru*]. Their awesomeness challenged the magical powers of the gods and knights, my ancestors in *wayang* stories. [*Kehebatannya menandingi kesaktian para satria dan dewa nenek-moyangku dalam cerita wayang*]. Trains—carriages without horses, without cattle, without buffalo—had been witnessed now for over ten years by my people [*sebangsaku*]. And astonishment [*keheranan*] remains in their hearts even today.[4]

In an echo of Abdullah's *Hikayat* (note the generous use of "*heran*" and "*ajaib*"), the applications of science and technology symbolize to Minke the promise of a utopian reenchantment of the world ("magical powers" is the phrase used to approximate the archaic "*sakti*"). It is as if something has changed in the very core of his being, and it is from this perspective that the content *trains* the reader into occupying the normative reading position that has been prepared for her. The reader of this text is exhorted to denigrate the "accumulation" of footsteps of those insignificant souls who dig themselves deeper in to the historical grave, metonymically represented by the labile "village" (*kampung*). However, the peremptory tone of the young man has a counterproductive effect on the implied reader, who becomes momentarily unsympathetic inasmuch as he or she resents being lectured at. Failing or refusing to resonate correctly with Minke's message, the reader may well learn to counterfocalize, that is, to take up a "mistaken" point of view, in which the declared oppositions between light and dark, modern and premodern, progressive and backward are seen as provocations to think and feel for absent others, rather than the bases of proper valuation or judgment.[5] Such is the waywardness of the literary text: it does more than it says; in doing so, it encourages us to learn to read. In light of this transaction, the reader may yet train herself to read in a tentative yet self-conscious way, not in order to produce a nostalgic account of the village or to recuperate an authentic lifeworld of the people, but to displace the terms in which such "reporting" takes place, to make space for other, less vanguardist configurations. The counterfocalized reading invited by the rhetoric of Pramoedya's text allows for other perspectives and conceptions of agency in a style akin to how Conrad's staging of Marlow's intricate description of his encounter with Jim outside the courtroom is interrupted and reconstellated by the wayward movement of the yellow dog. This approach would retain the sense of encounter—and its sense of the unfamiliar or unexpected—embedded in the Malay word that is translated as "discovery" (*penemuan*) in the passage above.[6]

A reading of the global is not content to naturalize its perspective. Other agents may be discerned who do not or cannot imagine history in the same way but whose disruptive effects enrich what would otherwise remain a univocal saying. Another way to elaborate a style of reading open to its own displacement emerges through a famous Indian nationalist's invocation of the peasant. Writing in the form of letters from prison to his daughter in 1944, the anticolonial leader Jawaharlal Nehru describes his attempts to inculcate in the Indian peasants he encounters an imagination of the nation. He presents this as the fusing together of the message of the nationalist leader with the desires of his peasant audience; he imparts to them an idiom or vocabulary by which they, too, can become "nationalists" in the proper sense of the term. In doing so, he provides an insight into two ways of conceiving the global operation. First, as part of a literal series of nations in the world and, second, as the metaphorization of an organic and living being:

> I tried to make them think of India as a whole, and even to some little extent of this wide world of which we were a part. I brought in the struggle in China, in Spain, in Abyssinia, in Central Europe, in Egypt and the countries of Western Asia. I told them of the wonderful changes in the Soviet Union and of the great progress made in America. . . .
>
> Sometimes as I reached a gathering, a great roar of welcome would greet me: *Bharat Mata ki Jai*—"Victory to Mother India." I would ask them unexpectedly what they meant by that cry, who was this Bharat Mata, Mother India, whose victory cry they wanted? My question would amuse them and surprise them, and then, not knowing exactly what to answer, they would look at each other, and at me. I persisted in my questioning. At last a vigorous Jat, wedded to the soil from immemorial generations, would say that it was the *dharti*, the good earth of India, that they meant. What earth? Their particular village patch, or all the patches in the district or province, or in the whole of India? And so question and answer went on, till they would ask me impatiently to tell them all about it. I would endeavor to do so and explain that India was all this that they had thought, but it was much more. The mountains and the rivers of India, and the forests and the broad fields, which gave us food, were all dear to us, but what counted ultimately were the people of India, people like them and me, who were spread out all over this vast land. *Bharat Mata*, Mother India, was essentially these people. You are parts of this *Bharat Mata*, I told them, you are in a manner

yourselves *Bharat Mata*, and as this idea slowly soaked into their brains, their eyes would light up as if they had made a great discovery.[7]

The "discovery" comes with all the force of an aesthetic shock; the peasants realize that their beings and bodies are in an organic and therefore fundamental manner linked to (their possession of) "Mother India." As "parts of" Mother India, they are not merely discrete elements within that nation, which, in turn, exists in an "unbounded series" (to use Benedict Anderson's term) with other nations like Abyssinia; they constitute its essential character.[8]

The seeing performed is global in the sense I have described it; Nehru's technique of artistic representation aims to induct his reader into a mode of thematization whose operations are not, for all their ideological differences, formally dissimilar to that employed by the eighteenth-century writers such as William Marsden, John Millar, or Adam Smith. The nationalist's achievement is to communicate this way of seeing to the peasant, as an act of general empowerment, a making-literate in the lingua franca of global political struggle. The world is made available in a comprehensive manner from a single and absolute perspective: in Nehru's case, it is used to valorize a "local" (peasantry) that is implicitly being oppressed by a "global" (colonialism)—but, as is clear, local and global are not so much opposed as complicit within this nationalist mode of representation. The plasticity of the global mode of thematization finds a different but equally powerful use with that suggested by the likes of John Millar. There it served the power of a comprehension in the context of a colonial capitalist Britain. Here it is in the service of national liberation, a fictive moment (staged as "truth") that is used to interpellate the reader into a particular way of reading the world and, as it were, operating it.

The global mode of thematization also switches between the registers of "historical" and "fictive" discourse. Nehru writes in the discourse of history, of course, but to grasp the representational "trick" by which this passage operates—again not unrelated to the way the global functions—it is necessary to note that the addressee is not the peasants, although the action comes through the putative reaction of the peasants ("their eyes would light up"), but rather a particular English-speaking reader. Nor do the peasants "exist." They are part of the "reality effect" by which the reader produces for herself an imaginary conception of an India that she can claim as self-evident.[9] Nehru deploys the conditional instead of the simple past tense to invoke the encounters with the peasants: "they would," "I would." This points to a *repetition* of events that took place in a historically indeterminate past, which produces a reality effect; "this happened *all the time*" becomes, "this is what it is really like *out there*."

In this way Nehru's prose shifts imperceptibly from the register of historical discourse to that of fiction in order to secure its claim to veracity, a telling instance of which is, "at last a vigorous Jat, wedded to the soil from immemorial generations, *would* say." This fictive invocation of a "real" person is the means by which a reality effect is created. Fiction is used to secure the discourse of historical truth. The Jat is surely not present at each speech Nehru gives; such a literal interpretation would require us to imagine the (in any case implausible) appearance of a Jat with raised hand at every such occasion. The potentially comic implications of such a repetitive appearance would fatally undermine the sober epiphany toward which the passage builds. A "competent" reading of this passage necessarily views the Jat as figurative, not literal, and it is by way of the aesthetic effect so generated by this figure that an effect of the real is produced: *this actually happened* ("their eyes lighted up"). The figure of the Jat reveals how the conditional tense is used to forge the referential illusion, in which words dissolve into the things they point at.[10]

It is, after all, essential that the passage be coded as "history" and not "fiction." This is the reason the reader is so deeply moved to imagine herself as part of this community. The figurative appearance of a Jat produces the referential illusion; his presence gives substance to the received idea of a "real" peasant and enables the metropolitan reader to identify with the "discovery" as it is registered in the equally immediate, "lighted up" eyes of the peasants. The figure of the Jat therefore begins the crucial aesthetic effect of making available an "authentic" subject position that is thought to underwrite and justify the reader's feelings. That is to say, for truth to be successfully produced here, the reader must not think that the Jat merely serves as straight man to Nehru's performance; she must think that the peasants Nehru addresses do indeed come to imagine "India" as the nationalist leader himself asserts India and "Mother India" ought to be imagined.

The "peasants" are a rhetorical means to that global end. In this consolidating move, history as truth is produced as the other is effaced through instrumentalization. Historical discourse is set to work by the rhetorical device called "peasants." The point of this discussion is not to expose this maneuver as false or objectionable; rather, it is to show how truth is neces-

sarily produced through a mobilization of a peculiar way of seeing and saying. This effect is produced *for the reader* in the willful link made between
two claims: "you are in a manner *Bharat Mata*," and, "as this idea slowly
soaked into their brains, their eyes would light up as if they had made a
great discovery." It is in this manner that the implied reader of this passage,
the English-speaking reader (not the peasant), sutures her own desires to
the normative imagination of the nation laid forth in the global rhetoric of
the nationalist. The figure of the peasants—coded as authentic, organic—
enables this achievement as truth or justice—evidence of which, if any were
needed, is to be found in the irrefutability of their shining eyes. This is the
reflex by which history is produced and the frame of seeing and its rules of
operation are enacted and communicated to the reader of the *Discovery of
India*. The seeing is finessed as the seen.

I take as my example the figure of the mobilized yet effaced *figure* of the
peasant here to validate a sympathetic yet distinct mode of reading. This is
an imaginative exercise for cultural criticism that does not try to subsume
the claims of difference—not least because, as Nehru and Pramoedya show,
the global perspective is an indispensable tool in the empowerment of the
poor and the disenfranchised.[11] An interruptive mode of reading does not
relinquish that awareness even as it alerts the reader to the heterogeneity
that the global perspective covers over or appropriates. In this way, a historical imagination attentive to its own limits and open to its interruption
informs the critical practice I have elaborated in this book.

By defamiliarizing this powerful and indispensable mode of truth production, we ask how representation—and the habits and presuppositions
that operate representation—can be interrupted and redirected. One way of
trying to imagine this is by learning to see other spaces as textured—here
figured by the effaced "peasants" (Nehru) or "ancestors" (Minke)—and not
simply as deficient peoples awaiting induction into the global perspective.
Even if the condition of global representation is the representation of objects in the world as "self-consolidating"—Heidegger's *Weltbild*—an attention to the rhetorical dimensions of language can teach humility and creativity; in this way, we open ourselves to the possibility of being interrupted,
turned in other directions, and perhaps we even learn to read in ways that
we do not yet think possible.

NOTES

INTRODUCTION: HOW TO READ THE GLOBAL

1. "The history of writing will conform to a law of mechanical economy: to gain the most space and time by means of the most convenient abbreviation; it will never have the least effect on the structure and content of the meaning (of ideas) that it will have to vehiculate" (Derrida, "Signature Event Context," 312). By asking if such "vehiculation" can be effective, Derrida illustrates a way of thinking history through the matter of representation.

2. For a sampling of approaches that conceive of globalization as an "objective, empirical process" (Pieterse, *Globalization and Culture*, 16), see Appadurai, "Disjuncture and Difference"; Pieterse, *Globalization and Culture*; Cooper, "What Is the Concept of Globalization Good For?"; Mazlish, "Global History and World History"; Osterhammel and Petersson, *Globalization*; Scholte, *Globalization: An Introduction*.

3. Scholte, *Globalization: An Introduction*, 24.

4. Bayly, "'Archaic' and 'Modern' Globalization," 48–49. Hereafter cited as "Archaic."

5. "Cannibalized" is a term Bayly borrows from Appadurai, "Disjuncture and Difference."

6. For a modern Sino-Malay "agent" who takes up this homogeneous relay, see Lee, *The Singapore Story*. Lee's "Asian values" might be cast as the result of such cannibalization. In chapter 3 I discuss one of Lee's precursors, Abdullah Munshi, who composed his "autobiography" in the context of what Bayly would call "archaic globalization."

7. My use of "activate" is indebted to Walter Benjamin's description of what it is to "articulate the past": "To articulate the past historically does not mean to recognize it 'the way it really was' (Ranke). It means to seize hold of memory as it flashes up at a moment of danger. Historical materialism wishes to retain that image of the past which unexpectedly appears to man singled out by history at a moment of danger. The danger affects both the content of the tradition and its receivers. The same threat hangs over both: that of becoming a tool of the ruling classes. In every era the attempt must be made anew to wrest tradition from a conformism that is about to overpower it" (Benjamin, "Theses on the Philosophy of History," in *Illuminations*, 257).
8. For instance, see Moretti, "Conjectures on World Literature."
9. A good example of this is Benedict Anderson's peculiar use (in *Imagined Communities*) of Walter Benjamin's phrase (from "Theses on the Philosophy of History"), "homogenous, empty time." Anderson instrumentalizes this phrase in the exact sense that Benjamin's warns against; he takes for granted the very perspective that Benjamin calls into question.
10. Mazlish, "Global History and World History," 18.
11. Mazlish, "Global History and World History," 18.
12. Mazlish, "Global History and World History," 20.
13. Epistemic presuppositions frame and confine the way the world is practically brought into view, from the kind of examples invoked, the metaphors or analogies drawn, to the lines of argument by which policy proposals and legal regimes are shaped. Objective methods are inextricably tied to valuations in practice. Vandana Shiva argues that "the engineering paradigm of biotechnology is based on the assumption that life can be made. Patents on life are based on the assumption that life can be owned because it has been constructed." The global intellectual property rights regime that is set up to enforce this precomprehension is incapable of regarding nature or "non-Western knowledge systems" as creative (Shiva, *Biopiracy*, 24). The global perspective taken for granted by students of the humanities and social sciences cannot properly take into account the forms of life that do not compute with the global perspective.
14. Mazlish, "Global History and World History," 20. Carl Pletsch's critique of homogenizing frameworks within which such studies operate, as well as their unacknowledged commitment to modernization theory, remains relevant here. See Pletsch, "The Three Worlds."
15. Frank, *ReOrient*, 7.
16. Markley, *The Far East and the English Imagination*, 8–9.
17. Markley, *The Far East and the English Imagination*, 2.
18. Foucault, *The Archaeology of Knowledge*, 91.
19. Wong, *China Transformed*, 281.

20. Partha Chatterjee notes the origins of such thinking in nationalism. "The claims of western civilization were the most powerful in the material sphere. Science, technology, rational forms of economic organization, modern methods of state-craft—these had given the European countries the strength to subjugate the non-European peoples and to impose their dominance over the whole world. To overcome this domination, the colonized people had to learn those superior techniques of organizing material life and incorporate them within their own cultures" (Chatterjee, *The Nation and Its Fragments*, 119–20).

21. World Bank, *The East Asian Miracle*, 79–80.

22. For a more cautious assessment of the Asian "miracle," see Anderson, "From Miracle to Crash." Marking the context of postwar decolonization of the former European colonies, and communism's appeal to the masses, Anderson notes the political conditions in which "growth" was encouraged: "To shore up the line of teetering dominoes, Washington made every effort to create loyal, capitalisti-cally prosperous, authoritarian and anti-Communist regimes [in this region]—typically, but not invariably, dominated by the military." Elsewhere, Anderson insightfully criticizes the unreflective use of categories like "kinship" because it does not depict "historical subjectivities, [but] actually represents a certain con-temporary vision of cosmopolitanism based on a quasi-planetary dispersion of bounded entities. Wherever the 'Chinese' happened to end up—Jamaica, Hun-gary or South Africa—they remain countable Chinese, and it matters very little if they also happen to be citizens of those nation-states" (Benedict Anderson, "Nationalism, Identity, and the Logic of Seriality," in *The Specter of Comparisons*, 45.) This way of counting, institutionalized by "imperial state machineries," con-tinues to dominate the thinking of identitarian diasporics, ethnic nationalists at "home," not to mention authors of World Bank reports.

23. It is of some interest to note that until the 1960s, both colonial and develop-ment literature characterized parts of this region—here described by the Cold War category "Southeast Asia"—as "backward, changeless societies with weak ephemeral political structures, despotic, often rapacious, rulers, endemic disease, almost uniform poverty and internecine warfare," and "for advocates of 'mod-ernization theory' the traditional societies of the pre-colonial, colonial and post-colonial periods were static, bounded and conservative. In the more extreme views such societies were presented as lacking economic logic" (Dixon, *South East Asia in the World Economy*, 35). Both this view and that of the World Bank are drawn from a global perspective, although it appears to be true that the lat-ter relies chiefly on the role of port cities and ignores the hinterland in order to evoke a precolonial world that was already tending toward producing a society run along the lines of "economic logic."

24. Clifford, "Traveling Cultures," in *Routes*, 30. It is worthwhile distinguishing my position from Clifford's, whose many examples of "constructed and disputed

historicities, sites of displacement, interference, and interaction" do not address the global perspective by which he brings these diverse figures into view. Failing to put into question this perspective, Clifford's essay ends up giving the impression that the global is merely one way of seeing among many, to be juxtaposed against the dynamic local perspectives of, say, the "Asian indentured laborer" who fetches up on the Orinoco coast in the nineteenth century, or "diasporic and migrant cultures" in the North American metropolis in the twentieth (35). My point is that we need to recognize that the global frames the discursive terms and material conditions within which agency can be institutionally validated, not least because, and Clifford's essay is an example of this, it is the naturalized perspective through which even "resistance" is configured by producers of modern knowledge.

25. Heidegger, "Age of the World Picture," 60. This is a translation of "Die Zeit des Weltbildes."

26. Smith, *Wealth of Nation*, 4.7.c.80.

27. The global is in this manifestation a mode of discursive thematization produced in the context of state-sponsored international commerce geared toward "the ruthless drive to accumulate." Its characteristics are a systemic focus on armed trade: coercion, plunder, and monopolies. This program is by historical convention not deemed to apply to the Asian empires on the peripheries of which networks of commodity production and exchange thrived from the twelfth century A.D. (Curtin, *Cross-Cultural Trade in World History*, 149, 151–57). By definition, therefore, these empires did not produce the material conditions for a "global" perspective. For an interesting elaboration of the operative differences in these terms, see Palat and Wallerstein, "What World-System," 38. For a theoretical consideration of contexts in which trade and production were not designed to become global in the manner celebrated by Smith, see Chaudhuri, "Reflections on Premodern Trade."

28. These complex formations are explored in Forbes, *Africans and Native Americans*. Smith was not ignorant of the prior cultural interactions of Amerindians, either, or of the fact that the spice trade was carried on by Asians long before the historical advent of European armed trade (see, respectively, *Wealth of Nations*, 4.1 and 4.7.c.100). My simple point is to highlight the epistemic underpinnings of "discovery." In short, it is not simply an "empirical" question of "who came first."

29. Bayly, "The First Age."

30. Marshall, *A Free Though Conquering People*, 10. See also Ballantyne, "Empire, Knowledge, and Culture," 117–26.

31. Ballantyne, "Empire, Knowledge, and Culture," 126–28. In this connection, it is worth digressing from the substance of Ballantyne's informative essay to dispense with an unfortunately typical misconception of "postcolonial studies."

Ballantyne declares that, "Far from being a foreign imposition created by the 'willed activity' of foreign invaders (*pace* Edward Said), colonial knowledge was the product of 'cultural negotiation,' a 'dialogic' process whereby both British and local understandings 'altered continuously' in mutual modification ... fashioning a new body of information and understandings that were truly hybridized: neither 'European' nor 'indigenous'" (128). Because Ballantyne does not distinguish between "knowledge" and "knowledge production," he concerns himself exclusively with *empirical* instances of native elite (his examples are exclusively Indian) participation in colonial knowledge production. As such, he fails to grasp the epistemic challenge posed by scholarship produced in the wake of Said's *Orientalism*. As I have noted elsewhere in this chapter, the uncritical celebration of "agency" and "hybridity" (or is it hybridity *as* agency?), whether it takes place in colonial history or postcolonial studies, has not always been salutary.

32. Guha, *A Rule of Property for Bengal*; Bastin, *The Native Policies of Sir Stamford Raffles*.

33. Kratoska, Raben, and Nordholt, "Locating Southeast Asia," 3.

34. Skinner, "Transitional Malay Literature."

35. Shklovsky, "Art as Device."

36. "If in informative prose a metaphor aims to bring the subject closer to the audience, or drive a point home, in poetry it serves the opposite function. Rather than translating the unfamiliar into the terms of the familiar, the poetic image 'makes strange' the habitual by presenting it in a novel light, by placing it in an unexpected context" (Ehrlich, "Russian Formalism," 629).

37. "The aim of poetry is to make perceptible the texture of words in all its aspects" (quoted in Ehrlich, "Russian Formalism," 631).

38. Spivak, *Critique of Postcolonial Reason*, 49.

39. "If we forget the productive unease that what we do with the utmost care is judged in the margins, in the political field one gets the liberal pluralism of repressive tolerance and sanctioned ignorance, and varieties of fundamentalism, totalitarianism, and cultural revolution; and in the field of writing about and teaching literature, one gets the benign or resentful conservatism of the establishment and the multiculturalist masquerade of the privileged as the disenfranchised, or their liberator, both anchored in a lack of respect for the singularity and unverifiability of 'literature as such'" (Spivak, *Critique of Postcolonial Reason*, 175–76).

I. ADAM SMITH AND THE CLAIMS OF SUBSISTENCE

1. From the 1760s, "Britain's empire of the seas had become an empire of extended territory as well. An empire of conquest now coexisted alongside the old empire of trade and settlement. Consequently, politicians and administrators were

confronted by a series of new imperial problems related to questions of authority, liberty, and the ways in which alien non-Protestant or non-Christian peoples
should be governed within the empire" (Bowen, "British Conceptions of Global
Empire," 7). In the period until "the American Revolution and beyond the British were in the collective grip of agoraphobia, captivated by, but also adrift and
at odds in a vast empire abroad and a new political world at home which few of
them properly understood. It was a time of raised expectations, disorientation
and anxiety" (Colley, *Britons*, 105).

2. Bayly, "The First Age"; H.V. Bowen, "British Conceptions of Global Empire."
3. Hyam, "The Primacy of Geopolitics," 31.
4. "By uniting, in some measure, the most distant parts of the world, by enabling
    them to relieve one another's wants, to increase one another's enjoyments, and to
    encourage one another's industry, their general tendency would seem to be ben-
    eficial" (4.7.c.80). Smith was not the first writer to describe the world as a single,
    interconnected entity, developing in common time. He drew upon this insight
    to configure the British empire as the world-historical facilitator of universal
    "liberty" and "justice" worldwide.
5. P. J. Marshall, "Britain Without America: A Second Empire?" 576–95; See also
    Vincent T. Harlow, *Founding of the Second British Empire*, 1:62.
6. Winch, *Classical Political Economy and the Colonies*; Stevens, "Adam Smith and
    the Colonial Disturbances." Jennifer Pitts speculates briefly on Smith's views
    on the colonial expansion in India that was well underway (*A Turn to Empire*,
    55–56).
7. "A rich country [for the mercantilists], in the same manner as a rich man, is
    supposed to be a country abounding in money; and to heap up gold and silver in
    any country is supposed to be the readiest way to enrich it. For some time after
    the discovery of America, the first inquiry of the Spaniards, when they arrived
    upon any unknown coast, used to be, if there was any gold or silver to be found
    in the neighbourhood? By the information which they received, they judged
    whether it was worth while to make a settlement there" (4.1.2). The so-called
    "mercantilists" are straw figures that Smith caricatures in order to elaborate his
    vision of imperial reform (as noted by many, including A. W. Coats, *On the His-
    tory of Economic Thought*, 140.)
8. Webster, *Gentlemen Capitalists*, 27–31.
9. And most famously: "The discovery of America, and that of a passage to the
    East Indies by the Cape of Good Hope, are the two greatest and most impor-
    tant events recorded in the history of mankind" (4.7.c.80). I discuss this passage
    in the introduction.
10. Dutch and French support for the Americans during the War of Independence
    meant that Dutch-controlled Malay ports were closed to the British at a time
    when access to the China trade was especially critical, even as the French were

seeking to restore their position (after their defeat by the British in 1763) in the Indian subcontinent. Although Smith adopts the disinterested tone of the social scientist, his observation more obviously reflects a widespread official desire for a port in the Malay Archipelago to secure British military and commercial interests at a time of intense hostilities worldwide (see Ryan, *A History of Malaysia and Singapore*, 90–92). The first British naval base in Malaya, Penang, was founded in 1786. Malacca was seized in 1795, Batavia held from 1811 to 1817, and Singapore founded in 1819. The crucial importance Smith assigns these ports finds an echo in British and French strategies during the Napoleonic wars. Soon after the Netherlands fell to Napoleonic France, Britain seized Dutch Malacca in an attempt to forestall French expansion in the Malay Archipelago. The French in turn claimed that victory over the Netherlands gave them the right to "have full use of Dutch naval bases around the world, for example, the Cape of Good Hope, Ceylon and Java as well as Malacca" (Ryan, *A History of Malaysia and Singapore* 97–98).

11. See P. J. Marshall, "Britain Without America," 2:575–77.

12. The latter impulse is discernible in Colley, "Imperial Trauma," 209; Fleischacker, *On Adam Smith's* Wealth of Nations, 261; Pitts, *A Turn to Empire*, 26.

13. Schumpeter, *History of Economic Analysis*, 186.

14. Smith defines subsistence as "revenue" (4.1.1), and he uses it at different moments to refer to quantitatively calculated entities, such as wages (1.5.15; 5.2.131), profits (1.7.43), cost of living (1.8.25–26; 5.2.158), standard of living (5.1.228), and so on. But these uses of subsistence are always embedded within the prior and contingent context of social and historical relations (5.1.228; 5.1.181; 5.1.54; 3.1.5). This indicates that subsistence does not possess for Smith the reductively quantitative sense it has in the age of neoclassical economics. And it certainly does not have the pejorative connotations the word has acquired in the wake of modernization theory ("subsistence economies"—like "Third World"—being synonymous today with backwardness and misery). It is not clear when "subsistence" comes to connote poverty. Such usage is not common in the eighteenth or nineteenth centuries, going by the entries in the *Oxford English Dictionary*. (The *OED* notes the increase of such reductively quantitative uses of the word in the late nineteenth century, but the greatest number appear after 1945.) Smith also uses subsistence interchangeably with "plentiful revenue" in 4.1.1, implying that subsistence is the condition for any examination of abundance rather than its opposite.

15. Smith uses the East India Company's abuses of power as an associative template for "mercantilist" abuses from the past. One of the most striking instances of this conflation occurs when he refers simultaneously to the natives of "the East and West Indies" who have suffered under the yoke of their European masters, at one stroke bringing into view a vision of global suffering that spans space and

time: Amerindians from the fifteenth century, African slaves to the Americas in the sixteenth and seventeenth centuries, and Indian and Malay peasants in the eighteenth all forced to toil within an unfree market system. "*To the natives however, both of the East and West Indies,* all the commercial benefits which can have resulted from [the discovery of America and a passage to the East Indies by the Cape of Good Hope] have been sunk and lost in the dreadful misfortunes which they have occasioned" (4.7.c.80; emphasis added).

16. History for Smith has its basis in rhetoric, in how language is the condition and effect of the way we are trained to see and act in the world. In his *Lectures on Rhetoric and Belles Lettres* (1748), Smith notes, for instance, that the psychological intensity of Tacitus's prose is calculated to produce "effects" that act upon the "dispositions" of Romans who live in an imperial era of unprecedented prosperity and peace (112). In the case of Livy, the Latin historian Smith admired most, historical representation is less focused on "accuracy" (109) than on instigating a set of affects: representation here assumes a more instructional character and is more easy in its acknowledgement of the intimate relation between the description of events and the will to engineer a proper response from its audience (108–9). One scholar offers the interesting detail that Smith's lectures were delivered before thirteen- or fourteen-year-old boys, children of the Scottish bourgeoisie already inducted into commercial or industrial activity linking Glasgow to the British empire in, among other places, Asia (Phillipson, "Adam Smith as Civic Moralist," 179, 181). For a reading attentive to the rhetorical dimensions of Smithian "historiography," see Pocock, "Adam Smith and History."

17. This polemic is necessarily premised upon an unhistorical view, as is conceded elsewhere by Smith when he tacitly notes that far from destroying the market, mercantile imperialism actually laid the conditions for it (1.11.g.26; 4.7.b.7). Indeed, the condemnation of exclusive companies would not seem as egregious had Smith distinguished between their present corruption and their historical necessity. By treating monopoly as a kind of historical original sin, he contradicts his own point that only exclusive companies could have raised the capital and borne the enormous risks attendant upon such distant ventures (4.7.c.95 ff; 5.1.e.26–30).

18. The metaphor of "opening" is worth a note that cannot be pursued here: on the one hand, it is suggestive of an organic or natural process, as in birth or metamorphosis. On the other, "opening" suggests an enclosed entity that has to be prized open. In his study of Smith's materialist theory of historical development, Andrew Skinner notes that exchange economies—where production is for sale in the market—are unique to the commercial societies that arrive at the ends of the four historical stages defined by hunting, pasturage, farming, and commerce (Skinner, "Historical Theory," 77, 87). Elsewhere in the text, Smith suggests that the simple, subsistence economies of the natives were not likely to

have "naturally" been capable of participating in market exchange to any great or systematic extent.

19. In book 3 of *The Wealth of Nations*, Smith argues that the natural or "proportioned" development of Europe as it was guided by agriculture was subverted by the growing power and influence of the merchants. I discuss this further below.

20. I agree with Keith Tribe's observation that self-interest in *The Wealth of Nations* is inflected by Smith's *Theory of Moral Sentiments*: human beings are formed within "a general system of social reciprocity: each one of us judges others as a spectator, while others do likewise to us ... the Smithian conception of self-interest is not an injunction to act egoistically ... it is embedded within a framework of social reciprocity that allows for the formation of moral judgment" (Tribe, "Adam Smith: Critical Theorist?" 621).

21. "As sovereigns, [the East India Company's] interest is exactly the same with that of the country which they govern. As merchants their interest is directly opposite of that interest" (4.7.c.103): Smith's rhetoric anticipates the animating spirit of Pitt's India Act of 1784 and Lord Cornwallis's reforms of the 1790s. Cornwallis is a figure symbolic of both imperial ends and beginnings. The defeat of the army he led at the battle of Yorktown was decisive to Britain's surrender of the American colonies. Soon after he was put in charge of reforming the East India Company with the aim of instituting Enlightenment ideals of imperial rule.

22. Here is one such account of the untroubled, almost insensible development from nonmarket to market society that Smith provides. This is the continuist ideology that underpins the natural or unforced shift from "subsistence" to "exchange" economy: "But when a society becomes numerous they would find a difficulty in supporting themselves by herds and flocks. Then they would naturally turn themselves to the cultivation of land and the raising of such plants and trees as produced nourishment fit for them. . . . And by this means they would gradually advance into the age of Agriculture. As society was farther improved, the severall arts, which at first would be exercised by each individual as far as was necessary for his welfare, would be separated; some persons would cultivate one and another others, as they severally inclined. *They would exchange with one another what they produced more than was necessary for their support, and get in exchange for them the commodities they stood in need of and did not produce themselves. This exchange of commodities stands in time not only betwixt the individuals of the same society but betwixt those of different nations . . . Thus at last the Age of commerce arises.*" (Smith, *Lectures on Jurisprudence*, 1.27–32; emphasis added). Note also that subsistence—what "was necessary for their support"—connotes "self-sustaining." In the discussion of market price and wages below, subsistence will mean "bare survival." Smith's alternation between these two meanings of subsistence (to legitimize his discourse) already points to the irreducibly hybrid character of the "system of natural liberty," or what I call the market system,

as simultaneously being a derivation from and a superseding of the nonmarket economies by which it is "naturally" preceded.

23. Citing Smith's *Theory of Moral Sentiments*, Donald Winch observes that "self-interest is bound up with and overlaid by other psychological propensities" that only emerge within the learned habits formed through "social interaction" (Winch, "Adam Smith," 106). And "economic transactions based on mutual need are 'so strongly implanted by nature that they have no occasion for that additional force which the weaker principles need' (*Lectures on Jurisprudence* [1763–64], 527). . . . What Smith had to explain was how the progress of opulence had been retarded or distorted, rather than how it ever got started" (Winch, "Adam Smith," 107). This partly explains why free trade is deemed natural and bears affinities to the nonmarket societies of Asia and America, whereas the merchants are categorically excluded from any link to either free-trade or nonmarket economies. Needless to say, Smith's assumptions make no sense in historical terms, but they frame the kind of historical narrative and truth claims produced in *The Wealth of Nations*.

24. Reinhart Koselleck argues that Smith's work is underwritten by the impulses of a "vanquished" group "who perceive themselves surpassed by history or who have set themselves the goal of catching up with or surpassing the development of things." Koselleck further notes that key figures of the "Scottish Enlightenment" were members of a peripheral elite within the metropolitan core who produced the legitimating discourses for the market systems of the core that would in turn be repackaged and exported by the metropole as the dominant formula of colonial capitalist "improvement." "Coming as they did from a country that had been left behind, England's progress was the primary experience of Kames, Hume, Robertson, Ferguson, Smith, Millar and Stewart, so much as to elevate this temporal differentiation to the methodological starting point for their new history . . . the Scots consciously included hypothesis and conjectures in their arguments. The production of theory became an imperative of method" ("Transformations of Experience and Methodological Change: A Historico-Anthropological Essay," in *The Practice of Conceptual History*, 80, 81).

25. I cannot pursue that suggestion here, for my aim is to attend to the lessons of reading Smith's *Wealth of Nations* as a framing text for the book as a whole. I will, however, follow through on this proposal in the chapters that follow. For an instructive style of engaging empirical scholarship, see Spivak's discussion of Kant's invocation of "*der rohe Mensch*" (man in the raw) in the *Critique of Judgment*: "But if in Kant's world the New Hollander (the Australian Aborigine) or the man from Tierra del Fuego could have been endowed with speech (turned into the subject of speech), he might well have maintained that, this innocent but unavoidable and indeed, crucial example—of the antinomy that reason will supplement—uses a peculiar thinking of what man is to put him out of it." (Spivak, *Critique of Postcolonial Reason*, 26).

26. The term "self-regulating market" is taken from Polanyi, *The Great Trans-formation*.

27. These terms are drawn from the first chapter of Marx, *Capital*, vol. 1. Smith refers to these practices in the European context when he refers to the lavish feasts thrown by the duke of Warwick, or when nails are exchanged for beer in the Scottish Highlands (1.4.3). Smith also notes that "among the Tartars, as among all other nations of shepherds, who are generally ignorant of the use of money, cattle are the instruments of commerce and the measures of value" (4.1.2). Similarly, in the slave plantations of North America, the articulation of nonmonetized economies with global production and exchange for the market is another form taken by the "total or expanded form of value." In chapter 3, I rely on Gayatri Spivak's redeployment of these categories to show the ways in which the cultural and the economic interrupt each other most striking-ly in the colonial or precapitalist context. See Spivak, *Outside in the Teaching Machine*, 75–76.

28. In Britain, the threatened subsistence of the exploited farmer (1.10.14–20) mo-tivates Smith's criticism of merchant and manufacturing guilds, just as he dis-courages the participation of smaller European economies in the carrying trade because it comes at the expense of the sustenance of the local industry (4.7.c.97). The controversial distinction Smith establishes between "productive" and "un-productive labor" is similarly based upon whether or not an activity is thought to promote subsistence.

29. Veblen, "Preconceptions of Economic Science," 408.

30. Istvan Hont and Michael Ignatieff argue that although Smith was far from indifferent to the needs of the laboring poor, he believed laissez-faire and free trade the best means of securing the "adequate subsistence" of the poorest. It follows that Smith's system of natural liberty necessarily excludes "'distributive justice' from the appropriate functions of government in a market society. Smith insisted that the only appropriate function of justice was 'commutative'; it dealt with the attribution of responsibility and the punishment of injury among in-dividuals" ("Needs and Justice," 24–25). Assuming even that this formulation is adequate to the market societies of eighteenth-century Britain, it would be pre-cipitate to elevate it to the status of a universal principle (whose roots lie in the natural liberty of human beings and societies or in conjectures about homoge-neous stadial development). Historical conditions are diverse, and "subsistence" does not possess a self-identical or unchanging form in space and time.

31. In Smith's account, the proper name "Europe" is not taken to signify a historical exception or norm. See, for instance, the metonymization of a "hospitality"—a markedly nonmarket trait—in the earl of Warwick, an "Arabian chief" and the "highlands of Scotland" (3.4.509). To an extent, the relation between marketized and nonmarketized economies, absent the interference of the state, suggests

material conditions characterized by heterogeneous economic formations. The market system does not automatically universalize itself—it needs the supervening force of the state or conquering army to do so. Because Smith is opposed to such "violent operations," the natural development of markets can be situated in a context of internal differences within Europe as well as between Europe and non-Europe.

32. Smith displays a quite traditional prejudice towards the trader and his lack of attachment to the land: "A merchant, it has been said very properly, is not necessarily the citizen of any particular country. It is in a great measure indifferent to him from what place he makes his trade; and a very trifling disgust will make him remove his capital, and together with it all the industry which it supports, from one country to another. No part of it can be said to belong to any particular country, till it has been spread as it were over the face of that country, either in buildings, or in the lasting improvement of lands" (3.4.519).

33. Smith hastens to add that such stories are the exception that proves the rule: "In the modern history of Europe, their extension and improvement have generally been posterior to those which were the offspring of foreign commerce. England was noted for the manufacture of fine cloths made of Spanish wool, more than a century before any of those which now flourish in the places above mentioned were fit for foreign sale" (3.3.20).

34. The discussion of China occurs in the chapter in which he tacitly acknowledges his debt to the physiocrats, who saw in land the natural source from which all value derived—an indication of the "animism" spoken of earlier (Smith himself declares: "in agriculture nature labors alongside with man" [1.5]). But Smith, of course, settled on labor as the basis of value and, unlike the physiocrats, held that manufacture counts as productive labor. Smith also believed China's development to have been curtailed by its resolute hostility to foreign trade (4.9.41).

35. "In her present condition, Great Britain resembles one of those unwholesome bodies in which some of the vital parts are overgrown, and which, upon that account, are liable to many dangerous disorders scarce incident to those in which all the parts are more properly proportioned" (4.7.c.43).

36. Smith appears to have Aristotle in mind when he distinguishes between the natural or morally bounded acquisition of wealth (*oikonomeia*), in which the subsistence of the household is served and the unnatural or limitless acquisition of wealth is an end in itself (*chrematistike*). The Greeks acquired colonies in accordance with the first law and modern Europeans, the second. Aristotle provides a crucial source for the way Smith uses the word "natural": "One kind of property acquisition is a *natural* part of household management, then, in that a store of goods that are necessary for life and useful to the community or city-state or household either must be available to start with, or household manage-

ment must arrange to make it available. At any rate, true wealth seems to consist in such goods" (*Politics*, 1256 b26–30).

37. Spivak, *Critique of Postcolonial Reason*, 49. I discuss the passage in which this phrase occurs in the introduction.

38. The same is already true of the America Columbus "discovered": the ability to engage and set this perspective to work is a task for reading, that is, an approach that troubles the perspective of conventional history. See Forbes, *Africans and Native Americans*, 6–24.

2. OPIUM CONFESSIONS

1. See the important study by Guha, *A Rule of Property for Bengal*, 93–200.

2. De Quincey, *Confessions of an English Opium-Eater and Other Writings*. The other works collected in this volume are *Suspiria de Profundis* (1845), "On the Knocking at the Gate in Macbeth" (1823), and "The English Mail Coach" (1849).

3. Amin, "The Ancient World-Systems," 247–48. Amin notes the fundamental distinction between capitalist and noncapitalist (or tributary) systems in the way that production is made available as meaningful activity to its agents: "No society prior to modern times was based on [the principles of economistic alienation and the dominance of economics]. All advanced societies from 300 BC to 1500 AD are, from one end of the period to the other, of a profoundly similar nature, which I call tributary in order to show this essential *qualitative* fact; namely, that the surplus is directly tapped from peasant activity through some transparent devices associated with the organization of the power hierarchy (power is the source of wealth, while in capitalism the opposite is the rule). The reproduction of the system therefore requires the dominance of an ideology—a state religion—which renders opaque the power organization and legitimizes it" (248).

4. Nigel Leask has argued that De Quincey's representation of the "pains and pleasures of opium upon his sensitive nervous system [are] a metaphor (or a symbol, in the Coleridgean sense) for the effects of capitalism, in its newly developed imperialist phase, upon the body politic. . . . De Quincey's apologia for opium is also an apologia for imperialism as the means of stimulating a torpid and internally fissured national culture, and of displacing domestic anxieties onto an oriental Other" (*British Romantic Writers*, 171). I am indebted to Leask's investigation of the material correlates of De Quincey's writing, but rather than "the [British] body politic," I am interested first of all in emphasizing the international or non-European dimensions of De Quincey's rhetoric of opium. I do not simply take this as evidence of a national predicament. For this reason I do not focus on how the fragmented European self is "healed" or seek, for that matter, to expose the displaced ideological or racialist strategies by which this

recuperation takes place. Instead, I follow the track of the dispersive or "centrifugal" forces unleashed as a means to the textual activation of unfamiliar imaginative possibilities. The *pull* of an Asia construed by De Quincey through a burgeoning colonial archive is most instructive in this regard. I focus on one instance of this vector through the encounter with the Malay, not least as it opens up a pocket in which De Quincey, by a curious reversal, dreams of how he might become an object for the Malay's imagination.

5. I am indebted for this insight to Barrell, *The Infection of Thomas De Quincey*.

6. In De Quincey, *Works*, volume 18.

7. Having feathered his nest in Dove Cottage with Ricardo, Kant, and comfortable furniture in 1816, De Quincey names tea and opium—two commodities secured by means of the imperial economy—as stimulants essential to the consummation of domestic bliss (*Confessions*, 60–61).

8. Blue, "Opium to China."

9. De Quincey, "On the Knocking at the Gate in Macbeth," in *Confessions*, 83n.

10. De Quincey would have been aware that his consumption of opium was itself circumscribed by the terms of generalized commodity exchange, in which the incalculable heteronomy of use value (for which "drug" is a placeholder term) appears as an effect of the quantitative reduction by which exchange value ("commodity") is defined. See *Logic of Political Economy*, reprinted in *Works*, volume 14. In this essay, which is an elaboration of David Ricardo's labor theory of value, De Quincey notes that in political economy use value has significance only as it helps determine price (14:196; 14:237–38). However, and without contradiction, he notes also that use value as it is "disengaged" from political economy is a kind of "wealth" (14:195). In the *Confessions* this heterogeneous conception of wealth appears in the polyvalent agencies of the drug as it plays out within (and as it revalues) the regime of the commodity. Elsewhere in this chapter, my use of terms such as "making equivalent" is authorized by De Quincey's definition of exchange value as the power "to command an equivalent" (14:195). See also Robert Maniquis's discussion of De Quincey's relation to Ricardo in "Lonely Empires," 118–27.

11. For the wider context of the search for the Northwest Passage, see Glyndwr Williams, "The Pacific," 556–62.

12. See also the citation in the *Confessions* of Wordsworth, *The Excursion*, 2:834–37: "The appearance, instantaneously disclosed, / Was of a mighty city—boldly say / A wilderness of building, sinking far / And self-withdrawn into a wondrous depth" (*Confessions*, 71). The Wordsworth passage goes on to describe this wilderness as being composed of "diamond, and of gold, / With alabaster domes and silver spires" (71).

13. Cain and Hopkins, *British Imperialism*, 53–104.

14. Using Piranesi's "Antiquities of Rome" as a template, De Quincey evokes a surreal image of such administrative and legislative organs through "the vast Goth-

ic halls" in which are housed "all sorts of engines and machinery . . . expressive of
enormous power put forth, and resistance overcome" (*Confessions*, 70). But the
point of this anecdote is also that Piranesi is confounded by the thing he seeks
to represent; similarly, the artist who thinks he has penetrated the workings of
institutional authority is baffled by its intricacies, condemned by ignorance to
see the same thing repeated everywhere; hence the imagery of vegetal life, or the
"same power of self-reproduction and endless growth" (70).

15. Livingstone, *The Geographical Tradition*, 32–62, 103, 216–18.

16. Chung, "The Britain-China-India Trade Triangle." The enormous profits gener-
    ated by opium exports to China had disastrous social and political effects which
    were well-known to the British (see 423–24). British manufacturers also came to
    depend on the profitability of opium because Indian workers ensured a market
    for their products in India. For the crucial role played by the port cities of the
    Malay Archipelago in creating an effective commercial structure that formed the
    basis of the British Empire in Asia, see Webster, "British Export Interests."

17. This notion of the opium trade acting as a heteronomous stimulant of the na-
    tional economy is taken up from a fascinating perspective by Nigel Leask. Leask
    notes that "De Quincey's apologia for opium is also an apologia for imperialism
    as the means of stimulating a torpid and internally fissured national culture,
    and of displacing domestic anxieties onto the oriental Other" (*British Romantic
    Writers and the East*, 171). See also Greenberg, *British Trade and the Opening of
    China*. Greenberg observes that opium was "probably the largest commerce of
    the time in any single commodity" (105). When the Chinese authorities sought
    to end the drug trade in 1839, Britain declared war on China. The Opium War
    resulted in the forced opening of Chinese markets to imported opium; his-
    torians estimate there were 40 million opium addicts in China alone by that
    century's end (see Pomeranz and Topik, *The World That Trade Created*, 103.)

18. On the Northwest Passage, and the futile attempts beginning in the sixteenth
    century to find a shortened route to the Spice Islands, see Glyndyr Williams,
    Voyages of Delusion.

19. De Quincey's enthusiasm for colonial expansion perhaps reflects the fact that
    he belonged to a generation that was shaped by successful imperial wars and a
    growing awareness of the immense profitability of colonies. In his journalism
    De Quincey shows himself to be well informed about the details and outcomes
    of battles in places as far-flung as India, the Malay Archipelago, and the West
    Indian islands, not to mention Latin America and the Near East. Following
    the end of the Napoleonic wars, the countless skirmishes against native forces
    conducted through the nineteenth century were part of what De Quincey took
    for granted as the fabric of normality: not just imperialism, but war, as a way of
    life. See Duffy, "World Wide War," 184–206, for an account of how the British
    were left as the dominant global power at the end of these wars. "The enlarged

British Empire of 1815 was not the triumphant fulfillment of any detailed master plan. Events in Europe became the main preoccupation, while Imperial strategic planning chiefly looked westward: initially to acquire an enlarged Empire in the Caribbean; thereafter to acquire an Empire of trade and trading bases on the American mainland, particularly in Latin America. Yet in the event by far the biggest expansion of Empire was not in the West but in the East, and these wars indeed mark the real, unplanned, and unintentional, 'swing to the East' of British Imperial development" (Duffy, "World Wide War," 184).

20. See Cowan, "Early Penang and the Rise of Singapore"; and Bassett, "British Commercial and Strategic Interest."

21. Webster, "British Export Interests," 138–74.

22. Opium was "the one element in a larger system upon which the entire system [of colonial and capitalist relations] came to rest. . . . If we look at the trading world of Asia as a system of interdependent relationships, the role of opium emerges as a pivotal agent of change. For most of the nineteenth century, the drug was the major export from India to China, pushing aside Indian textiles as the most valuable of India's products. At the same time, the drug revenue was the second most important source of income for the Indian government" (Trocki, *Opium, Empire, and the Global Political Economy*, 58).

23. Quoted in Andaya and Andaya, *A History of Malaysia*, 100. One historian gives an estimate of the sums involved: "By the end of the [eighteenth century] the quantity sold annually in Java had risen to thirty-five tonnes at a selling price of nearly two million Spanish dollars. John Crawfurd [an eminent E.I.C. official and historian] reckoned the supply to all the rest of the Indonesian archipelago as another 350 chests or twenty-two tonnes. . . . For the Dutch and British companies who imported the opium, however, the profits were 168 per cent over the Bengal buying price, and 3000 per cent over the Bengal cost price" (Reid, "Economic and Social Change," 500.)

24. Polanyi, *The Great Transformation*, 68–76.

25. This point may be extended to include the Chinese laborers in Southeast Asia, whose "economy" until the eighteenth century was embedded with native modes of production. Carl Trocki argues for a rupture that takes place in the late eighteenth century, when opium played a more active role in the transformation of Malay society and in the management and control of Chinese labor. Its effects on the Chinese economy mark another instance of the role played by opium in shaping native society as an effect of the colonial capitalist economy. To this extent, Trocki's assertion that "the product of Chinese labor was increasingly *being drawn into* the channels of western commerce" (italics added) requires a theoretical elaboration that adopts a skeptical distance from the naturalizing effect of "transition" narratives, one that I cannot provide here: "The expanding colonies of Chinese laborers came to be prime markets

for Indian opium and Singapore rapidly organized itself to provide them with it. It was not long before the provision of opium to the coolies became the central function of every Chinese *kongsi*. . . . control of the opium commerce and the opium revenue farming system were the key levers of colonial control in the early days of the nineteenth century" (Trocki, "Chinese Pioneering," 98–99).

26. De Quincey, "Ceylon" (1843), in *Works*, 14:173. De Quincey was unaware that the restoration of the colonies was part of a British strategy of building up the weak Dutch as a buffer against any resurgent French threat in Asia (Mills, *British Malaya*, 48–50).

27. De Quincey suspects that the Malay walked from London. For a discussion of East Indian seamen left in varying states of destitution in London, see Lahiri, "Contested Relations," 169–83. Grevel Lindop notes that "Malay" sailors passed through the port city of Liverpool, situated less than forty miles from De Quincey's residence (*The Opium-Eater*, 218).

28. This inmixing bears some relation to the precolonial era, in which the Malay appears embedded or part of a historically and culturally mixed legacy. Miscegenation surely cannot be far from Tomé Pires's mind in his sixteenth-century list of the visitors to and residents of the Melaka Sultanate: "Moors from Cairo, Mecca, Aden, Abyssinians, men of Kilwa, Malindi, Ormuz, Parsees, Rumes, Turks, Turkomans, Christian Armenians, Gujaratees, men of Chaul, Dabhol, Goa, of the kingdom of Deccan, Malabars and Klings, merchants from Orissa, Ceylon, Bengal, Arakan, Pegu, Siamese, men of Kedah, Malays, men of Pahang, Patani, Cambodia, Champa, Cochin China, Chines, Legueos, men of Brunai, Lucoes, men of Tamjompura, Laue, Banka, Linga (they have a thousand other islands), Moluccas, Banda, Bima, Timor, Madura, Java, Sunda, Aru, Bata, country of the Tomjano, Pase, Pedir, Maldives" (Tomé Pires, *Suma Oriental*, 1:268, quoted in Curtin, *Cross-Cultural Trade in World History*, 130).

29. Richard Winstedt, ed., *Malaya*. London, 1923, 86–87, quoted in Emerson, *Malaysia*, 14 n). See also the illuminating essays in Barnard, ed., *Contesting Malayness*.

30. "All these [language] analyses always refer back to two principles, which were already those of *general grammar*: that of an original or common language which supposedly provided the initial batch of roots; and that of a series of historical events, foreign to language, which, from the outside, bend it, wear it away, refine it, make it more flexible, by multiplying or combining its forms (invasions, migrations, advances in learning, political freedom or slavery, etc.)" (Foucault, *The Order of Things*, 234). Read together with De Quincey's interpellation of the Malay, one wonders if the "archaic" fellowship posited by De Quincey through the common root of all languages is not related to the claim of a "natural" civil society instituted through colonial production and exchange.

31. Originating in the eighteenth century, such scholarship was in part directed at "locating India's civilization in the larger world of European classical antiquity." (For an overview of this tradition of scholarship as it served the exigencies of colonial rule, see Metcalf, *Ideologies of the Raj*, 6–14, 80–92. On the influence of linguistics and comparative philology on De Quincey's writings, see Mc-Donagh, *De Quincey's Disciplines*, 91–99.) De Quincey imagined the Malay as a kind of "Indian"; the Malay Archipelago was at the time commonly referred to as "India" or "Further India," as, for instance, in John Crawfurd's *History of the Indian Archipelago* (1820). Adam Smith included the Malay Archipelago as part of the "East Indies."

32. Here is a representative instance that draws together the various aspects of a social crisis that had become normalized and were to serve as the point of historical departure for the gradual establishment of colonial rule that prided itself on ethical governance and universal improvement: "The opium traffic quickly became the mainstay of Riau's international as well as local commerce. The *Tuhfat* [*al-Nafis*] mentions ships carrying opium from Bengal as early as 1740. By the 1760s, it was so well established that Daing Kemboja obtained half the cargo of a British opium ship on credit in order to pay the Dutch indemnities demanded for the Linggi wars. The proceeds from that sale amounted to $77,754" (Trocki, *Prince of Pirates*, 22).

33. Marsden, *A Dictionary and Grammar of the Malay Language* (1812). Grevel Lindop speculates that the Malay in the *Confessions* may have been drawn from the figure on the frontispiece of Marsden's *History of Sumatra* (1811) (Lindop, *The Opium-Eater*, 218).

34. Montesquieu's use resonates with this sense of the word: "Amongst the Malays where no form of reconciliation is established, he who has committed murder, certain of being assassinated by the relations or friends of the deceased, abandons himself to fury, wounds and kills all he meets" (*The Spirit of Laws*, 24.17[3]). With a similarly reasonable view, Steelkilt, in Herman Melville's *Moby-Dick* (1851), "proposes" to "run a muck from the bowsprit to the taffrail; and if by any devilishness of desperation possible, seize the ship" (277).

35. For a study of the colonial context in which native languages and practices were codified and transmitted by Europeans, see Cohn, "The Command of Language and the Language of Command," 276–329.

36. Russell Jones, introduction to the *Dictionary*, x–xi. See also John Bastin's discussion of Marsden's reputation as a historian, "English Sources for the Modern Period of Indonesian History," 256–57 and passim.

37. See Kiernan, *Colonial Empires and Armies*, 24. In Kiernan's account, British technological superiority made the invasion of Java (1811) so one-sided that it may as well have been a massacre.

38. For a fictional account of these one-sided battles that continued well into the nineteenth century, see Conrad, *An Outcast of the Islands* (1896). The characterization of the defeated but defiant Babalatchi, with his implacable hatred of the white man, is a case in point.

39. Raffles, *The History of Java*, 250. Raffles also served as lieutenant governor of Java from 1811 to 1816, when he returned to London to be knighted for his services to the Crown. The *History* was reviewed in that same year in prominent publications such as the *Edinburgh Review*, the *Quarterly Review*, and the *Asiatic Journal*. De Quincey is likely to have been aware of the work.

40. A dictionary compiled by a contemporary of Raffles gives, "AMUK. The muck of the writers of Queen Anne's time, who introduced the word into our language" (Crawfurd, *A Descriptive Dictionary*).

41. Wilkinson, *A Malay-English Dictionary*; emphasis added. The start of Wilkinson's entry reads as follows: "**amok.** Furious attack; charge; amuck. Of desperate onslaughts in old romances: *Hikayat Sang Samba, Hikayat Indera Jaya,* Crawfurd's *Malay Grammar, Dissertation on the Malay language* page 78, *Malay Annals,* cf also Sundanese **ngamuk** (to fight furiously), **pamuk** (great fighter)." Wilkinson's entry also point to the literary contexts ("old romances") in which the word appears. I cannot pursue that insight here.

42. This reversal looks back to that earlier revaluation of the colonial period. See Volosinov, *Marxism and the Philosophy of Language*, 65–70.

43. Guha, "The Prose of Counter-Insurgency." In modern Malay, colloquial uses of the word draw in part on *amuk* as indiscriminate violence, but the racially pejorative definitions of the word are likely the result of the instrumentalities of colonial tutelage. In the concise dictionary compiled by the most eminent colonial scholar of Malay of the twentieth century, Richard Winstedt, who also served as the British resident of Perak, that authority may be heard in the neatly dismissive definition of *amuk*: "frenzied attack; attack madly." The different connotations of the word, in particular that of "desperate resolution," circumspectly recorded by William Marsden in a less secure moment for the British, had evidently been expunged by the time of late colonial rule. See Winstedt, *A Practical Modern Malay-English Dictionary*.

44. Spivak, "How to Teach a Culturally Different Book," 249.

45. My primary source for the various European uses of "amuck" is *Hobson-Jobson: A Glossary of Anglo-Indian Phrases of Kindred Terms, Etymological, Historical, Geographical, and Discursive* (1882), compiled by Colonel Henry Yule and A.C. Burnell.

46. Two quick points about the "*amuk*" entry here. Produced in the late nineteenth century, *Hobson-Jobson* relies on British colonial scholarship for its primary native derivation and definition of *amuk*. The compilers cite Oxley and Crawfurd,

and they quote the well-known scholar Skeat, who describes *amuk* as "the Malay national method of committing suicide, especially as one never hears of Malays committing suicide any other way." Needless to say, this statement resonates with De Quincey's hilarious mock-scholarly claims about various racial "others" scattered across the *Confessions*. Such forms of death, the reader is told, often involve the murders of the members of the suicide's own family. As noted previously, this does not seem to have been the principal definition of *amuk* before the nineteenth century. Second, this glossary has elements in it that enable it to be read against the grain of the univocal imagination. *Hobson-Jobson* entertains the possible historical relation lying beneath or before the shifts between the uses of the Malay word "*amuk*" and its putative cognates in Malabari (*amouchi* or *amuco*), Malayalam (*amar-kkan*), Sanskrit (*amokshya*), Javanese (*amuco*), Gujarati (*amaucos*), Arabic (*ahmak*) and so forth, suggesting the lineaments of a fabular and open-ended taxonomy accreting around the word in each non-European language, "true" or "fictive." The colonial archive here points to the possibilities of different, wayward, lateral organizations of the word that turn away from the European scholarly fixation with containing native violence, rational or otherwise. This chapter tracks the imaginative possibility of the word in its Malay form, keeping in mind the other paths suggested by these (putatively) related uses as they too have been shaped and transformed by the impress of their own historical scripts.

47. In the seventeenth-century *Sejarah Melayu*, one Malay chief challenges or invites another to "*mengamuk*" (Shellabear, ed., *Sejarah Melayu* [Malay annals], 131), as in a duel. A similar use of the word, in the sense of a deadly fight, is found in another famous work, this one from the nineteenth-century: "*Ada pun orang2 Siak merampas-lah perahu panglima kedua itu dengan segala senjata-senjatanya, dan mana2 orang yang tertinggal itu; beramok-lah bermati-matian*" (Raja Ali Haji, *Tuhfat al-Nafis*, 89). See also a sixteenth-century Portuguese source quoted by Raffles: "[The Javans] are a brave and determined race of men, and for any slight offence will run amok to be revenged" (Diogo de Couto, *Decad.* 4.3.1, quoted in Stamford Raffles, *History of Java*, xxv.)

48. The change in meaning is puzzled over by colonial authors. C.B. Buckley: "Mr. John Crawfurd says that the word ... [means] a desperate and furious charge or onset, either of an individual or body of men. The charge of the English at Waterloo, or the French over the bridge at Lodi would be considered, he says, by a Malay as illustrious *pengamoks*. Dr. Johnson in his *Dictionary* says he 'knows not from what derivation the word is made to mean to run madly and attack all he meets'" (Buckley, *Anecdotal History of Old Days in Singapore*, 100–101, 102).

49. There is one mention from the seventeenth century of an opium-related murder in *Hobson-Jobson* that corresponds superficially to the nineteenth-century British definitions of *amuk* as irrational or mindless violence. But the entry turns

out to be both anomalous and mysterious; it starts by pointing to the violence as "mad" but then points out that the *muck* is regarded by locals as an "invincible hero" who has to be made an example of by the Dutch colonial authorities: "(1659) 'I saw this month of February at Batavia, the breasts torn with red-hot tongs off a black Indian by the executioner; and after this he was broken on the wheel from below upwards. This was because through the evil habit of eating opium (according to the godless custom of the Indians) he had become mad and raised the cry of *Amocle* (misp. for **Amock**) . . . in which mad state he had slain five persons. . . . This was the third **Amock**-cryer whom I saw during that visit to Batavia (a few months) broken on the wheel for murder. . . . Such a murderer and **Amock**-runner has sometimes the fame of being an invincible hero because he has so manfully repulsed all who tried to seize him. . . . So the Netherlands Government is compelled when such an **Amock**-runner is taken alive to punish him in a terrific manner'" (Schulzens, *Ost-Indische Reise-Beschreibung*, German ed., 19–20, 227). The violence committed under the influence of opium appears to cause anxiety to the colonial state: stated in crudely presentist terms, "criminality" shades into "terrorism."

50. See, for example, the words in an unrelated context, of Frank Swettenham, *About Perak* (1893): "It is this state of blind fury, this vision of blood, that produces the amok" (quoted in OED online, s.v. "amok"). In this connection it is worth reflecting on the descriptions of, for instance, "ethnic" and "religious identity" taken for granted in textbooks of social science on the formerly colonized world.

51. *Kamus Dewan.*

52. "*Amuk* can mean 'to sweep over, to knock down': *amuk hidung*: [excitement at the smell of] mouthwatering (food); *diamuk asmara*: to be head over heels in love. *Diamuk lindu*: to be swept over by an earthquake" (Stevens and Schmidgall-Tellings, *Comprehensive Indonesian-English Dictionary*).

53. Echols and Shadily, *An Indonesian-English Dictionary.*

54. See, for instance, Munshi, *Hikayat Abdullah* (1849), 269.

55. De Quincey, "Ceylon" (1843), *Works*, 14:175.

56. Bayly, *Imperial Meridian*, 193–216.

3. NATIVE AGENT

1. The most reliable English translation is that of A. H. Hill (1970). I have at times modified Hill's translation. Quotations from this work will be followed by page citations from the English and Malay editions.

2. This influential view is reflected in Milner, *The Invention of Politics in Colonial Malaya*, 10–54. Milner reads Abullah's work as "form[ing] a point of departure for a liberal critique of the *kerajaan* [this is Milner's general term for precolonial forms of native rule] which proposed new ways of thinking about political life

and urged the primacy of 'race' over raja [*ruler*] as a focus of communal loyalty and identity" (31). He reads Abdullah as following in the path blazed by the economic liberalism of Adam Smith. Whereas Milner argues that Abdullah performs ideology critique and that his "I" (*saya*) underscores the individualistic worldview of the *Hikayat*, I concentrate on the epistemic dimensions of the text, that is to say, how its formal or "literary" dimensions make available the *way* it presents the world and, conversely, how this reflex of representation can be turned to engage other, less familiar, ways of seeing.

3. "Melaka" is sometimes spelled "Malacca" in quotations in this chapter. The inconsistencies in the spelling of some Malay words—hikayat/hikajat; rosak/rusak; jalan/djalan etc.—are all also an unavoidable feature of this chapter given the variant spellings of Malay words over time. Where I refer to or use Malay words, I have adhered to the convention followed in the Malaysian dictionary *Kamus Dewan*.

4. Duffy, "Worldwide War and British Expansion," 184–207.

5. For a discussion of the importance of port cities to the consolidation of European imperialism in Asia, see McPherson, "Port Cities as Nodal Points of Change."

6. A graphic picture of the atmosphere of geopolitical calculation, intrigue, and destabilization of hostile native rulers is captured in the instructions received by Stamford Raffles from Governor-General Hastings on November 28, 1818. Quoted in Wurtzburg, *Raffles of the Eastern Isles*, 461–67. For a recent discussion, see Locher-Schulten, *Sumatran Sultanate and Colonial State*, chapters 1–2.

7. Siti Hawa Haji Salleh, *Kesusasteraan Melayu pada abad kesembilan belas*, 177; Pramoedya Ananta Toer, ed., *Tempo Doeloe*, 11; Skinner, "Transitional Malay Literature."

8. Abdullah was not quite at home in his own home; this much is clear from the extraordinary love that he expresses for the Malay language and his attempts on occasion to distinguish himself from the Malays. See also Traill, "An Indian Protagonist of the Malay Language." A.C. Milner notes the tensions inhering to this "more fluid, ethnic situation": "It should be noted that 'Malay' is a category which, as we shall see, was subject to redefinition. For centuries, people of foreign origin had been accepted into particular Malay communities. By changing oneself in such areas as language, dress, customs and religion, it was possible to 'become Malay'" (*The Invention of Politics in Colonial Malaya*, 12). Later, the colonial administration and then Malay nationalism would give ethnicity "important new connotations," turning it into a "less porous category" (12).

9. For a discussion of the traditional *hikayat* that indirectly throws light on Abdullah's relationship to classical Malay literature, see Errington, "Some Comments on Style in the Meanings of the Past." For an analysis of Raja Ali Haji, a contemporary who wrote with a chasteness unlike Abdullah's hybridized Malay, see

Andaya and Matheson, "Islamic Thought and Malay Tradition." See also Henk Maier's discussion of Abdullah's central yet ambiguous position in Malay literary history in *We Are Playing Relatives*, 13–19.

10. The first institute of higher education in colonial Malaya, Sultan Idris Training College, was established in 1924 to train teachers for rural schools. The Malay peninsula lacked a middle class of the kind created in British India by the nineteenth century (Roff, *Origins of Malay Nationalism*, 142–47). One is struck by the stark differences between a relatively lone figure like Abdullah in mid-nineteenth-century Melaka and the cultural and material resources enabled by formal British rule that obtained where Bengali writers composed their work. See, in this regard, David Kopf, *British Orientalism and the Bengal Renaissance*. Neither Abdullah nor any inhabitant in the Malay Archipelago had the kind of institutional access to English education analyzed by Gauri Viswanathan in *Masks of Conquest*, and they were therefore in little danger of being "raised out of one class of society without having a recognized place in any other class [of colonial society]" (Adam, *Report of Education in Bengal and Bihar*, quoted in Viswanathan, *Masks of Conquest*, 149).

11. "Abdullah, a Malay only in the sense of being Muslim, wrote for a European postulated audience, thus one with which a Malay reader would find it impossible to identify" (Sweeney, *Authors and Audiences in the Malay World*, 7). At the other extreme, see Siti Hawa, who takes for granted that Abdullah is "Malay" (*Kesusasteraan Melayu pada abad Kesembilan Belas*, 158–64).

12. Abdullah is generally regarded as one of the most important writers in the canon of Malay letters; his *hikayat* (prose narrative) is a pioneering example of the modern vernacular. But he has been criticized by anticolonial nationalists for his wide-eyed admiration for the British and for his harsh criticisms of the Malays. Sweeney asserts that Abdullah had no intention of "reforming" the Malays because he makes no attempt to "establish common ground" with them and, because he lacked "Malay humility," his text would have had a "jarring effect" on native readers. My aim is to focus on how the formal conduct of Abdullah's text communicates a mode of thematization, a style of depiction. To that extent, the *Hikayat* must be read as an experimental work (whether or not this was its author's intention). It enacts a new kind of seeing. Anthropological facts are of secondary concern here since I do not think that writers or texts ought to be evaluated on how completely they conform to social-scientific definitions of their "culture." See Sweeney, *Reputations Live On*, 17.

13. The context for this judgment is the Siamese king's apparently insulting reply to the friendly overtures of the East India Company. Here, as elsewhere, I have modified Hill's translation as necessary.

14. Raffles to William Marsden, January 21, 1822, quoted in Wurtzburg, *Raffles of the Eastern Isles*, 620.

15. Marx, *Capital*, 1:138–77.

16. Marx, *Capital*, 1:162.

17. It is instructive to contrast Abdullah's interminable list with the translator Hill's nicely schematized footnote to these pages of the *Hikayat*: "Abdullah's list of the terms used in the very extensive demonology of Malaya requires a word of introduction. Historians recognize three phases in the cultural development of the Malay people: (1) the period of primitive paganism, of beliefs in the spirits of the sea, mountains, trees, etc. (2) the period of Indian influence, which introduced the mythology of the Hindus, (3) the period of Islamic influence which added *jinns*, whose existence the Koran admits, the four Archangels and various prophets. But at best this is a definitive classification of cultural influences that became interwoven" (Abdullah, *Hikayat Abdullah*, 114 n).

18. Marx, *Capital*, 1:155. Marx notes the "defects" of this value form: "Firstly, the relative expression of the value of the commodity is never complete, because the series of its representations never comes to an end. The chain, of which each equation of value is a link, is liable at any moment to be lengthened by a newly created commodity, which will provide the material for a fresh expression of value. Secondly, it is a motley mosaic of disparate and unconnected expressions of value. And lastly, if, as must be the case, the relative value of each commodity is expressed in this expanded form, it follows that the relative form of value of each commodity is an endless series of expressions of value which are all different from the relative form of value of every other commodity" (1:156).

19. Marx, *Capital*, 1:154.

20. Spivak, "In a Word: Interview," in *Outside in the Teaching Machine*, 12, 61.

21. For a discussion of how improving programs in the colonies were underpinned by imperial "tribute" masking itself as free trade, see Habib, "The Colonialization of the Indian Economy, 1757–1900," in *Essays in Indian History*, 319–26. As much as the native societies over which it sought control, the colonial institution was a hybrid form, its actions activated by means of both the total or expanded and the universal equivalents forms of value.

22. Spivak, *Critique of Postcolonial Reason*, 101.

23. Needless to say, this distinction is itself a heuristic device to help grasp the unevenness in which such an encounter took place; far from serving as empirical explanation, my aim is to defamiliarize the standard metropolitan accounts in which such encounters are coded in the conformist language of subsumption or "transition." A rhetorical reading requires that we avoid the historically tendentious narratives in which texture is effaced.

24. Contrast this notion of *kelebihan*, which may be described as individual excellence, with Abdullah's discussion of grandeur (*kebesaran*; 68; 71), which in its negative forms of self-aggrandizement (*membesarkan diri*) he associates with

high-ranking people (*orang kaja atau besar*). It is *kelebihan* (instead of the more conventional *kebesaran*), as excellence in the field of study or the conscientiousness of rulers, that Abdullah makes the condition for the highest achievement in this world, whether or not one becomes rich and powerful: a good name (*nama jang baik*; 68; 71) in the eyes of the community.

25. Spivak argues that whereas it is possible for capital to be represented as the "mysterious reproduction of money" in advanced capitalist societies, "in the case of foreign trade ... such passages in Marx as 'foreign trade cheapens ... the necessary means of subsistence into which variable capital [labor power] is converted,' and 'the use of slaves and coolies, etc.,' allow us to supplement Marx's analysis by suggesting that, especially in that branch of foreign trade which is 'colonial trade,' one of the reasons why the 'money-form' as an explanatory model is particularly misleading is because, relative to the social productivity of 'the privileged country,' the 'total or expanded form of value' is still operative in the colonies.... [T]his form, comprised of 'chain[s] ... [or] endless series...of disparate and unconnected expressions of value,' is particularly rich for the analysis of expressions of the value form in appearances other than economic" (Spivak, *Critique of Postcolonial Reason*, 100–101). The terms, "money form" and "total or expanded form of value" are taken from Marx's discussion (in *Capital*, vol. 1) of the various forms in which exchange may take place.

26. Abdullah arranges for his deceased daughter and his wife to be buried in a Tamil Muslim cemetery (*dimasdjid Keling*; 365, 395). But note also that he refers to Malay as "my language [*bahasa diriku*]" and, even as "our language [*bahasa kita*]." The question of identity is complex in the *Hikayat*. The ahistorical, Orientalist classifications engineered by the postcolonial Malaysian state—indigene versus immigrant (*bumiputra, pendatang*, etc.)—stops any thoughtful discussion of these questions.

27. The study of globalization assumes capitalist teleology. Cultural studies ought to study the global not simply as the universalizing of the general equivalent (a reflex assumption of the social sciences to which many literary and cultural critics tacitly conform), but rather as a manner of suggesting the ways in which the global is opened up by "value codings" that presuppose the mediation between different expressions of the value form. The economic and cultural cannot be opposed. Spivak crosses Foucault's attempts to think diverse recodings on the order of the everyday—his notion of "power" is another name for the total or expanded form—with Marx's attempt to undo capitalism from within by the workers' reading themselves into the idiom of general equivalence. See Spivak, *Critique of Postcolonial Reason*, 103–4.

28. According to the treaties between the British and the Malays, the British could claim no right to territory, were subject to the sovereign authority of the Sultan Husain, and were only granted the right to establish a trading factory on the

island. C. M. Turnbull offers an account of the various treaties in *A History of Singapore*.

29. There is already a texture that is glossed over: in Abdullah's report of this story, the Pangeran uses the word "*sengadja*" to assert that the Sayid has the funds but is deliberately withholding payment. This suggests the possibility of a personal relationship between the two men, and the Pangeran is using the colonial state to do his will. The Sayid refers to himself as a foreigner ("*anak dagang*") who is from the interior. Farquhar may well have been manipulated by his personal friendship with the Pangeran. Later, when the Pangeran sends for help, it is, quite unusually, the magistrate Farquhar (and not the chief of police, Andrews) who comes to the Pangeran's aid. There is much more to this story than meets the eye, obviously.

30. The connotations of wanton or indiscriminate violence are not apparent in Abdullah's uses of the word, although Hill almost always translates it in this way. Where Abdullah writes of stabbings and violent fights—"*Maka pada tiap2 hari ada orang bertikam dan mengamuk*" (225)—Hill translates as follows: "men daily engage in stabbing affrays and run *amok*" (178). ("*Mengamuk*" is similarly mistranslated elsewhere: 179, 227, and 345–46).

31. For a discussion of the lexicographic recoding of *amuk* that takes place in the colonial era, in which the Malay meaning of "being violent" is recast as "frenzied or indiscriminate violence," see my discussion of the word in chapter 2.

32. The urgent and overwhelming nature of Raffles's response suggests perhaps a fear that the East India Company's already legally dubious claim to Singapore would be further undermined by any native unrest. This explains why even after it becomes clear that the Sayid has nothing to do with native opposition to the British presence, Raffles chooses to make an example of the Sayid by having his corpse displayed publicly and branding him a traitor and a rebel when he meets the sultan.

33. Miller, "Letters of Colonel Nahuijs," 195.

34. The Sayid's burial ground became a shrine (*keramat*). For a history of *keramat* in the Malay Archipelago, see the articles collected in Chambert-Loir and Reid, eds., *The Potent Dead*.

35. Buckley, *An Anecdotal History of Old Times in Singapore*, 100. Buckley fails to note, however, that such sentiments, if they existed, may have been informed by the official positions of both the "Hindoo" and the "Nazarene" (Christian), both of whom would have been viewed as representatives of an alien and oppressive colonial power. Racial or religious feelings need not have been dominant. For a discussion of the precolonial "multicultural" aspects of sainthood (*keramat*) in the region, see Mandal, "Popular Sites of Prayer."

36. It may not be far-fetched to argue that the ethnocentric rhetoric of anti-colonial nationalists in both Singapore and Malaysia derives from complex *re*-recodings

of value such as this. Abdullah's presentation of the British revaluation of Malay practices sets the formal outline in which a normative "Malaysian" national identity is imagined. This is not merely to reiterate the (persuasive) argument for the "construction" of communalist politics in the period of colonial rule and anticolonial nationalism. It is to point to native agency in the making of modern national forms, in which the critique of colonial revaluation goes together with a wholesale adoption of its mode of perspectivizing. This distinction between ideology and episteme is put into play by Abdullah's reading of the encounter between Raffles and the sultans. My larger point is that this native elite value coding can be turned through an interrogation of its assumptions and "reflexes." Critical and pedagogical practices can make available other imaginative possibilities.

37. The word for treason against the ruler, "*menderhaka*," is a term derived from the Sanskrit that harks back, according to some historians, to inscriptions of the Srivijayan empire (Andaya and Andaya, *History of Malaysia*, 27; see also Milner, *Kerajaan*). It is worth noting that this charged word—going back in the region at least to the seventh century C.E.—is invoked by a functionary of a European trading company that is, by its own admission in the treaties it drafted and signed with the Malay rulers, to have no legal authority, let alone pose as the sovereign power of the land. Here we see an inverted parallel with the activation of the English "amuck," discussed in the last chapter.

38. See Abdullah, *Hikajat Abdullah*, 178–79 (Hill's translation). For a different reading of this exchange, see Trocki, *Prince of Pirates*, 49–60. Trocki tries to interpret events from a local point of view: he argues that the native elite sought to rely on the British to reestablish an older Malay trading empire, in the tradition of Melaka and Srivijaya. Indeed, according to the famous Bugis account written by a contemporary, Raja Ali Haji (*Tuhfat al-Nafis*), Riau was a thriving native port in the late eighteenth century until it was destroyed by a Dutch attack in 1784. In Raja Ali's account, William Farquhar says in 1818 that it is the British intention to make good on their promise to "'restore Riau to His Excellency Sultan Mahmud, the late ruler. If [the Dutch] want to use force to take Riau, then take up arms to oppose them and send word quickly to us. The English Company will come to help as best it can, because the Dutch intend to revoke the English Company's gift to the Malay king'" (Raja Ali Haji, *Tuhfat al-Nafis*, trans. Matheson and Andaya, 223). When the British established themselves in Singapore, it quickly became clear that they had no intention of restoring the Malay authorities to their rightful place. Instead they sought to curtail the powers of the local elite and to marginalize them from decision making. As a consequence, relations with the Malay elite deteriorated. From the latter group's point of view, Singapore was a Malay port; the British publicly endorsed this view but were using Malay "sovereignty" solely to keep the Dutch at bay, even as they worked to undermine Malay authority from within. With the signing

of the Anglo-Dutch treaty (1824) the duplicity could end. Singapore became a British possession, and the old Malay political and social networks were broken up into European "spheres of influence"; today they are known as "Malaysia," "Singapore," and "Indonesia."

39. Here the total or expanded form of value intersects with the general equivalent. Although discontinuous, the figure of the dead Sayid as martyr resonates for the colonial recoding of *amuk* as amuck, which had long been used by the Portuguese, Dutch, and British to code native "resistance" since the seventeenth century. For evidence of amuck as a term charged with political, that is, anticolonial valency, see the entry on "amuk" in Yule Burnell, *Hobson-Jobson*.

40. See Carl Trocki's discussion of the local context in *Prince of Pirates*, 30–55. Trocki has little to say about subaltern perspectives in the native world; he is interested in the viewpoint of the Malay elites.

41. The word *"heran"* occurs in many places, especially when Abdullah witnesses some new western invention: daguerreotype (285), the printing press, electricity, and so on. The British steamship *Sesostris* stops in Singapore on its way to bombard Canton: "When I saw the ship all the limbs of my body shook with astonishment [*heran*] at such a wonderful sight" (297). In modern usage, *heran* (or *hairan*) often means feeling mystified or confounded at seeing or hearing something (inexplicable or out of the ordinary): *"berasa pelik atau ganjil ketika melihat atau mendengar sesuatu, takjub, kagum"* (*Kamus Dewan*). Abdullah's amazement sometimes carries this connotation too, albeit in a less pronounced manner.

42. Abdullah's impatience with those natives who fail to grasp this point is revealed in his remonstration with the Chinese in Singapore about the outcome of the First Opium War. The Chinese refuse to believe that China can be defeated by the puny English. When the outcome of the war proves the invincibility of the English, Abdullah silently mocks his Chinese interlocutors even as they express a newfound awe at the power of British arms and technology. Some Chinese passengers who came to Singapore on a ship the day before say, "'We are amazed [*heran*] at how clever the English are,' and they went on, while we listened, 'There is an island in the river near Canton. For the last two years our countrymen have been working on it. Eight hundred guns were mounted on it. It was very strongly fortified. But when the English came sixteen of their warships formed up in line and shelled the fort. In two hours the fort was blown completely to bits.' I said to [the Chinese gentlemen], 'Now you know what the gentleness of the English really means' and they replied, 'It was true, Enche, what you told us some time ago, and we are completely stunned (*heran sunggoh*)'" (307; 416).

43. Hill underscores the terms of colonial epistemic revaluation by translating *"pandai"* (cleverness, intelligence or knowledge) with the charged term "enlightenment."

44. In modern Malay, "*rosak*" signifies a discomposition or derangement from the order proper to things: no longer unified, but shattered, decomposed. The *Kamus Dewan* defines *rosak* as "*sudah tidak baik, sudah bercerai-cerai (tidak tersusun, pecah-pecah, dll)*."

45. Quilty, *Textual Empires*.

46. On the training of docile bodies, see Foucault, *Discipline and Punish*, 137–38, 169, 190–93. "This new type of power, which can no longer be formulated in terms of sovereignty, is, I believe, one of the great inventions of bourgeois society. It has been a fundamental instrument in the constitution of industrial capitalism and of the type of society that is its accompaniment. This non-sovereign power, which lies outside the form of sovereignty, is disciplinary power" (Foucault, *Power/Knowledge*, 105). The contrast with the beatings that Abdullah receives in childhood (*Hikayat*, 46 [Hill trans.]) and with the implements of pedagogic torture that he describes in such detail (43–44; 23-25) could not be starker. Abdullah again tries to convey the fact that he is witnessing something qualitatively new to the Malay world.

47. The colonial episteme holds sway in the mainstream thinking of postcolonial societies like Malaysia and Singapore today. Identitarian and reactionary forms of self-assertion in the former colony—especially those that "challenge" the West— amount to little more than an instance of the "derivative" deployment of this episteme. There is perhaps no better instance of this mode of seeing than arguments for Asian exceptionalism, as seen most obviously in the debate over "Asian values," which is at best a form of reverse Orientalism: Asiatic essence posited by rich but intellectually challenged native elites. On the complicity between the "exceptionalist" or elite identitarian positions and the "universal forms of the modern regime of power," see Chatterjee, *The Nation and Its Fragments*, 13.

48. See the discussion in Siegel, "The 'I' of a Lingua Franca," in *Fetish, Recognition, Revolution*, 15–16.

49. Alfred North, letter attached to 1843 MS of the *Hikayat Abdullah*. North's agenda—that the book would be for a European readership—should not be confused with Abdullah's motivations or with the effects produced by the text.

50. I make no claim that this project is consistently undertaken by Abdullah, only that it is achieved at the level of the text. There is no question that Abdullah intends it at an obvious level, but it should also be said, for instance, that his resort to "*nasihat*" (advice or "morals") often reveals a startling disjunction between the complexity of events and the platitudes he draws from them. In the Raffles story just cited, for instance, Abdullah's "*nasihat*" is bland: "virtues are expensive to buy. . . . If you do not make careful and thorough enquiries into them, be sure that you will repent your folly, as did Mr. Raffles, but what good did it do him?"

51. On the varieties of trade that did not conform solely to exchange determined by prices and integrated markets, I have relied on Renfrew, "Trade as Action at a

Distance." Evidence of many of the kinds of trade described by Renfrew that are not based on the logic of capital accumulation characteristic of colonial capitalism—including "emissary" trade, "down the line" trade, and "central place location" redistribution and market exchange—are noted in passing in the *Hikayat* (342, 176, etc. [Hill trans.]). A different but homologous account could be given of the "Chinese economy" in Southeast Asia well into the nineteenth century. See Trocki, "Chinese Pioneering in Southeast Asia."

52. Abdul Kadir's "work" was both to teach and trade; the two activities happened side by side, in one temporal register: "*Hatta, dengan beberapa lamanja ia disana, pekerdjaanja sambil berniaga sambil mengadjar orang2 hulu itu, dari pada hal mengadji dan sembahjang dan sebagainja dari hal perkara Islam. Maka dengan hal jang demikian kasihlah mereka itu sekalian akan dia, lalu diperisterikan oranglah ia disana, serta didjadikannja akan dia chatib dalam kampung jang bernama Lubuk Keping* [After being there for some time, he traded at the same time as he taught the local upcountry people about prayer and study of matters relating to Islam. The people grew fond of him and he married and became khatib in the village called Lubuk Keping]" (31; 6). Abdul Kadir's role as a trader would have been tied to his appointment as *khatib* in the local mosque.

53. Ashin Das Gupta, "Introduction II: The Story," 38–40.

54. Arasaratnam, "The Eastward Trade of India," 212–15; Ashin Das Gupta, "India and the Indian Ocean," 147.

55. Subrahmanyam, "The Coromandel-Melaka trade in the Sixteenth Century."

56. Chaudhuri, *Trade and Civilization in the Indian Ocean*, 12. On the socialized origins of credit and "contract" before its enveloping by the modern legal institution, and the interplay between "trust" and "deceit," see Hicks, *Theory of Economic History*, 33–37; 77–79; Curtin, *Cross-Cultural Trade in World History*, 128.

57. Historians argue that the spread of Islam (from the twelfth century) in the Malay Archipelago was closely linked to trade and shipping (Meilink-Roelofsz, "Trade and Islam in the Malay-Indonesian Archipelago," 143–53; Ricklefs, *A History of Modern Indonesia*, 5–11). There is a history linking different Muslim merchant communities—Tamils, Bengalis, Arabs, Gujaratis—to the hinterland. These groups settled and became indigenized.

58. On the contextually determined character of the "I," demonstrated in the argument that "shifters are distinguished from all other constituents of the linguistic code solely by their compulsory reference to the given message," see Jakobson, "Shifters, Verbal Categories, and the Russian Verb," 132. For the distinction I am making between the two modes in which the "I" is deployed, I have adapted Emile Benveniste's distinction between the first- and third-person pronouns, the dispersed "instance[s] of utterance" by which the personal "I" is produced and the "I" which is an "abbreviation" of a system or economy of thematization (see "The Nature of Pronouns," 220–21).

59. Abdullah, *Kesah Pelayaran Abdullah*, 56. This work has been translated into English as *The Story of the Voyage of Abdullah* (A. E. Coope, trans.). Henk Maier notes that "the term *bahasa* . . . refers not only to what we would call language, or 'discursive configuration,' but also to 'culture.' *Bahasa* refers not just to the networks of words that are spoken and written, but also to appropriate behaviour, a set of manners that are relevant and effective enough to allow a group of people, no matter how different to live together in some degree of harmony" (Maier, *We Are Playing Relatives*, 6).

60. This is perhaps intimated in the Sayid Yasin case. The plaintiff in the case against Sayid Yasin, Pangeran, appears similarly to have had a personal relationship with the former. He claims that he knows that the Sayid has money but is deliberately refusing to pay. The word the Pangeran uses, "*sengadja*," implies perhaps that the Sayid is acting in bad faith. In ruling against the Sayid, Farquhar may have taken the side of one party in what may have been a personal dispute. Another reading is suggested by Trocki, who points out that the ruling against Sayid Yasin may have been related to the colonial state's general policy of taking the side of the Melaka, as opposed to the Johor, men. Whether the Sayid was linked to Temenggong cannot be ascertained, but it is striking that the latter takes charge of his funeral.

61. Skinner, "Creolized Chinese Communities"; Trocki, "Chinese Pioneering."

62. Abdullah, *The Story of the Voyage*, 10.

4. ANIMALITY AND THE GLOBAL SUBJECT IN CONRAD'S *LORD JIM*

1. "But there are degrees of feeling—the muffled, the faint, the just sufficient, the barely intelligent, as we may say; and the acute, the intense, the complete, in a word—the power to be finely aware and richly responsible. It is those moved in the latter fashion who 'get most' out of all that happens to them. . . . We care, our curiosity and our sympathy care, comparatively little for what happens to the stupid, the coarse, and the blind; care for it, and for the effects of it, at the most as helping to precipitate what happens to the more deeply wondering, to the really sentient" (James, preface to *The Princess Casamassima*, 62).

2. The abnormality of the helmsmen's behavior is compounded by the fact that a big storm is seen heading toward the already doomed ship (*Lord Jim*, 62) and that the whites jump in full view of the ship into the lifeboat (67) and call repeatedly for the engineer to join them.

3. This episode in Lord Jim is based on the actual desertion in 1881 of the pilgrim ship *Jeddah* by its European captain and officers. The "Report on the Action for Salvage brought against the Jeddah," *Straits Times Overland Journal*, October 22, 1881, states that the chief officer of the *Antenor*, which towed the *Jeddah* to Aden

after the desertion by its officers, "steered the Jeddah himself until he had taught two of the crew of the Jeddah to steer" (quoted in Sherry, *Conrad's Eastern World*, 55). There is no mention of native helmsmen, and it is clear that the ship could be steered. Conrad was familiar with the details of the "*Jeddah* affair"; why then the apparently gratuitous inclusion of the two Malays in the scene on the Patna? Why have them remain at the wheel of a ship that—unlike the *Jeddah*—has "lost its steerage-way" (61)?

4. Although J.H. Stape rightly disagrees with Tony Tanner's assertion that the Malay helmsman belongs to Conrad's "elect" or "blessed," he fails to indicate the extent of the Malay's circumscription in describing the latter's passivity as "a strict, automatic adherence to the code of seamanship and to the unthinking performance of the immediate task, the helmsman is simply unable to conceive of an alternate ordering of his activities" (Stape, "Lord Jim," 72).

5. Albert Guerard mistakes this for heroism: "And the evidence [the old Malay steersman] gives—if we attend to it as we do on later readings—pricks Jim's balloon. Not the man on the rack and tortured sinner but the old Malayan helmsman devoted and formed by the honest traditions of the sea is heroic" (quoted in Conrad, *Lord Jim*, ed. Moser, 410). Just a few lines earlier, however, Guerard (more accurately) described the two Malays as "thoughtless, immobile figures, not even part of our moral universe" (409). This striking inconsistency is perhaps symptomatic of the manner in which the Malays have been simultaneously summoned and dismissed in Conrad scholarship.

6. My use of "impoverished" draws on Jacques Derrida's discussion of animality in the work of Martin Heidegger (Derrida, *Of Spirit*, 43–50). I am indebted to Gayatri Chakravorty Spivak's meditation upon the implications of Derrida's essay for postcolonial studies (Spivak, "Responsibility"). Because the figure of the animal in *Lord Jim* has a provenance distinct from Derrida's object, however, I cannot for reasons of space elaborate upon my debt to and divergence from the complex itineraries of his and Spivak's essays. Suffice it to say that their general approach gives me a framework with which to explore the hierarchy between the human and the animal in Conrad's novel. As it appears in this essay, the animal is an anthrocentric metaphor that generally indexes a hierarchy or division within the general category of the "human."

7. This is also why the Malays' staying on the *Patna* cannot be called courageous. Courage is an act of calculation, which in any event presupposes imagination: "For the man who flies from and fears everything and does not stand his ground against anything becomes a coward, and the man who fears nothing at all but goes to meet every danger becomes rash" (Aristotle, *Nicomachean Ethics*, 1104a20–24). Like the animal, the Malay does not calculate—because he cannot.

8. In our day Marlow's racialism finds expression in more acceptable discursive forms. Daphna Erdinast-Vulcan turns Marlow's European-native relation into

a story that pits "modern" against "mythic" worldviews. For this critic, interiority is the exclusive preserve of the "modern" subject. Hence the shift to the world of Patusan is described as a "regression," an undoing of both individual autonomy and historical being. The prejudices of the colonial-capitalist nineteenth century are thereby transmuted into the enlightened schemata of a revived modernization theory, which takes as the subject of history the privileged metropolitan subject of global capitalism. At "the end of history," a powerful parochialism effaces otherness in the name of an ethical reading: "My own view is that, while [*Lord Jim*] is undoubtedly foregrounded against the spiritual and ethical malaise of modernity, it is not merely a reflection of the modern temper but an active, if desperate, attempt to defeat it by a regression to a mythical mode of discourse. This regression, effected by the transition to Patusan, is at the core of the structural rift of the novel" (Erdinast-Vulcan, *Joseph Conrad and the Modern Temper*, 35).

9. This is consistent with the description of the Muslim pilgrims when they are chanced upon by the French gunboat returning from colonial Réunion: "[On the *Patna*] the decks were packed as close as a sheep-pen: there were people perched all along the rails, jammed on the bridge in a solid mass; hundreds of eyes stared, and not a sound was heard when the gunboat ranged abreast, as if all that multitude of lips had been sealed by a spell" (83).

10. The natives are qualitatively distinct from the "pilgrims" in *Heart of Darkness* who can but refuse to work. They are also quite unlike the European sailors Jim encounters during his convalescence in the opening pages of the novel, who make clear their determination to "lounge safely through existence." The animal stands as an anthropomorphic division therefore: that undefinable quality that separates Europeans from natives. A civilizational and a racial hierarchy informs Marlow's valorization of discipline: "Haven't I turned out youngsters enough in my time, for the service of the Red Rag, to the craft of the sea, to the craft whose whole secret could be expressed in one short sentence, and yet must be driven afresh every day into young heads till it becomes the component part of every waking thought—till it is present in every dream of their young sleep?" (27).

11. See Ian Watt's discussion of these terms in *Conrad in the Nineteenth Century*, chapter 3. For all his meticulous research in other aspects of Conrad's Malayan writings, however, Watt fails to note the centrality of the merchant marine service to the consolidation of British imperialism in Southeast Asia. Watt instead settles on a romanticized description of the merchant seaman's labor: "the exercise of independent authority whose goal was not economic advantage but collective survival." The ship's officer, Watt continues in the same vein, was "an important and needed member of a community rather than someone who merely worked for a living; and the moral essence of his life remained the discharge of traditional responsibilities within a defined hierarchy" (20). Marlow's code of

honorable and professional conduct was not removed from the pressures of the historical moment.

12. See also Cowan, *Nineteenth-Century Malaya*, 165.

13. See, for instance, the reference in "The End of the Tether" (1902) to "the mail boats of the subsidized companies calling on the veriest clusters of palm-thatched hovels along the coast" (in Conrad, *Youth; Heart of Darkness; The End of the Tether*, 242).

14. Steinberg et al., *In Search of Southeast Asia*, chapter 22, 212–14. Toward the end of the novel, Jim informs Marlow that he wishes to set himself up as a coffee grower. Coffee was one of many lucrative crops that were in demand in the industrializing West.

15. Marlow gives us a picture of this in *Lord Jim* when he stops at "a little place on the coast about 230 miles south of Patusan River. Stein's schooner, in which I had my passage, put in there to collect some produce, and going ashore, I found to my great surprise that the wretched locality could boast of a third class deputy-resident, a big, fat, greasy fellow of mixed descent with turned out shiny lips" (170). Needless to say, this "Government official" (170) wants to be a trader and makes a proposition to Marlow the merchant sailor.

16. The situation is not unlike Marlow's at once moving and risible obsession with repairing the damaged boat in the Central Station, not allowing himself to think too deeply about the corruption and brutality of the company he works for. This is how Marlow pretends that the rectitude of "work" staves off the animality of historical reality.

17. Resink, "The Eastern Archipelago under Joseph Conrad's Western Eyes," in *Indonesia's History Between the Myths*, 322. Resink's essay deals primarily with the parts of the Malay Archipelago that fell within the Dutch sphere of influence. Nonetheless, his essay effectively evokes the conditions of "informal empire" that obtained in the British-dominated Malay states and Borneo; as importantly, he demonstrates that it was this conception of empire that most decisively influenced Conrad's vision of the Malay world.

18. Owen, ed., *The Emergence of Southeast Asia*, 174.

19. Furnivall, *Netherlands India*.

20. See in this regard Fredric Jameson's assertion that "these Mecca-bound pilgrims might just as easily have been replaced by Indian emigrants to South Africa, say, or by a group of families of overseas Chinese" (*The Political Unconscious*, 246.)

21. Andaya and Andaya, *A History of Malaysia*, 168.

22. From a statement by Sir Frederick Weld (quoted in Andaya and Andaya, *A History of Malaysia*, 177). Marlow's depiction of the impoverished existence of the natives in Patusan obliquely complements the normative arguments of Frank Swettenham, British resident and an architect of colonial policy in Malaya in the late nineteenth century. With the emergence of the anticolonial Indian national-

ist movement immediately in view, Swettenham warns of the dangers of exposing the Malay peasant to the discipline or "craft" (Conrad, *Lord Jim*, 27) that produces the "inward" (132) being. (This is in marked contrast to Lord Macaulay's influential 1835 "Minute on Indian Education." See Macaulay, *Selected Writings*, 235–52). Speaking of the newly Federated Malay States, Swettenham advocates "avoid[ing a system of education] likely to create an imitation, however remote, of the occasionally startling, sometimes grotesque, and often pathetic product of the British Indian schools" (Swettenham, *British Malaya*, 259). Conrad's friendship with Swettenham and familiarity with the latter's work is well known. Early in his writing career, Conrad was introduced to Swettenham by Hugh Clifford, who was also a colonial authority on Malaya (Najder, *Conrad: A Chronicle*, 290).

23. This view, all the more powerful for not being explicitly articulated in the novel, is studied as a cultural phenomenon in Adas, *Machines*, 134–65.

24. For a triumphalist example of the former, see Kurtz, "Democratic Imperialism"; for a conflicted expression of the latter see the interview given by the prime minister of Malaysia, Mahathir bin Mohamed, before his retirement (bin Mohamed, "We Should Not Pamper the Malays"). In the era of the New World Order, this upwardly mobile subject, trained in the sciences or in the humanities, is conditioned to view as normative or necessary the institutionalized politico-economic hierarchy that separates rich from poor nations. The absence of a just international economic order in the postcolonial era is reflected in the fact that today the World Trade Organization fails to represent the diversity of social needs of its member countries. Rather than seeking to adjudicate from the perspectives and needs of individual countries, it seeks in top-down fashion to "integrate" all countries into the global economy. This is only one of many pernicious ways in which the structural inequities of Free Trade masquerade as development. See Rodrik, "Global Governance of Trade."

25. In the context of a rapidly industrializing East and Southeast Asia in the 1980s and 1990s, an alternative to the (interiorized) discourse of human rights was proposed within the framework of a spurious "Asian values." Here the assertion of immutable differences between Asian and European "culture" mimicked by reversal Marlow's racial rhetoric. Predictably enough, the advocates of "Asian values" are votaries of the modern ideology introduced by colonial capitalism. In this respect, little distinguishes this position from Marlow's attitude toward "immobility."

26. See Stiglitz, *Globalization and Its Discontents*, 53–80.

27. As demonstrated by the fact that official government positions on development in postcolonial Indonesia, Malaysia, and Singapore—the successor states of colonial Malaya—reflect the narrow economic ideology of colonial capitalist "progress." See Anwar, *Asian Renaissance*. For a critical assessment, see Heryanto, "The Development of 'Development,'" 1–24.

28. As Marlow tells his listeners at another point, "All this happened in much less time than it takes to tell, since I am trying to interpret for you into slow speech the instantaneous effect of visual impressions" (30). At one level my reading here attempts to follow the animal's heteronomously induced attentiveness only to what is immediately present, not resolving "impressions" into "interpretation." Thus a virtue is made of (animal) necessity. This animal reading catches at and diverts the "instantaneous effects" even as they are uplifted by Marlow into the terms of causality and narrative.

29. In the very first sentence of the novel Jim is compared to an animal—a bull, in fact. "He was an inch, perhaps two, under six feet, powerfully built, and he advanced straight at you with a fixed from-under stare which made you think of a charging bull" (3). Read alongside the passage in which Marlow fears that Jim is beside himself with fury and that he may be insensible to appeals of reason (44), Jim begins to resemble the figure of *amuk* as I discuss it in chapter 2.

30. This scene parallels in reverse the theme of Abdullah's *Hikayat*. Whereas Abdullah seeks to induct himself into the ability to see and represent adequately, Jim is momentarily "stripped" of that capacity. There is a different kind of communication between Jim and the natives invisible to the text in this moment of defamiliarization.

31. The sight of the dog "reconstellates" that earlier memory. Walter Benjamin suggests the transvaluatory possibilities of such a relation: "To articulate the past historically does not mean to recognize it 'the way it really was' (Ranke). It means to seize hold of memory as it flashes up at a moment of danger" ("Theses on the Philosophy of History," in *Illuminations*, 257).

32. Because Jim's "immobility" here belies his struggle in the situation, it is perhaps no longer shocking to suggest that the stillness of the two helmsmen may conceal as complex a reaction. Between Marlow's representation and "Europe's way" of seeing that has dominated critical studies of the novel, each Malay helmsman is effaced: "There was such a great gulf fixed between [the helmsman's] perception of how to play his role in a theater of responsibility and the structure into which he was inserted that there was no hope for a felicitous performance from the very start. In order to hear him 'Europe' would need him to represent responsibility, by reflex, in 'Europe''s way. In other words, he would have to change his mind-set. That is how the old colonial subject was shaped. When we do it, we call it education" (Spivak, *Critique of Postcolonial Reason*, 61). What Spivak refers to here as "Europe's way" is another term for the educated or "inward" subject as described by Marlow. Conversely, the ethical task for "us" is learning to read otherwise.

33. The phrases in quotation marks are drawn from Nietzsche, *On The Genealogy of Morality*, 40.

34. For a historical account linking British metropolitan agendas to the gradual consolidation of the Malay Archipelago by the 1900s, see Webster, *Gentlemen Capitalists*, chapters 1–3.

35. See Wang, "Migration Patterns."

36. Jim dies by submitting to the anger of a native. "Lord Jim" is in one sense the title given to a migrant by other migrants. On a different note, Conradian ex-patriates like Almayer (*Almayer's Folly*) and Willems (*An Outcast of the Islands*) hold themselves apart from the Malays in a manner that contrasts sharply with Jim's life in Patusan. Whereas these men fall short of Marlow's (and Europe's) ideal of work, Jim's life in Patusan testifies to a different vision of work and belonging: Patusan is in this sense a space opened up by Europe that is not of Europe. Jim calls to be read and evaluated with a different eye.

37. In James Siegel's fascinating discussion of Dutch Indonesia in the early twenti-eth century, "Malay" is imagined less in ethnic or racial terms than as a commu-nity forming around and bound by the common use of the lingua franca of the Malay Archipelago. The category "Malay" is opened up and reimagined through the expanding (sometimes "improper") everyday use of the Malay language by creolized writers of popular fiction. This must have been the language in which Jim learned to communicate with those around him, including Jewel, who is born and raised in the archipelago. See Siegel, *Fetish, Recognition, Revolution*, 32. At the other extreme, it is impossible to know what language the aborigines sing in when they are freed from Sherif Ali's stockade (191). Outlined here is a different form of creolization (creoles before creolization in the modern sense), that escapes the purview of my analysis; little in the novel enables study of this foreclosed track.

38. Patusan might be studied in terms of "an example of the way a redistributive economy operated on the periphery of the global economy of Asia in its heyday, before it fell under the complete domination of the West. The key articulating unit in this seemingly small, inconsequential economic network was a strong regional sultanate; in the case of Sulu, it was set in a political and ecological framework that served to integrate the economic activity and resources of eth-nically diverse and often politically divided groups, and smaller sub-regions, that would supply the larger markets in China and the West with exotic marine and forest commodities" (Warren, *Sulu Zone*, 10). These commodities—Marlow names "edible bird's nest" (157) as one—were much sought after by European middlemen like Stein. In a section on the institutionalized violence of "free trade," Warren explores the impact of these movements of capital and labor on the ecology and the living conditions in this part of Southeast Asia. The "historical" model for Patusan, Berau, is named by Warren as one of the places greatly affected by these upheavals (*Sulu Zone*, 31).

39. In the post–Cold War era this viewpoint appears to have become hegemonic. See, for instance, Thomas Friedman's celebration of a U.S.-led "globalization" homologous to the relationship established by nineteenth-century Britain to its "informal empire" (Friedman, *Lexus and the Olive Tree*). For a discussion of "informal empire" see Gallagher and Robinson, "The Imperialism of Free Trade."

40. For the Malaysian case, see Abraham, *Divide and Rule*.

41. It is this assimilation of Jim to Patusan that makes Marlow liken him to an "undiscovered country" early on: "The views he let me have of himself were like those glimpses through the shifting rents in a thick fog—bits of vivid and vanishing detail, giving no connected idea of the general aspect of a country" (77).

CONCLUSION

1. This sentence is drawn from Arjun Appadurai, "Disjuncture and Difference," 30. *Pace* Appadurai, who is exercised by this tension, the point is that agency is imagined discursively and subjectively within the template given by the global perspective. The problem here is epistemic, not empirical, for this reason. Appadurai's proliferation of examples from around the world only engages the empirical phenomenon: it does not show how the global is a univocal template in which the agents all over the world have to imagine themselves. This serves to reinforce the very mode of perspectivizing that needs to be put in question. Thus, when Appadurai claims that "the complexity of the current global economy has to do with certain fundamental disjunctures between economy, culture, and politics that we have only begun to theorize," he confirms the epistemic conformism by which the global perspective is conflated with seeing as such.

2. Derrida, "This Strange Institution Called Literature," 64.

3. Spivak, "Subaltern Talk: An Interview with the Editors," in *The Spivak Reader*.

4. Pramoedya, *This Earth of Mankind*, 17 (translation modified slightly); Pramoedya, *Bumi Manusia*, 3.

5. See Bal, *Narratology*, 159–60.

6. *Penemuan* derives from *temu*, which means to meet with, to encounter someone or something.

7. Nehru, *The Discovery of India*, 60–61.

8. Benedict Anderson, *Specter of Comparisons*, 31. Like the implied reader of Nehru's passage, Anderson appears to conflate the content of the nationalist Haji Misbach's speech with how the listening Javanese peasants react to what Misbach says. Anderson implies that there takes place a homogeneous or transparent transfer of a "semantic load" from the speaker to his audience.

9. Barthes, "The Reality Effect."

10. The referential illusion occurs when "a historian claims to let a referent speak for itself." It operates a direct and unmediated link between word and thing. Barthes, "The Discourse of History," 132.

11. In his reading of this passage in the *Discovery of India*, Dipesh Chakrabarty criticizes Nehru's "mentalist" or "conceptual" reduction of the peasants' use of the phrase "*Bharat Mata*." In Chakrabarty's view, the phrase indexes for the peasants "practices sedimented into language itself and not necessarily to concepts either that the mind elaborates or that contain experiential truths" (*Provincializing Europe*, 177). He posits an opposition between the "aesthetic moment" of the peasants and the "realism of history" that is a trait of Nehru's speech. My reading avoids the kind of representational claim Chakrabarty makes. Unlike Chakrabarty, I do not see how a reading of *The Discovery of India*, in which "peasants" exist solely as textual representations serving the broader rhetorical aims of the artwork, authorizes extrapolations to how peasants *as such* really think and feel.

BIBLIOGRAPHY

PRIMARY WORKS

Conrad, Joseph. *Almayer's Folly*. 1895. Harmondsworth: Penguin, 1984.

———. *Lord Jim*. 1900. Ed. Thomas Moser. New York: Norton, 1968.

———. *An Outcast of the Islands*. 1896. Harmondsworth: Penguin, 1975.

———. *Tales of Unrest*. 1898. New York: Gordon Press, 1974.

———. *Victory*. New York: Modern Library, 1921.

———. *Youth; Heart of Darkness; The End of the Tether.* Ed. Robert Kimbrough. Oxford: Oxford University Press, 1984

De Quincey, Thomas. *The Collected Writings of Thomas De Quincey.* Ed. David Masson. 14 vols. London: Adam and Charles Black, 1889–1890.

———. *Confessions of an English Opium-Eater and Other Writings.* Ed. Grevel Lindop. London: Oxford University Press, 1985.

———. *Confessions of an English Opium-Eater.* Ed. Alethea Hayter. Harmondsworth, Eng.: Penguin Books, 1971.

———. *Recollections of the Lakes and the Lake Poets.* Ed. David Wright. Harmondsworth, Eng.: Penguin Books, 1970.

———. *Selected Essays on Rhetoric.* Ed. Frederick Lorrain Burwick. Carbondale, Ill.: Southern Illinois University Press, 1967.

———. *The Works of Thomas De Quincey.* 20 vols. Ed. Grevel Lindop. London: Pickering, 2001.

Abdullah bin Abdul Kadir. *Hikajat Abdullah.* Ed. Datoek Besar and R. Roolvink. Djakarta: Penerbit Jambatan, 1954.

——. *Hikayat Abdullah.* Trans. A. H. Hill. Kuala Lumpur: Oxford University Press, 1970.

——. *Kesah Pelayaran Abdullah.* Ed. A. H. Edrus. Singapore: Qalam Publishers. 1960.

——. *The Story of the Voyage of Abdullah bin Abdul Kadir Munshi.* Ed. and trans. A. E. Coope. Singapore: Donald Moore, 1949.

Smith, Adam. *Lectures on Jurisprudence.* 1763–64. Ed. R. L. Meek, D. D. Raphael, and P. G. Stein. New York: Oxford University Press. 1978.

——. *Lectures on Rhetoric and Belles Lettres.* 1748. Ed. J.C. Bryce. London: Oxford University Press, 1983.

——. *Theory of Moral Sentiments.* 1759. Ed. Knud Haakonsen. New York: Cambridge University Press, 2002.

——. *The Wealth of Nations.* 1776. Ed. R. H. Campbell, A. S. Skinner, and W. B. Todd. 2 vols. Oxford: Oxford University Press, 1975.

SECONDARY WORKS

Abraham, C. E. R. *Divide and Rule: The Roots of Race Relations in Malaysia.* Kuala Lumpur: INSAN. 1997.

Abu-Lughod, Janet. *Before European Hegemony: The World-System, 1250–1350.* New York: Oxford University Press, 1989.

Adam, William. *Adam's Report of Education in Bengal and Bihar in 1835 and 1838.* Ed. A. N. Basu. Calcutta: University of Calcutta Press. 1941.

Adas, Michael. *Machines as the Measure of Men.* Ithaca, N.Y.: Cornell University Press. 1989.

Alatas, Syed Hussein. *Myth of the Lazy Native.* London: Frank Cass, 1977.

Anwar, Ibrahim. *Asian Renaissance.* Singapore: Times Books International, 1996.

Amin, Samir. "The Ancient World-Systems Versus the Modern Capitalist World-System." In *The World System: Five Hundred Years or Five Thousand?* ed. Andre Gunder Frank and Barry Gills, 247–77. London: Routledge, 1993.

Andaya, Barbara, and Leonard Andaya. *A History of Malaysia.* London: Macmillan, 1982.

Andaya, Barbara, and Virginia Matheson. "Islamic Thought and Malay Tradition: The Writings of Raja Ali Haji of Riau (ca. 1809–ca. 1870)." In *Perceptions of the Past in Southeast Asia,* ed. A. Reid and D. Marr, 108–28. Singapore: Asian Studies Association of Australia, 1979.

Anderson, Benedict. "From Miracle to Crash." *London Review of Books,* April 16 1998.

——. *Imagined Communities: Reflections on the Origin and Spread Nationalism.* 2nd ed. London: Verso, 1990.

——. *The Specter of Comparisons.* London: Verso, 1998.

Appadurai, Arjun. "Disjuncture and Difference in the Global Cultural Economy." In *Modernity at Large*, 27–47. Minnesota: University of Minneapolis Press, 1996.

Arasaratnam, S. "The Eastward Trade of India in the Eighteenth Century." In *Politics and Trade in the Indian Ocean World: Essays in Honour of Ashin Das Gupta*, ed. Rudrangshu Mukherjee and Lakshmi Subramanian, 210–26. Delhi: Oxford University Press, 1998.

Aristotle. *Nicomachean Ethics*. Trans. W. D. Ross. Oxford: Oxford University Press, 1978.

——. *Politics*. Trans. C. D. C. Reeve. Indianapolis: Hackett, 1998.

Baines, Jocelyn. *Joseph Conrad: A Critical Biography*. Harmondsworth, U.K.: Penguin, 1986.

Bal, Mieke. *Narratology: Introduction to the Theory of Narrative*. Toronto: University of Toronto Press, 1997.

Ballantyne, Tony. "Empire, Knowledge, and Culture: From Proto-Globalization to Modern Globalization." In *Globalization in World History*, ed. A.G. Hopkins, 116–30. London: Pimlico, 2002.

Barnard, Timothy P., ed. *Contesting Malayness: Malay Identity Across Boundaries*. Singapore: Singapore University Press, 2004.

Barrell, John. *The Infection of Thomas De Quincey: A Psychopathology of Imperialism*. New Haven, Conn.: Yale University Press, 1991.

Barthes, Roland. "The Discourse of History." In *The Rustle of Language*, trans. Richard Howard, 127–40. New York: Hill and Wang, 1986.

——. *Mythologies*. Trans. Annette Lavers. New York: Hill and Wang, 1972.

——. "The Reality Effect." In *The Rustle of Language*, trans. Richard Howard, 141–49. New York: Hill and Wang, 1986.

Bassett, D.K. "British Commercial and Strategic Interests in the Malay Peninsula During the Late Eighteenth Century." In *Malayan and Indonesian Studies*, ed. J. Bastin and R. Roolvink, 122–40. Oxford: Clarendon, 1964.

Bastin, John. "English Sources for the Modern Period of Indonesian History." In *An Introduction to Indonesian Historiography*, ed. Mohammad Ali Soedjatmoko, G. J. Resink, and G. McT. Kahin, 252–71. Ithaca, N.Y.: Cornell University Press, 1965.

——. *The Native Policies of Sir Stamford Raffles in Java: An Economic Interpretation*. Oxford: Clarendon Press, 1957.

——. "Problems of Personality in the Reinterpretation of Modern Malaysian History." In *Malaysian and Indonesian Studies: Essays Presented to Sir Richard Winstedt on His Eighty-fifth Birthday*, ed. J. Bastin and R. Roolvink, 141–55. Oxford: Clarendon Press, 1964.

Bayly, C.A. "'Archaic' and 'Modern' Globalization in the Eurasian and African Arena." In *Globalization in World History*, ed. A.G. Hopkins, 47–73. London: Pimlico, 2001.

———. *Birth of the Modern World, 1780–1914: Global Connections and Comparisons.* Malden, Mass.: Blackwell, 2004.

———. "The First Age of Global Imperialism, c. 1760–1830." *Journal of Imperial and Commonwealth History* 26 (1998): 28–47.

———. *Imperial Meridian: The British Empire and the World, 1780–1830.* London: Longman, 1989.

Benjamin, Walter. *Illuminations.* Trans. Harry Zohn. New York: Schocken, 1969.

Bennett, Tony. *Formalism and Marxism.* London: Routledge. 1989.

Benveniste, Emile. "The Nature of Pronouns." In *Problems in General Linguistics,* trans. M. E. Meek, 217–22. Coral Gables, Fla.: University of Miami Press, 1971.

Black, Joel D. "Confession, Digression, Gravitation: Thomas De Quincey's German Connection." In *Thomas De Quincey. Bicentenary Studies,* ed. Robert Lance Snyder, 308–38. Norman: University of Oklahoma Press, 1981.

Blaut, James. *The Colonizer's Model of the World.* New York: Guilford, 1993.

Blue, Gregory. "Opium for China: The British Connection." In *Opium Regimes: China, Britain, and Japan, 1839–1952,* ed. Timothy Brook and Bob Tadashi Wakabayashi, 31–54. Berkeley: University of California Press, 2000.

Bowen, H. V. "British Conceptions of Global Empire, 1756–83." *Journal of Imperial and Commonwealth History* 26, no. 3 (September 1998): 1–27.

Buckley, C. B. *Anecdotal History of Old Days in Singapore.* Singapore: Oxford University Press, 1984.

Burke, Edmund. *A Philosophical Enquiry Into the Origin of Our Ideas of the Sublime and Beautiful.* Ed. James T. Boulton. Notre Dame, Ind.: University of Notre Dame Press, 1968.

———. *Reflections on the Revolution in France.* Ed. J.G.A. Pocock. Indianapolis: Hackett, 1987.

Cain, P. J., and A. G. Hopkins. *British Imperialism: Innovation and Expansion, 1688–1914.* London: Longman, 1993.

Chakrabarty, Dipesh. *Provincializing Europe: Postcolonial Thought and Historical Difference.* Princeton, N.J.: Princeton University Press, 2000.

Chambert-Loir, Henri, and Anthony Reid, eds. *The Potent Dead: Ancestors, Saints, and Heroes in Contemporary Indonesia.* Honolulu: University of Hawaii Press, 2002.

Chatterjee, Partha. *Nationalist Thought and the Colonial World: A Derivative Discourse?* New York: Zed Books, 1986.

———. *The Nation and Its Fragments.* Princeton, N.J.: Princeton University Press, 1993.

Chaudhuri, K. N. *Asia Before Europe: Economy and Civilization of the Indian Ocean from the Rise of Islam to 1750.* Cambridge: Cambridge University Press, 1990.

———. "Reflections on Premodern Trade." In *Political Economy of Merchant Empires,* ed. James D. Tracy, 221–42. Cambridge: Cambridge University Press, 1991.

——. *Trade and Civilization in the Indian Ocean: An Economic History from the Rise of Islam to 1750.* Cambridge: Cambridge University Press, 1985.

Chung, Tan. "The Britain-China-India Trade Triangle, 1771–1840." *Indian Economic and Social History Review* 11, no. 4 (December 1974): 411–31.

Clifford, James. *Routes: Travel and Translation in the Late Twentieth Century.* Cambridge, Mass.: Harvard University Press. 1997.

Cohn, Bernard. "The Command of Language and the Language of Command." In *Subaltern Studies IV,* ed. Ranajit Guha, 276–329. Delhi: Oxford University Press, 1985.

Coleridge, Samuel Taylor. *Biographia Literaria.* Ed. James Engell and W. Jackson Bate. Bollingen series, no. 75. Princeton, N.J.: Princeton University Press, 1983.

Colley, Linda. *Britons: Forging the Nation, 1707–1837.* New Haven, Conn.: Yale University Press, 1992.

——. "Imperial Trauma: The Powerlessness of the Powerful: Part 1." *Common Knowledge* 11, no. 2 (Spring 2005): 198–214.

Cooper, Frederick. "What Is the Concept of Globalization Good For? An African Historian's Perspective." *African Affairs* 100, no. 399 (April 2001): 189–213.

Cowan, C.D. "Early Penang and the Rise of Singapore, 1805–1832." *Journal of the Malayan Branch of the Royal Asiatic Society* 22, no. 2 (1950).

——. *Nineteenth-Century Malaya: The Origins of British Political Control.* London: Oxford University Press, 1961.

Crawfurd, John. *Descriptive Dictionary of the Indian Islands and Adjacent Countries.* London: Bradbury & Evans, 1856.

Curtin, Philip. *Cross-Cultural Trade in World History.* Cambridge: Cambridge University Press, 1984.

Das Gupta, Ashin. "India and the Indian Ocean in the Eighteenth Century." In *India and the Indian Ocean, 1500–1800,* ed. Ashin Das Gupta and M. N. Pearson, 131–61. Calcutta: Oxford University Press, 1987.

——. "Introduction II: The Story." In *India and the Indian Ocean, 1500–1800,* ed. Ashin Das Gupta and M. N. Pearson, 25–45. Calcutta: Oxford University Press, 1987.

De Man, Paul. *Allegories of Reading: Figural Language in Rousseau, Nietzsche, Rilke, and Proust.* New Haven, Conn.: Yale University Press, 1979.

——. *Blindness and Insight: Essays in the Rhetoric of Contemporary Criticism.* 2nd rev. ed. Minneapolis: University of Minnesota Press, 1983.

Derrida, Jacques. *Of Spirit: Heidegger and the Question.* Trans. Geoffrey Bennington and Rachel Bowlby. Chicago: Chicago University Press. 1989.

——. "Signature Event Context." In *Margins of Philosophy,* trans. Alan Bass, 307–30. Chicago: University of Chicago Press, 1982.

———. "'This Strange Institution Called Literature': An Interview with Jacques Derrida." In *Acts of Literature*, ed. Derek Attridge, 33–75. New York: Routledge, 1992.

Dixon, Chris. *South East Asia in the World Economy: A Regional Geography*. Cambridge: Cambridge University Press, 1991.

Duffy, Michael. "World Wide War and British Expansion, 1793–1815." In *Oxford History of the British Empire*, ed. P. J. Marshall, 2:184–207. Oxford: Oxford University Press, 1999.

Echols, John M., and Hasan Shadily. *An Indonesian-English Dictionary*. Cornell, N.Y.: Cornell University Press, 1961.

Emerson, Rupert. *Malaysia: A Study in Direct and Indirect Rule*. Kuala Lumpur: University of Malaya Press, 1937.

Erdinast-Vulcan, Daphna. *Joseph Conrad and the Modern Temper*. Oxford: Oxford University Press. 1991.

Erlich, Victor. "Russian Formalism." *Journal of the History of Ideas* 34, no. 4 (1973): 627–38.

Errington, Shelly. "Some Comments on Style in the Meanings of the Past." *Journal of Asian Studies* 38, no. 2 (1979): 231–44.

Fernando, Lloyd. "Conrad's Eastern Expatriates." *PMLA* 91 (1976): 278–90.

Fleischacker, Samuel. *On Adam Smith's* Wealth of Nations*: A Philosophical Companion*. Princeton, N.J.: Princeton University Press, 2004.

Forbes, Jack D. *Africans and Native Americans: The Language of Race and the Evolution of Red-Black Peoples*. Urbana: University of Illinois Press, 1993.

Foucault, Michel. *The Archaeology of Knowledge*. Trans. A. M. Sheridan Smith. London: Tavistock, 1972.

———. *Discipline and Punish*. Trans. Alan Sheridan. New York: Vintage, 1979.

———. *The Order of Things: An Archeology of the Human Sciences*. New York: Pantheon, 1971.

Frank, Andre Gunder. *ReOrient: Global Economy in the Asian Age*. Berkeley: University of California Press, 1998.

Friedman, Thomas. *The Lexus and the Olive Tree*. New York: Farrar, Strauss, Giroux. 1999.

Furnivall, John S. *Netherlands India: A Study of Plural Economy*. Cambridge: Cambridge University Press, 1944.

Gallagher, John, and Ronald Robinson. "The Imperialism of Free Trade." *Economic History Review*, 2nd series, no. 6 (1953): 1–13.

GoGwilt, Christopher. *The Invention of the West: Joseph Conrad and the Double Mapping of Europe and Empire*. Stanford, Calif.: Stanford University Press, 1995.

Greenberg, Michael. *British Trade and the Opening of China, 1800–42*. Cambridge: Cambridge University Press, 1969.

Guerard, Albert J. *Conrad the Novelist.* Cambridge, Mass.: Harvard University Press, 1965.

Guha, Ranajit. "The Prose of Counter-Insurgency." In *Subaltern Studies II*, ed. Guha, 1–42. Delhi: Oxford University Press, 1983.

———. *A Rule of Property for Bengal: An Essay on the Idea of Permanent Settlement.* 1963. Durham, N.C.: Duke University Press, 1990.

Gullick, J. M. *Malay Society in the Late Nineteenth Century: The Beginning of Change.* Singapore: Oxford University Press, 1987.

Habib, Irfan. *Essays in Indian History.* Delhi: Tulika, 1995.

Harlow, Vincent T. *The Founding of the Second British Empire, 1763–1793.* Vol. 1. London: Longman, 1952.

Hayter, Alethea. *Opium and the Romantic Imagination: Addiction and Creativity in De Quincey, Coleridge, Baudelaire, and Others.* Wellingborough, U.K.: Crucible, 1988.

Heidegger, Martin. "Age of the World Picture." In *Off the Beaten Track*, ed. and trans. Julian Young and Kenneth Haynes, 57–85. Cambridge: Cambridge University Press, 2002.

———. "Die Zeit des Weltbildes." In *Holzwege*, ed. Vittorio Klostermann. Frankfurt: Vittorio Klostermann, 1952.

Heryanto, Ariel. "The Development of 'Development.'" Trans. Nancy Lutz. *Indonesia* 46 (1988): 1–24.

Hicks, John. *Theory of Economic History.* London: Oxford University Press. 1969.

Hont, Istvan, and Michael Ignatieff, "Needs and Justice in the *Wealth of Nations*: An Introductory Essay." In *Wealth and Virtue: The Shaping of Political Economy in the Scottish Enlightenment*, ed. Hont and Ignatieff, 1–44. Cambridge: Cambridge University Press, 1983.

Hopkins, A. G., ed. *Globalization in World History.* London: Pimlico, 2001.

Hurgronje, C. Snouck. *Mekka in the Latter Part of the Nineteenth Century.* Leiden: Brill, 1970.

Hyam, Ronald. "The Primacy of Geopolitics: The Dynamics of British Imperial Policy, 1763–1963." *Journal of Imperial and Commonwealth History* 27, no. 2 (May 1999): 27–52.

Jakobson, Roman. "Shifters, Verbal Categories, and the Russian Verb." In *Selected Writings*, 2:130–47. Paris: Mouton, 1971.

James, Henry. *Art of the Novel.* New York: Scribner, 1937.

Jameson, Fredric. *The Political Unconscious: Narrative as a Socially Symbolic Act.* Ithaca, N.Y.: Cornell University Press, 1981.

———. "Third World Literature in the Era of Multinational Capitalism." *Social Text* 15 (1986): 65–88.

Johns, A. H. "Islam in Southeast Asia: Reflections and New Directions." *Indonesia* 19 (1975): 33–56.

Jordan. John E. *Thomas De Quincey, Literary Critic: His Method and Achievement.* Berkeley: University of California Press, 1952.

Kamus Dewan. Kuala Lumpur: Dewan Bahasa dan Pustaka. 1989.

Kathirithamby-Wells, J. "The Age of Transition: The Mid-Eighteenth to the Early Nineteenth Centuries." In *The Cambridge History of Southeast Asia*, ed. Nicholas Tarling, 1:576–612. Cambridge: Cambridge University Press, 1992.

Kiernan, V.G. *Colonial Empires and Armies, 1815–1960.* Montreal: McGill-Queens University Press, 1998.

Kipling, Rudyard. *Kim.* Ed. Edward Said. London: Penguin, 1989.

Koebner, Richard. *Empire.* Cambridge: Cambridge University Press, 1961.

Kopf, David. *British Orientalism and the Bengal Renaissance: The Dynamics of Indian Modernization, 1775–1900.* Berkeley: University of California Press, 1969.

Koselleck, Reinhart. *The Practice of Conceptual History.* Trans. Todd Samuel Presner. Stanford, Calif.: Stanford University Press, 2002

Kratoska, Paul H., ed. *Honourable Intentions: Talks on the British Empire in Southeast Asia Delivered at the Royal Colonial Institute, 1874–1928.* Singapore: Oxford University Press, 1983.

Kratoska, Paul H., Remco Raben, and Henk Schulte Nordholt. "Locating Southeast Asia." In *Locating Southeast Asia: Geographies of Knowledge and Politics of Space*, ed. Kratoska, Raben and Nordholt, 1–20. Singapore: Singapore University Press, 2005.

Kurtz, Stanley. "Democratic Imperialism: A Blueprint." *Policy Review* no. 118 (April–May 2003). http://www.hoover.org/publications/policyreview/3449176.html.

Lahiri, Shompa. "Contested Relations: the East India Company and Lascars in London." In *The Worlds of the East India Company*, ed. H.V. Bowen et al., 169–82. Suffolk: The Boydell Press, 2002.

Leask, Nigel. *British Romantic Writers and the East: Anxieties of Empire.* Cambridge: Cambridge University Press, 1992.

Lee Kuan Yew. *The Singapore Story: From Third World to First.* Singapore: Times, 1999.

Lindop, Grevel. *The Opium-Eater: A Life of Thomas De Quincey.* New York: Taplinger, 1981.

Livingstone, David N. *The Geographical Tradition.* London: Blackwell, 2003.

Macaulay, Thomas Babington. *Selected Writings.* Chicago: University of Chicago Press, 1972.

Maier, Henk. *We Are Playing Relatives: A Survey of Malay Writing.* Leiden: KITLV Press, 2004.

Maimunah, Mohd. Ungku Tahir. *Modern Malay Literary Culture: A Historical Perspective.* Singapore: ISEAS, 1987.

Mandal, Sumit. "Popular Sites of Prayer, Transnational Migration, and Cultural Diversity: Exploring the Significance of *Keramat* in Southeast Asia." Paper presented at the Workshop on Transnational Religion, Migration, and Diversity." Social Science Research Council Workshop, Kuala Lumpur, December 2–4, 2004.

Maniquis, Robert M. "Lonely Empires: Personal and Public Visions of Thomas De Quincey." Ed. Eric Rothstein and Joseph Anthony Wittreich. *Literary Monographs* 8:49–137. Madison: University of Wisconsin Press, 1976.

Markley, Robert. *The Far East and the English Imagination, 1600–1730.* Cambridge: Cambridge University Press, 2005.

Marsden, William. *A Dictionary and Grammar of the Malay Language.* 1812. Reprint, intro. Russel Jones. Singapore: Oxford University Press, 1983.

——. *The History of Sumatra.* 1783. Kuala Lumpur: Oxford University Press, 1966.

Marshall, P. J. "Britain Without America—a Second Empire?" In *Oxford History of the British Empire*, ed. P. J. Marshall, 2:576–95. Oxford: Oxford University Press: 1999.

——. *A Free Though Conquering People: Eighteenth-Century Britain and Its Empire.* Burlington, Vt.: Ashgate, 2003.

Marx, Karl. *Capital.* 3 vols. Trans. Ben Fowkes. New York: Vintage, 1977.

Mahathir, bin Mohamed. "We Should Not Pamper the Malays Too Much." *Straits Times* (Singapore), June 19, 2003.

Matheson, V., and A. C. Milner, eds. *Perceptions of the Haj.* Singapore: ISEAS, 1987.

Mazlish, Bruce. "Global History and World History." *The Global History Reader*, ed. Bruce Mazlish and Akira Iriye, 16–20. New York: Routledge, 2005.

McDonagh, Josephine. *De Quincey's Disciplines.* Oxford: Oxford University Press, 1994.

McPherson, Kenneth. "Port Cities as Nodal Points of Change." In *Modernity and Culture: From the Mediterranean to the Indian Ocean*, ed. C. A. Bayly and Leila Tarazi Fawaz, 75–95. New York: Columbia University Press, 2005.

Meek, Ronald. *Social Science and the Ignoble Savage.* Cambridge: Cambridge University Press, 1976.

Meilink-Roelofsz, M. A. P. "Trade and Islam in the Malay-Indonesian Archipelago Prior to the Arrival of the Europeans." In *Islam and the Trade of Asia*, ed. D. S. Richards, 137–58. Philadelphia: University of Pennsylvania Press, 1970.

Melville, Herman. *Moby-Dick.* 1851. New York: Penguin, 1992.

Metcalf, Thomas R. *Ideologies of the Raj.* Cambridge: Cambridge University Press, 1995.

Miller, H. E. "Extracts from the Letters of Colonel Nahuijs." *Journal of the Malayan Branch of the Royal Asiatic Society* 19, no. 2 (October 1941): 169–209.

Mills, L. A. *British Malaya, 1824–1867.* Oxford: Oxford University Press, 1966.

Milner, Anthony. *Kerajaan: Malay Political Culture on the Eve of Colonial Rule.* Tucson: University of Arizona Press, 1982.

——. *The Invention of Politics in Colonial Malaya.* Cambridge: Cambridge University Press, 1995.

Montesquieu, Charles de Secondat, Baron de. *The Spirit of Laws*. 1748. Ed. and trans. David Wallace Carrithers. Berkeley: University of California Press, 1977.

Moretti, Franco. "Conjectures on World Literature." *New Left Review* 1 (January–February 2000): 54–86.

Najder, Zdzislaw. *Joseph Conrad: A Chronicle*. New Brunswick, N.J.: Rutgers University Press. 1983.

Nehru, Jawaharlal. *The Discovery of India*. 1946. Delhi: Oxford University Press, 1985.

Nietzsche, Friedrich. *On The Genealogy of Morality*. Ed. Keith Ansell-Pearson. Trans. Carol Dieth. Cambridge: Cambridge University Press, 1994.

Ohlmeyer, Jane H., "'Civilizinge of Those Rude Partes': Colonization Within Britain and Ireland, 1580–1640s." In *Oxford History of the British Empire*, ed. Nicholas Canny, 1:124–47. Oxford: Oxford University Press. 1998.

Osborn, Jeremy. "India and the East India Company in the Public Sphere of Eighteenth-Century Britain." In *The Worlds of the East India Company*, ed. H.V. Bowen, Margarette Lincoln, and Nigel Rigby, 201–22. Suffolk: The Boydell Press, 2002.

Osterhammel, Jürgen, and Niels P. Petersson. *Globalization*. Princeton, N.J.: Princeton University Press, 2005.

Owen, David Edward. *British Opium Policy in India and China*. New Haven, Conn.: Yale University Press, 1934.

Owen, Norman G., ed. *The Emergence of Southeast Asia*. Honolulu: University of Hawaii Press, 2005.

Palat, Ravi Arvind, and Immanuel Wallerstein. "Of What World-System Was pre-1500 'India' a Part?" In *Merchants Companies and Trade: Europe and Asia in the Early Modern Era*, ed. Sushil Chaudhury and Michel Morineau, 38–41. Cambridge: Cambridge University Press, 1999.

Phillipson, Nicholas. "Adam Smith as Civic Moralist." In *Wealth and Virtue: The Shaping of Political Economy in the Scottish Enlightenment*, ed. Istvan Hont and Michael Ignatieff, 179–202. Cambridge: Cambridge University Press, 1983.

Pieterse, Jan Nederveen, *Globalization and Culture*. Lanham, Md.: Rowman and Littlefield, 2004.

Pitts, Jennifer. *A Turn to Empire: The Rise of Imperial Liberalism in Britain and France*. Princeton, N.J.: Princeton University Press, 2005.

Pletsch, Carl. "The Three Worlds, or the Division of Social Scientific Labor, Circa 1950–1975." *Comparative Studies in Society and History* 23, no. 4 (1998): 565–89.

Pocock, J.G.A. "Adam Smith and History." In *Cambridge Companion to Adam Smith*, ed. Knud Haakonsen, 270–87. Cambridge: Cambridge University Press, 2005.

Polanyi, Karl. *The Great Transformation: The Political and Economic Origins of Our Time*. Boston: Beacon Press, 1944.

Pomeranz, Kenneth, and Steven Topik. *The World That Trade Created: Society, Culture, and the World Economy, 1400–the Present*. London: M.E. Sharpe, 1999.

Pramoedya Ananta Toer. *Bumi Manusia*. Jakarta: Hasta Mitra, 1980.

——, ed. *Tempo Doeloe: Antologi Sastra Pra-Indonesia*. Jakarta: Hasta Mitra, 1982.

——. *This Earth of Mankind*. Trans. Max Lane. New York: Penguin, 1982.

Quilty, Mary Catherine. *Textual Empires: A Reading of Early British Histories of Southeast Asia*. Clayton, Vic., Australia: Monash Asia Institute, 1998.

Raffles, Stamford. *The History of Java*. 1817. Singapore: Oxford University Press, 1988.

Raja Ali Haji. *Tuhfat al-Nafis* (The precious gift). Trans. Barbara Andaya and Virginia Matheson Hooker. Oxford: Oxford University Press, 1982.

——. *Tuhfat al-Nafis: Sejarah Melayu dan Bugis*. Singapore: Malaysia Publications. 1965.

Reid, Anthony. "Economic and Social Change, c. 1400–1800." In *The Cambridge History of Southeast Asia*, ed. Nicholas Tarling, 1:460–507. Cambridge: Cambridge University Press, 1992.

——. "Nineteenth Century Pan-Islam in Indonesia and Malaysia." *Journal of Asian Studies* 26, no. 2 (1967): 267–83.

Renfrew, Colin. "Trade as Action at a Distance: Questions of Integration and Communication." In *Ancient Civilization and Trade*, ed. J. A. Sabloff and C.C. Lamberg-Karlovsky, 3–60. Albuquerque: University of New Mexico Press, 1975.

Resink, G.J. *Indonesia's History Between the Myths*. The Hague: W. Van Hoeve, 1968.

Ricklefs, M. C. *A History of Modern Indonesia Since c. 1300*. 2nd ed. Stanford, Calif.: Stanford University Press, 1993.

Rodrik, Dani. "The Global Governance of Trade as If Development Really Mattered." New York: United Nations Development Program, 2001.

Roff, William R. *The Origins of Malay Nationalism*. New Haven, Conn.: Yale University Press, 1967.

Ryan, N.J. *A History of Malaysia and Singapore*. Kuala Lumpur: Oxford University Press, 1976.

Said, Edward. *Culture and Imperialism*. Cambridge, Mass.: Harvard University Press, 1993.

——. *Orientalism*. New York: Vintage Books, 1979.

Scholte, Jan Aart. *Globalization: An Introduction*. New York: St. Martin's Press, 2000.

Schumpeter, Joseph. *History of Economic Analysis*. New York: Oxford University Press, 1954.

Shellabear, W.G., ed. *Sejarah Melayu* (Malay annals). Petaling Jaya: Fajar Bakti, 1975.

Sherry, Norman. *Conrad's Eastern World*. Cambridge: Cambridge University Press, 1966.

Shiva, Vandana. *Biopiracy: The Plunder of Nature and Knowledge*. Boston: Southend Press, 1997.

Shklovsky, Viktor. "Art as Device." In *Theory of Prose*, trans. Benjamir Sher, 1–14. Elmwood Park, Ill.: Dalkey Archive Press, 1990.

Siegel, James. *Fetish, Recognition, Revolution*. Princeton, N.J.: Princeton University Press, 1997.

Simmel, Georg. "The Stranger." In *Georg Simmel on Social Forms*, ed. Donald Levine, 143–49. Chicago: University of Chicago Press, 1971.

Siti Hawa Haji Salleh. *Kesusasteraan Melayu pada abad kesembilan belas*. Kuala Lumpur: Dewan Bahasa, 1997.

Skinner, Andrew. "Historical Theory." In *A System of Social Science: Papers Relating to Adam Smith*, 76–108. Oxford: Oxford University Press, 1996.

Skinner, C. "Transitional Malay Literature: Ahmad Rijaluddin and Munshi Abdullah." *Bijdragen tot de Taal-, Land-, en Volkenkunde* 134 (1978): 466–87.

Skinner, G. William. "Creolized Chinese Communities in Southeast Asia." In *Sojourners and Settlers*, ed. Anthony Reid with the assistance of Kristine Alilunas Rodgers, 51–92. New South Wales: Allen and Unwin, 1996.

Snyder, Robert Lance, ed. *Thomas De Quincey: Bicentenary Studies*. Norman: University of Oklahoma Press, 1981.

Spivak, Gayatri Chakravorty. *A Critique of Postcolonial Reason*. Cambridge, Mass.: Harvard University Press, 1999.

——. *In Other Worlds: Essays in Cultural Politics*. New York: Methuen, 1987.

——. *Outside in the Teaching Machine*. New York: Routledge, 1993.

——. "Responsibility." *Boundary* 2 (1994): 19–64.

——. *The Spivak Reader*. Ed. Donna Landry and Gerald Maclean. London: Routledge, 1996.

Stape, J. H. "Lord Jim." In *Cambridge Companion to Joseph Conrad*, ed. Stape, 63–80. Cambridge: Cambridge University Press. 1996.

Steinberg, David Joel, et al. *In Search of Southeast Asia*. New York: Praeger, 1971

Stevens, Alan M., and A. Ed. Schmidgall-Tellings. *Comprehensive Indonesian-English Dictionary*. Athens: Ohio University Press, 2004.

Stevens, David. "Adam Smith and the Colonial Disturbances." In *Essays on Adam Smith*, ed. Andrew Skinner and Thomas Wilson, 202–17. Oxford: Oxford University Press, 1975.

Stewart, Dugald. "Account of the Life and Writings of Adam Smith, L.L.D." 1793. In *Essays on Philosophical Subjects*, by Adam Smith, ed. W. P. D. Wightman and J. C. Bryce, 269–352. London: Oxford University Press, 1980.

Stiglitz, Joseph. *Globalization and Its Discontents*. New York: Norton, 2002.

Stokes, Eric. *English Utilitarians and India.* Oxford: Clarendon Press, 1959.

Subrahmanyam, Sanjay. "The Coromandel-Melaka Trade in the Sixteenth Century." In *Improvising Empire: Portuguese Trade and Settlement in the Bay of Bengal 1500–1700,* 16–46. Delhi: Oxford University Press, 1990.

Sweeney, Amin. *Authors and Audiences in the Malay World.* Berkeley: University of California Press, 1980.

——. *A Full Hearing: Orality and Literacy in the Malay World.* Berkeley: University of California Press, 1987.

——. *Reputations Live On: An Early Malay Autobiography.* Berkeley: University of California Press, 1980.

——. "Some Observations on the Nature of Malay Autobiography." *Indonesia Circle* 51 (1990): 21–36.

Swettenham, Frank. *British Malaya: An Account of the Origin and Progress of British Influence in Malaya.* 1906. London: Allen and Unwin, 1948.

Tarling, Nicholas, ed. *The Cambridge History of Southeast Asia.* 2 vols. Cambridge: Cambridge University Press, 1992.

——. *Piracy and Politics in the Malay World: A Study of British Imperialism in Nineteenth-Century South-East Asia.* Melbourne: F.W. Cheshire, 1963.

Teeuw, A. *Modern Indonesian Literature.* The Hague: Martinus Nijhoff, 1967.

Traill, H. F. O'B. "An Indian Protagonist of the Malay Language." *Journal of the Malayan Branch or the Royal Asiatic Society* 52, no. 2 (1979): 67–83.

Tregonning, K.G., ed. *Papers in Malayan History.* Singapore: University of Malaya Press, 1962.

Tribe, Keith. "Adam Smith: Critical Theorist?" *Journal of Economic Literature* 37, no. 2 (June 1999): 609–32.

Trocki, Carl. "Chinese Pioneering in Southeast Asia." In *The Last Stand of Asian Autonomies,* ed. Anthony Reid, 83–102. London: Macmillan, 1997.

——. *Opium, Empire, and the Global Political Economy.* London: Routledge, 1999.

——. *Prince of Pirates: The Temenggongs and the Development of Johor and Singapore, 1784–1885.* Singapore: Singapore University Press, 1979.

Turnbull, C.M. "The Origins of British Control in the Malay States before Colonial Rule." In *Malayan and Indonesian Studies: Essays Presented to Sir Richard Winstedt,* ed. J. Bastin and R. Roolvink, 166–83. Oxford: Clarendon Press, 1967.

——. *The Straits Settlements, 1826–67.* London: Athlone, 1972.

Van Leur, Jacob Cornelius. *Indonesian Trade and Society: Essays in Asian Social and Economic History.* The Hague: W. Van Hoeve, 1955.

Veblen, Thorstein. "Preconceptions of Economic Science." *The Quarterly Journal of Economics* 13, no. 4 (1899): 396–426.

Viswanathan, Gauri. *Outside the Fold: Conversion, Modernity, and Belief.* Princeton, N.J.: Princeton University Press, 1998.

————. *Masks of Conquest: Literary Study and British Rule in India.* New York: Columbia University Press, 1989.

Volosinov, V. N. *Marxism and the Philosophy of Language.* 1929. Trans. Ladislav Matejka and I. R. Titunik. Cambridge, Mass.: Harvard University Press, 1986.

Wallace, Alfred Russell. *The Malay Archipelago: The Land of the Orang-Utan, and the Bird of Paradise. A Narrative of Travel, with Studies of Man and Nature.* 2 vols. London: Macmillan, 1869.

Wang Gungwu. *Community and Nation: Essays on Southeast Asia and the Chinese.* Sydney: Allen and Unwin, 1981.

————. "Migration Patterns in History: Malaysia and the Region." *Journal of the Malaysian Branch of the Royal Asiatic Society* 58, no. 1 (1985): 43–58.

Warren, James Francis. *The Sulu Zone: The World Capitalist Economy and the Historical Imagination.* Amsterdam: VU University Press, 1998.

Watt, Ian. *Conrad in the Nineteenth Century.* Berkeley: University of California Press, 1980.

Webster, Anthony. *Gentlemen Capitalists: British Imperialism in Southeast Asia, 1770–1890.* London: Tauris, 1998.

————. "British Export Interests in Bengal and Imperial Expansion into South-East Asia, 1780–1824: The Origins of the Straits Settlements." In *Development Studies and Colonial Policy*, ed. Barbara Ingham and Colin Simmons, 138–74. London: Frank Cass, 1987.

Wilkinson, R. J. *A Malay-English Dictionary.* Romanized. 2 vols. Mytilene, Greece: Salavaopoulos and Kinderlis, 1932.

Williams, Glyndwr. "The Pacific: Exploration and Exploitation." In *Oxford History of the British Empire: The Eighteenth Century*, ed. P. J. Marshall, 2:552–75. New York: Oxford University Press, 1998.

Winch, Donald. "Adam Smith: Scottish Moral Philosopher as Political Economist." *The Historical Journal* 35, no. 1 (March 1992): 91–113.

————. *Classical Political Economy and the Colonies.* Cambridge, Mass.: Harvard University Press, 1965.

Winichakul, Thongchai. *Siam Mapped: A History of the Geo-Body of a Nation.* Honolulu: University of Hawaii Press, 1994.

Winstedt, Richard. *A History of Classical Malay Literature.* Kuala Lumpur: Oxford University Press, 1925.

————. *A Practical Modern Malay-English Dictionary.* Singapore: Kelly and Walsh, 1952.

Wolters, O. W. *History, Culture, and Region in Southeast Asian Perspectives.* Singapore: ISEAS, 1982.

Wong, R. Bin. *China Transformed: Historical Change and the Limits of European Experience.* Ithaca, N.Y.: Cornell University Press, 1993.

World Bank, The. *The East Asian Miracle: Economic Growth and Public Policy.* New York: Oxford University Press, 1993.

Wurtzburg, C.E. *Raffles of the Eastern Isles.* London: Hodder & Stoughton, 1954.

Yule, Henry, and A.C. Burnell. *Hobson-Jobson: A Glossary of Anglo-Indian Phrases of Kindred Terms, Etymological, Historical, Geographical, and Discursive.* 1882. London: John Murray, 1903.

INDEX

difference, 126–129, 144–145, 155–156, 159;
in anticolonial texts, 165–168, 173;
global mode of perspectivization
and, 167–168
discipline, 116–118, 203n. 46, 207n. 10
discovery, 170, 178n. 28; agents of as
European, 15, 178n. 27; of America,
36–38, 180n. 9; phases of, 14–16; violence and, 37–38, 51
Discovery of India (Nehru), 170–173
displacement: of autonomous "I," 128;
of global mode of perspectivization,
2, 5, 20–21, 23, 41, 46, 82, 108, 128,
166–167, 170; of native labor, 141–142;
subsistence and, 40–49. *See also* defamiliarization
Duffy, Michael, 189–190n. 19

East Asian Miracle, The (World Bank
Report), 10–11
East Indies, as geopolitical category,
17–18, 29, 31, 46
economy: exchange, 44, 68, 182n. 18,
183n. 22, 185n. 28, 188n. 10; growth
models, 145; internally differentiated, 44–46, 185–186n. 31; redistributive, 211n. 38; society as condition
for, 44; subsistence as ground of,
39. *See also* nonmarket economies;
subsistence
education, 197n. 10; Abdullah and,
96–98, 103–104, 120; dangers of colonial, 114–115
elites, native, 17, 77–78, 113, 161–162, 201n.
38
epistemological frameworks, 2, 16, 35,
38, 60–61, 176n. 13, 203n. 47, 212n. 1
equivalence/commensuration, 76, 91,
102–103
Erdinast-Vulcan, Daphna, 206–207n. 8
ethical subjectivity, 130–131, 133–134

ethnicity, 105, 120, 126–128, 196n. 8, 199n.
26
Eurocentrism, 6, 121; anti-Eurocentrism, 6–11
Europe: internally differentiated
economies, 44–46, 185–186n. 31; lack
of natural development, 47–48; as
mode of temporalization, 155; premodernity, image of, 89–90
everyday world, 133, 136
exchange economies, 44, 68, 182n. 18,
183n. 22, 185n. 28, 188n. 10
exteriority, 64–65, 67–68, 85, 87, 155

Farquhar, William, 106–113, 200n. 29,
201n. 38, 205n. 60
fictive discourse, 171–172
First Opium War, 202n. 42
foreign trade, 45, 63–64, 186n. 33, 34,
199n. 25
Foucault, Michel, 199n. 27
France, 14, 26; British victory over
(1815), 19, 60, 73, 97
Frank, Andre Gunder, 8
free choice rhetoric, 145
free trade, 158; De Quincey's argument
for, 63–64; diverse practices, 56–57;
improvement rhetoric, 18–19, 26–27,
35, 42; introduced to America, 50–52;
mercantilism vs., 38, 44; origins in
subsistence, 34–35, 38–39, 43, 47; premarket exchange and, 37; as remedy
for natural poverty of talent, 55–56;
rhetoric of, 18–19, 27; self-regulating
market, 44
Friedman, Thomas, 212n. 39

gender issues, 105, 124
general equivalence (monetary form),
43, 101–103, 112, 115, 129, 149, 199n. 25
geopolitical categories, 17–18, 29, 31, 46